Microsoft Office

Standard and Professional

PRISMA Computer Courses are structured, practical guides to mastering the most popular computer programs. PRISMA books are course books, giving step-by-step instructions, which take the user through basic skills to advanced functions in easy to follow, manageable stages.

Now available:

dBase IV
Excel 4.0 for Windows
Lotus 1-2-3
Lotus 1-2-3 for Windows
MS-DOS 3.3 to 5.0
MS-DOS 6.2
Novell Netware
UNIX
Windows
WordPerfect 6.0
WordPerfect for Windows
Visual Basic for Windows
Word 6.0 for Windows
Norton Desktop for Windows

Anita Koelma

Microsoft Office

Standard and Professional

PRISMA COMPUTER COURSE

Prisma Computer Courses first published in Great Britain 1992 by

Het Spectrum
PO Box 2996
London N5 2TA

Translation: George Hall
Production: LINE UP text productions

ISBN 1 85365 322 5

British Library Cataloguing-in-Publication Data.
A catalogue record for this book is available from the British Library.

Contents

Foreword

Microsoft Office is a package which consists of a series of advanced business applications, which all work in the same way. These applications are so uniform and their operating structure is so cohesive that it seems as if they form one program. They enable you to make integrated documents which are compiled out of elements created in the various different applications.

For example, you can create a form letter in Word into which you can insert the address data from an Access database so that each form letter receives a personal tint. Or you can add an Excel chart containing turnover figures to an annual report created in Word. If you are connected to a network on which Microsoft Mail is active, you can send documents along with messages to other network users. The facilities provided by each individual application, and by the applications in conjunction, are enormous.

Microsoft Office version 4.3 (Microsoft Office Professional) consists of the following components:

Microsoft Word

- the word processor Microsoft Word 6.0
- the spreadsheet program Microsoft Excel 5.0
- the presentation program Microsoft PowerPoint 4.0
- the database management system Microsoft Access 2.0
- a work station licence for Microsoft Mail 3.2 which is an electronic mail system for networks.

Microsoft Excel

Microsoft PowerPoint

Microsoft Access

Microsoft Mail

You can only use Microsoft Mail if you have the Server edition of Mail for PC networks.

Version 4.2 of Microsoft Office, Microsoft Office Standard edition, also consists of the applications mentioned above, with the exception of Microsoft Access 2.0. In this book, we shall deal with working with Microsoft Office Professional.

You will become familiar with the individual applications, with the facilities provided by Microsoft Office Manager and with the integration techniques, by means of description, examples and exercises.

This book has the following structure:

- Chapter 1 provides an overview of the possibilities of the Microsoft Office integrated package. The installation of the package is outlined and you can find out how to add and remove program elements using Office Setup after the installation has been carried out.
- Chapter 2 gives a description of working with Windows and Windows applications in general. You are instructed, for example, how to use the mouse, the toolbars, normal and shortcut menus, how to rearrange windows on the screen and how to make optimum use of the Help function.
- Chapters 3 to 6 give an introduction to working with Microsoft Word, Microsoft Excel, Microsoft PowerPoint and Microsoft Access.
- Chapter 7 demonstrates how to make practical use of Microsoft Mail to send messages to users either outside or within the network.
- Chapter 8 enables you to make acquaintance with the facilities provided by Microsoft Office Manager. You will find out how to start up applications by means of the Microsoft Office Manager, how to arrange application windows on the screen and how to adjust the toolbar to your own requirements.

- Chapter 9 gives an introduction to integration possibilities supplied by Microsoft Office. This includes information about copying, moving, linking, embedding, importing and exporting data, and other information about OLE techniques (object linking and embedding). In addition, this chapter provides an overview of other Microsoft Office facilities such as the insertion of objects, the Illustration gallery, WordArt and Graph. The insertion of images into a document is demonstrated.
- Chapters 10 to 13 deal with practical exercises in integration. You will make compilation documents in Microsoft Word, Microsoft Excel, Microsoft PowerPoint and Microsoft Access using fictional examples.

The following conventions apply in this book:

- A plus sign between two named keys means that you should press and hold down the first key, and then press the second key. Then release both keys. Therefore, if you read that you have to press Alt+B, press the Alt key, hold it down and then press B. Then release both keys.
- A comma between two keys means that you should press them consecutively. If, for example, you see that you should press **', e** to produce the **é**, you should first press the **'** and then the **e**.
- 'Clicking' means that you should place the mouse pointer on the object in question and then quickly press and release the left mouse button.
- 'Double clicking' means that you should place the mouse pointer on the object in question and then press the left mouse button twice in rapid succession.
- 'Dragging' means that you should place the mouse pointer on the object in question, press and hold down the left mouse button and then move the mouse pointer to the required position. Release the mouse button when you reach there.

- The names of menus, menu options, windows, window elements and command buttons are displayed in italics.
- Text that you should type yourself is shown in boldface.
- The names of files are shown in capitals.
- If you should click on a toolbar button to implement a command, the relevant button will be displayed in the margin.
- When we refer to 'Word', we mean 'Microsoft Word'. The same principle applies to Microsoft Excel, Microsoft PowerPoint, Microsoft Access and Microsoft Mail.

1 Introductory remarks
The Microsoft installation
Starting up the Office Manager

1.1 The advantages of an Integrated package

The functionality of Microsoft Office is formed not only by the excellent facilities provided by each individual application, but also by the uniformity of the applications in the package. In principle, all the applications are operated in a similar way. Therefore, when you have learned to work with one application, you will find it easy to master the others, since the toolbars, menus, commands and dialog windows in the diverse packages are all operated in the same way. The facilities are different but the structure is the same.

The virtue of Microsoft Office is the way in which the applications cooperate as it were. Although each individual application provides many ingenious functions, the functionality of the integrated package is greatly increased by the way in which application documents and parts of documents can be combined to form the required final product.

Because various applications can be active at the same time, you can switch quickly and conveniently from one application to the other. Accordingly, it is easy to move or copy data from one application to another. In addition, you can link, embed, import and export data with a few simple commands. If you place the application windows next to one another, you have a good overview of the source and target positions of data which are to be moved or copied.

1.2 The advantages of the Office applications

Each Microsoft Office application provides its own special facilities:

Microsoft Word

- Word is used to create text-based documents. These can be letters or memos or even books. Word provides advanced functions for checking and formatting the text, along with facilities such as styles and macros to automise the work.

Microsoft Excel

- Excel is suited to working with numbers and making calculations. The data are organised in worksheets and workbooks. In fact, the Excel functions are so extensive that this program is even used to make financial analyses for large companies. You can create charts and carry out 'what-if' analyses.

Microsoft PowerPoint

- PowerPoint is an application with facilities for creating presentations. You can make overhead transparencies, 35 mm slides, notation pages and handouts. You can insert Word documents or Excel charts, for example, into a presentation, which, of course, you can also combine with other applications.

Microsoft Access

- Access is an advanced application for managing data in databases. Forms ensure straightforward data input. You can also design reports and queries (reports based on specified search criteria).

1.2.1 An intelligent package

Microsoft Office has IntelliSense, which can be described as a kind of 'intelligence' which tries to understand what you are trying to do. This means that the application will automise many frequently-recurring actions and will simplify difficult tasks. Examples of these are:

- The AutoCorrect function in Word, which will automatically correct typing errors while you work. Words

which you regularly tend to type erroneously, or easy abbreviations which you quickly type, can be automatically replaced by the correct version of the word or term.
- The AutoFormat function in Word, which automatically assigns a professional layout to a document. Word recognises certain components of a document, such as headings, and creates a form for these based on the built-in styles available.
- The Excel Tips in Excel, which supplies tips and suggestions on how to execute your current tasks better and more quickly. In addition, it provides information about new functions available for this task.
- The PivotTable Wizard in Excel, which displays a series of interactive dialog windows from which you can select data to create a pivot table in which data are summarised.
- The AutoContent Wizard in PowerPoint, which assists you in creating a presentation.
- The Pick a Look Wizard in PowerPoint, which helps you to select an appropriate style for your presentation.
- The Word Mail Merge Report Wizard in Access, which helps you make a DDE (Dynamic Data Exchange) link between a Word document and an Access table or query so you can produce form letters or address labels.

1.2.2 Linking and embedding data

Microsoft Office also provides OfficeLinks, a function for exchanging data between one application and another. You can, for instance, drag data from one application to another to embed them. The OfficeLinks function and the OLE technique (Object Linking and Embedding) enable you to embed the data created in a file in one application in a file in another application. You can also link these data to the destination file, which means that if you change the data in the original file, they are also changed in the second file; this is ideal for financial data which undergo changes.

In addition, there are special toolbar buttons in the applications by means of which you can easily activate functions in other applications. In this way, if you are working on a task within an application which involves inserting elements from a different application, you can activate the functions of the other application by clicking on the corresponding button. Examples of these are:

Insert Microsoft Excel Worksheet

- The *Insert Microsoft Excel Worksheet* button on the Word standard toolbar, which enables you to insert a worksheet at the insertion position in a Word document.
- The *Insert Microsoft Excel Worksheet* button on the PowerPoint standard toolbar, which enables you to insert a worksheet into the presentation.

Insert Microsoft Word Table

- The *Insert Microsoft Word Table* button on the PowerPoint standard toolbar, which enables you to insert a Word table into the presentation.

Output to Form Letters

- The *Output to Form Letters* button on the Database toolbar in Access, which enables you to combine Access data with a Word document.

Analyze with Microsoft Excel

- The *Analyze with Microsoft Excel* button on the Database toolbar in Access, which enables you to save data as an Excel worksheet and subsequently open the file in Excel.

1.3 System requirements

In order to be able to work with Microsoft Office, you need the following hard- and software:

- a computer with a 386 microprocessor or higher
- 4 Mb working memory, but 8 Mb is preferable if you wish to have several applications simultaneously active
- 92 Mb free space on the harddisk for a full installation, 65 Mb for a standard installation and 31 Mb for a minimum installation of the Microsoft Office Professional version (for Microsoft Office Standard that is 77 Mb, 55 Mb and 23 Mb respectively)
- a 3.5 inch diskdrive or 5.25 inch diskdrive for high density diskettes
- a VGA screen adapter or screen adapter for higher resolution
- a mouse
- Windows NT or Windows NT Advanced Server version 3.1 or higher
  or
  MS-DOS version 3.1 or higher and Windows version 3.1 or higher
  or
  MS-DOS version 3.1 or higher and Windows for Workgroups version 3.1 or higher.

If you wish to make use of Mail, you should have the Server edition of Microsoft Mail for PC networks. A workstation licence is supplied along with Microsoft Office, but the main software for this is part of the Server edition.

If you install Microsoft Office on a network, the network should be compatible with the Windows environment. Suitable environments are:

- Microsoft Networks (Windows NT, Windows NT Advanced Server, Windows for Workgroups or LAN Manager)
- Novell NetWare
- LANtastic
- Banyan VINES.

1.4 Installing Microsoft Office

When installing Microsoft Office, you can select one of four options. Later, if you are not satisfied with the settings you have specified or if you wish to add or delete certain elements, you can use Setup again to make modifications. Section 1.5 deals with this in more detail.

The Setup program implements the installation of Microsoft Office almost completely automatically. The only thing you have to do is to select certain options during the installation procedure. In order to install Microsoft Office on your computer harddisk, proceed as follows:

1. Start up Windows. Ensure that any opened applications are closed down.
2. Insert Microsoft Office diskette 1 in diskdrive A or B.
3. Open the *File* menu and select the *Run* option in the Windows Program Manager.
4. Type **a:setup** in the Command Line box in the Run dialog window. If you insert the diskette into diskdrive B, you have to type **b** instead of **a**.
5. Click on the *OK* button.

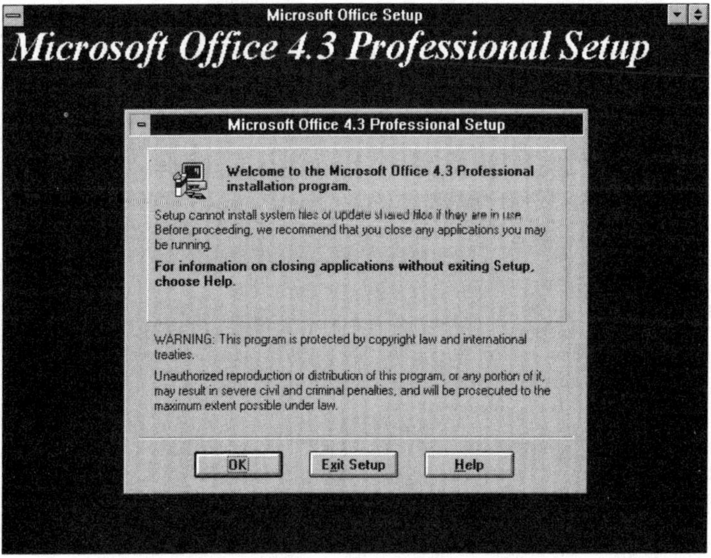

The *Welcome to Microsoft Office 4.3 Professional Setup* window appears, in which you are advised to close all other opened applications before proceeding.

6 Select *OK*. If you wish to gain information about closing applications, first click on the *Help* button.

Another window appears, in which you are requested to type your name and the name of your company. The company name is not obligatory.

7 Enter the name(s) and activate the *OK* button.

A window appears asking for confirmation of the name(s).

8 Select *OK* if the data are correct or *Change* if alterations have to be made.

The following window asks you to note the registration number on your registration card.

9 Enter this number and select *OK*.

The next window asks you to specify the path to the directory in which you wish to install the Microsoft Office Manager. Setup advises the C:\MSOFFICE directory for this.

10 Select *OK* if you are willing to accept this suggestion. Select *Change Directory* if you wish to install these files elsewhere.

Subsequently, dialog windows appear in which you are asked to specify directories for PowerPoint, Word, Excel and Access. Proceed as in step 10 above.

The following window will appear:

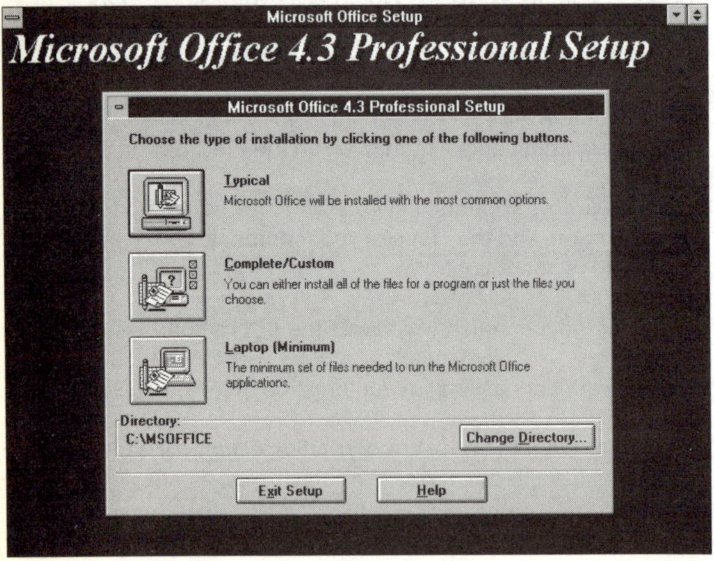

Here, you have to make a choice concerning the type of installation you require:

- The *Typical* option installs the most common components of the Microsoft Office package.
- The *Complete/Custom* option installs all components of the Microsoft Office package, or those you specify yourself.
- The *Laptop (Minimum)* option enables you to select applications from which only the files which are absolutely necessary will be installed.
- The *Workstation* option may also be available if you are installing Microsoft Office within a network.

11 Click on the required button.

If you choose the *Complete/Custom* option, the following window will appear.

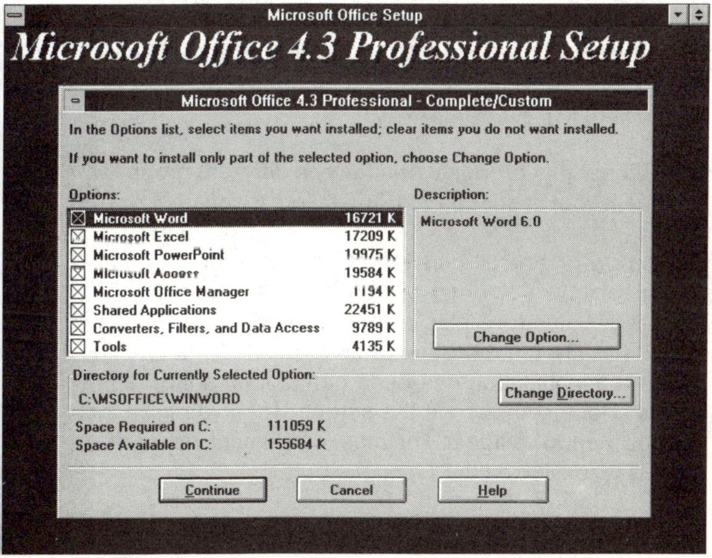

Click on the small squares to place crosses at the applications or components that you want to install. This also means that there should be no cross next to applications you do not wish to install. Even if you only wish to install a part of an application, you should place a cross in front of the application name.

12 If you want to install all applications, select *Continue*. If you wish to install a part of an application, select the appropriate name and click on the *Change Option* button. Place crosses in front of the components you wish to install and then click on *OK*. Then select the *Continue* button. Do the same for all components or applications that you wish to partially install.

The installation program continues, and you may have to reply to questions appearing on the screen. Eventually, you will be asked to choose the program group in which Microsoft Office is to be placed. Setup suggests the Microsoft Office group itself. Icons belonging to the Microsoft Office applications and components will be displayed in this group window.

13 Accept this proposal or specify a different group to meet your requirements, and select *Continue*.

Setup now begins to install the Microsoft Office files in the specified directories on the harddisk. Because of the sheer volume of files to be installed, this will take some time. Switch diskettes when requested.
When the installation has been completed, a message to this effect is shown on the screen. Then you have to start up Windows again. The most convenient way of doing this is to click on the *Continue* button.

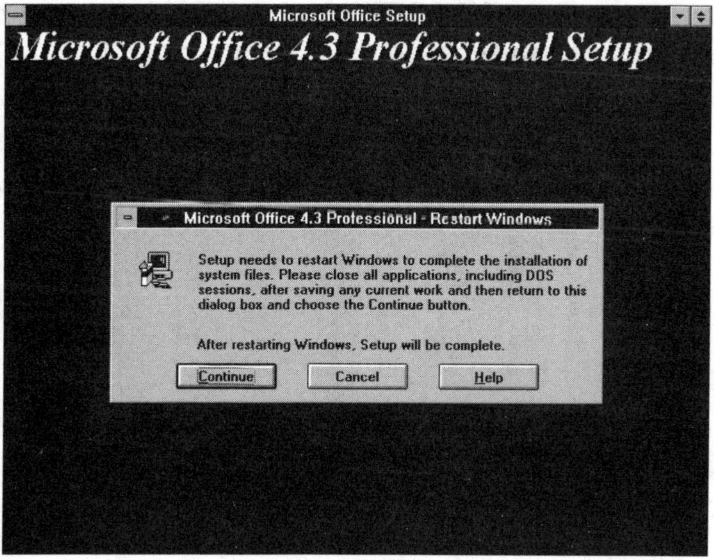

1.5 Running Office Setup again later

If Microsoft Office has been fully installed, the Office Setup program will also be available on the harddisk. The program icon is displayed in the Microsoft Office group of the Program Manager.

This program enables you to add or remove Microsoft Office applications or components. You can also install Office all over again if program files have somehow got lost; or you can remove all installed Office applications and components.

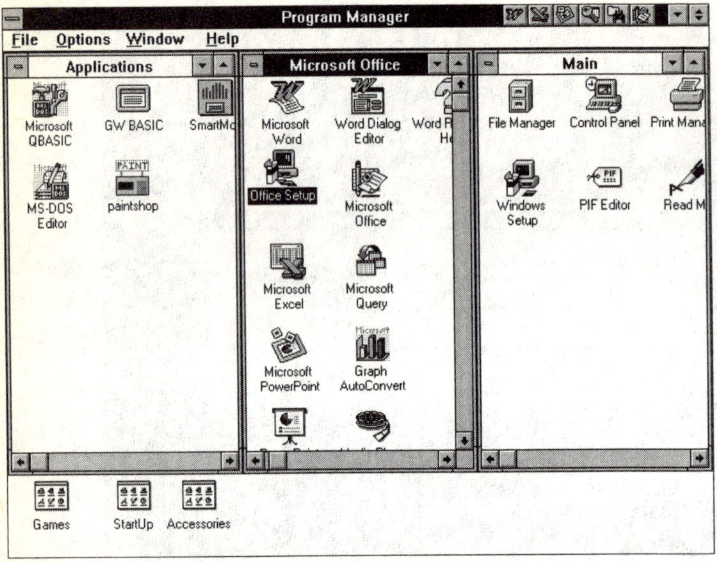

To start up Office Setup, proceed as follows:

1 When Microsoft Office has been started up, select the *Office Setup* option from the *Office* menu (see chapter 8). You can also click on the Office Setup icon in the Microsoft Office group of the Program Manager.

Note
If you are working with Microsoft Office in a network, it might be impossible to start up Office Setup. If you are using a workstation version, you can start up Setup from the workstation on which Office is installed.

When activated, Setup states that it is looking for the installed components. This may take a little time. If you have installed an application separately, a dialog window will appear first; select the appropriate application from this window by marking the name and clicking on *OK*.

The Office Setup opening screen then appears:

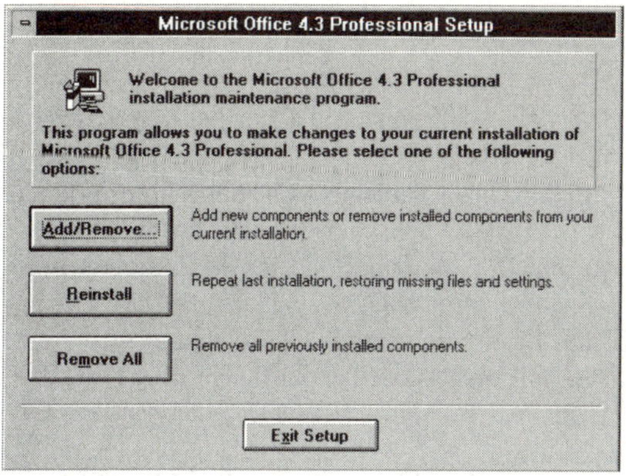

2 Activate one of the following buttons:

- *Add/Remove* if you wish to add or remove components or applications from the current setup.
- *Reinstall* if you wish to execute the installation again, in cases of damaged files for example.
- *Remove All* if you wish to undo the entire installation.

The window that appears when you select *Add/Remove* operates in exactly the same way as that which appears if you select *Complete/Custom* during the first Microsoft Office installation (see steps 11 and 12 in section 1.4).

Ensure that crosses are placed next to the applications you wish to install or retain. Remove the crosses next to the applications to be deleted. If you wish to add or remove components of an application, select the name of the corresponding application and select *Change Option*. Ensure that the name of the application itself is not switched off, otherwise you will not be able to modify it.

Place crosses next to the components to be retained and remove the crosses next to the components to be removed. Then select the *Continue* button.

1.6 Starting up the Microsoft Office Manager

During the installation, Microsoft Office is automatically placed in the StartUp group of the Program Manager. This means that the Microsoft Office Manager is automatically activated when Windows is started up. The Microsoft Office Manager toolbar in the upper right-hand corner of the screen indicates that the Microsoft Office Manager is active.

If the Microsoft Office Manager is not started up, you can double click on the Microsoft Office icon in the Microsoft Office group of the Program Manager. The Microsoft Office Manager toolbar will then appear.

You can copy the Microsoft Office icon to the StartUp group by dragging the icon from the Microsoft Office group while holding down the Ctrl key. If you wish to remove the icon from the StartUp group, click on it once to mark it and press Del.

The Microsoft Office Manager toolbar enables you to activate and close down applications, arrange application windows on your screen, search for certain files and to open the Microsoft Office menu. Chapter 8 deals with this in more detail.

2 Working with Windows and Windows applications

All Microsoft Office applications are operated in a similar way, due to their uniformly standardised structure. All these applications provide toolbars, menus, scroll bars, dialog windows and other screen elements which display great likenesses. This chapter discusses how to work with Windows and Windows applications. In addition, you will learn about the utilities provided within the applications, such as the Help function, the indicators and the button info, which all help to facilitate working with the applications.

2.1 Working with the mouse

To operate Windows and the Windows applications, a mouse is practically indispensible. Many actions and commands can actually be implemented more quickly using the keyboard, but nevertheless a mouse is essential for some aspects, such as working with the buttons on the toolbar.

Because of its increasing popularity, availability and convenience, we presume that you will be working with the mouse. However, in this chapter, we shall give a brief outline of how to specify commands using the keyboard. If you prefer this method, you can continue using it yourself.

The symbol on the screen indicating the current position of the mouse pointer can assume a number of shapes. The shape displayed depends on the application or program in use and on the position of the mouse pointer.

various mouse pointer shapes

2.2 Starting up Windows

If Windows has not yet been started up, type the following behind the DOS prompt:

```
win
```

Then press Enter.

The Windows Program Manager will probably appear, although this will depend on the programs installed on your computer, the way in which the programs and icons have been arranged and on the contents of the StartUp group. Normally, the opening screen will look something like this:

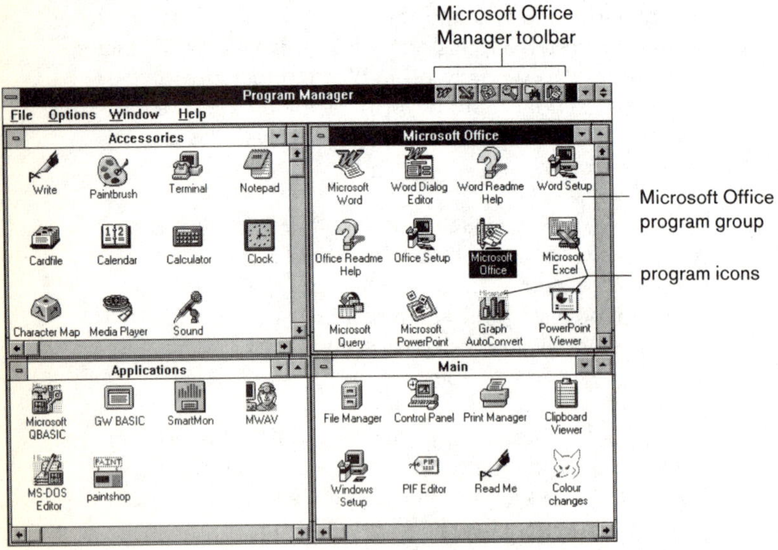

2.3 Using the Program Manager to start up applications

You can start up the Microsoft Office applications from the Program Manager, or you can use the Microsoft Office Manager toolbar (this method will be discussed in more detail in chapter 8). In order to start up a Microsoft Office application from the Program Manager, proceed as follows:

- Ensure that the Microsoft Office group window is opened and the icons are clearly visible.
- Double click on the application to be activated.

2.3.1 Switching between applications

One of the major advantages of Windows is that it is possible to have several applications open simultaneously. Once you have opened one application, you can switch to the Program Manager to open another if required. If the Microsoft Office toolbar is displayed on the screen, you can also use it to activate another application.

There are several ways of switching to the Program Manager:

- Press and hold down the Alt key and press the Tab key a number of times. Each time you press Tab, the name of an opened application will appear. When *Program Manager* appears, release both keys. The Program Manager is then displayed.
- Press Ctrl+Esc to activate the Task List. Select the *Program Manager* and then activate *Switch To*.
- Open the Control menu (Alt+Spacebar) of the currently active application and select *Switch To*. Select *Program Manager* from the subsequent list and then activate the *Switch To* button.

You can also switch to any other opened application in this way. Simply select the name of the required application instead of the *Program Manager*.

Exercise

Just for practice, we shall activate the Excel and Word applications. The Word window should then remain visible on the screen.

Procedure:

1 Ensure that the Program Manager and the Microsoft Office program group are visible on the screen.

Microsoft Excel

2 Double click on the Microsoft Excel icon.

3 Press Alt+Tab or use the Task List to switch to the Program Manager. Ensure that the Microsoft Office program group is opened and clearly visible.

Microsoft Word

4 Double click on the Microsoft Word icon. When the *Tip of the Day* window appears, click on *OK*.

2.4 Working with windows

The window in which an application is displayed is referred to as an 'application window'. An application window contains – disregarding the menu bar and other supporting screen elements – a document, a worksheet, a presentation sheet, a table, a form or a report, depending on the application. The figure below displays a Word application window containing the empty opened document 'Document1'.

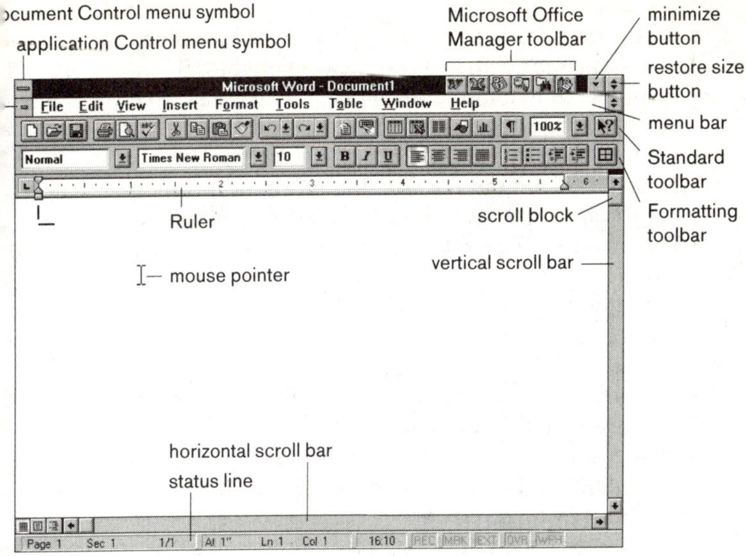

In this example, the document window fills the entire screen. This is also indicated by the fact that the name of the document is shown in the application title bar.

The window elements have the following functions:

- The application window is the window in which the application is displayed on the screen.
- The document window, worksheet window etc. is the window in which the currently active worksheet, document etc. is shown.
- The name of the currently active application is shown on the application title bar.
- The name of the currently active document is shown on the title bar of the document, workbook etc.
- The Microsoft Office Manager toolbar provides diverse facilities for starting up and closing down applications, arranging application windows, searching for files and opening the Microsoft Office menu. This tool-

bar can be adjusted to suit your own requirements. This will be dealt with in more detail in chapter 8.

- The menu bar displays the names of the menus which can be opened. You then select one of the options provided. This is dealt with in the next section.
- The Standard toolbar provides various buttons for executing common tasks. The Microsoft Office applications provide a large number of toolbars which resemble one another.
- The Formatting toolbar provides buttons for adjusting the layout of your documents.
- The Ruler enables you to quickly modify indentation, the margin widths, the column widths and the distance between the Tab stops.
- The vertical scroll bar and block enable you to move the contents of the screen upwards and downwards. Click on the arrow heads to move the screen one line at a time, or click above or below the scroll block to move the contents by one full screen page. You can also drag the scroll block to move quickly to a certain section of the document. In the Page Layout mode, there are additional buttons with double arrows which move you to the previous or following page when you click on them.
- You can move the contents horizontally by clicking on the horizontal scroll bar and block in a similar way. There are also, in certain applications, other special buttons on the horizontal scroll bar; these will be discussed in the sections dealing with these applications.
- The status bar displays specific relevant information about the current settings in the active document.
- The mouse pointer is the small symbol on the screen; this corresponds to the movements of the mouse.
- The Control menu is opened when you click on the Control menu button in the upper left-hand corner of the screen. This menu provides commands for enlarging, reducing, moving and closing the application win-

dow, and for switching to the Task List. You can also open the Control menu by pressing the key combinations Alt+Spacebar. If you double click on the Control menu button, the currently active application will be closed.

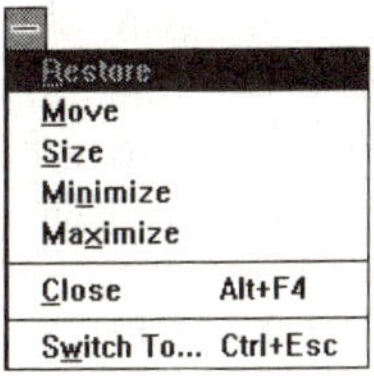

Application Control menu

- Similarly, if you click on the Control menu button of a document, workbook etc., you will open a menu enabling you to alter the size and position of the document window, worksheet window etc. This can also be done by pressing the key combination Alt+hyphen. A double click on this Control menu button will close the currently active document.
- Clicking on the *Restore* button restores the previous window size. Then the button changes into the *Maximize* button which enables you to increase the size of the window to fill the screen.
- Clicking on the *Minimize* button reduces the window to an icon. If you then double click on the icon, the window will regain its previous size.

The Help windows and dialog windows also have Control menus, although these normally only consist of the commands *Move* and *Close*.

In addition, you will also encounter screen components which are specific to their own applications. These will be outlined in the sections dealing with the applications in question.

2.4.1 Placing the windows next to one another

It is possible to arrange the position of the windows of the opened applications according to your own requirements. Chapter 8, dealing with the Microsoft Office Manager, discusses this in more detail.

Within an application, you can arrange the position of documents or workbooks etc. on the screen. You can use the commands in the *Window* menu to do this, or you can drag the window frames until they acquire the desired size. To relocate a window, drag the title bar of the window to the required position.

2.5 Working with menus

All the commands you can implement in an application are displayed in the menus. In order to give one of these commands, you must first open the menu containing the command in question. This is done by clicking on the name of the menu in the menu bar. Then activate the command by clicking on its name in the list of menu options. You can also click on the name of the menu, hold down the mouse button and move the mouse pointer to the required command; then release the mouse button. The selected option is then implemented.

To open a menu by means of the keyboard, press and hold down the Alt key and press the underlined letter displayed in the menu of your choice. Thus, to open the *File* menu in Word, you would press Alt+F. To open one of the menu options, press the corresponding underlined letter in the options list. You can also activate the required option by pressing the Cursor Down key to move the marking bar to it and then press Enter.

A menu option may also have submenus. In that case, a small triangle is shown behind the menu option. The same procedure applies to these as to menus and menu options.

2.5.1 Shortcut keys

You will notice that certain key combinations are shown next to many of the menu options. You can use these shortcut key combinations to execute the menu commands in one go instead of first having to open the menu and select the appropriate option. The disadvantage of these, of course, is that you have to remember them. You might also press the wrong letter by accident, so that a fully undesired procedure is carried out. Fortunately, these kind of procedures can often be easily undone. Word in particular provides a large range of facilities here.

2.5.2 Undoing commands

It is possible to undo the last command in all applications. When working in Word, a list is compiled of the last hundred commands executed during the current session, which can be undone.

Undo

If you wish to undo the previous command, click on the *Undo* button on the Standard toolbar (in Word, Excel and PowerPoint), or on one of the toolbars in Access which provides this option. You can also choose the *Undo* option from the *Edit* menu.

Redo/
Repeat

The *Redo* and *Repeat* buttons in Word and Excel enable you to restore the command you neutralised using the *Undo* command, and to repeat the last specified command. You can also activate these commands from the

Edit menu in the relevant application. The actual name of the command will depend on the last specified command.

The Undo function in Word provides considerably more facilities. An arrow is shown next to the *Undo* button. If you click on it, a list of all the commands specified during the current session is displayed (up to a maximum of 100). You can undo a whole series of modifications by dragging the mouse pointer across them and then releasing the mouse button. This can only be done with a consecutive series of commands, beginning with the last one (at the top). You can also simply select a command from the list. All the commands from that point onwards are undone.

The Repeat function in Word is just as extensive. You can repeat up to a maximum of 100 commands.

2.6 Working with dialog windows

Many commands are not implemented immediately; a dialog window appears first, in which you can determine additional parameters. Each menu option with three dots behind it will open a dialog window when activated.

The following figure displays the *Format Cells* dialog box (*Format* menu, *Style* option, *Modify* button) in *Excel*:

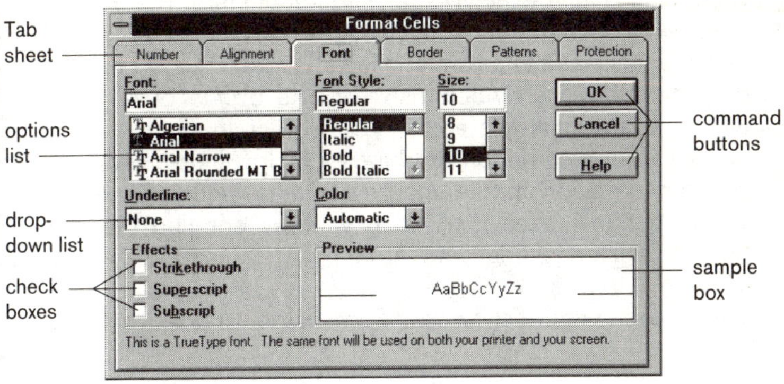

The components displayed have the following functions:

- A dialog window may consist of several Tab sheets. Each Tab sheet provides a category of options.
- An options list provides a series of options from which you can make a choice.
- A drop-down list provides a series of options from which you can make a choice once you have opened the list.
- A cross in a check box activates the corresponding option. Several check boxes may be active simultaneously. If no cross is displayed, the option is not active.
- The sample box (Preview) shows an example of the newly specified settings.
- The command is actually executed by means of the command buttons, or a new dialog window is activated. A button with three dots leads to a new dialog window.

Caution
When you click on the *OK* button, the command is activated along with the newly specified parameters. The dialog window is closed. In a dialog window containing Tab sheets, the settings are applied to all Tab sheets, not only the one currently being shown. The *Cancel* button will annul the changes and the dialog window is then closed. The *Help* button produces a Help window providing information about the current dialog window. The *Close* button closes the dialog window bringing the newly specified settings into force.

The following figure shows the *Print* dialog window from Word.

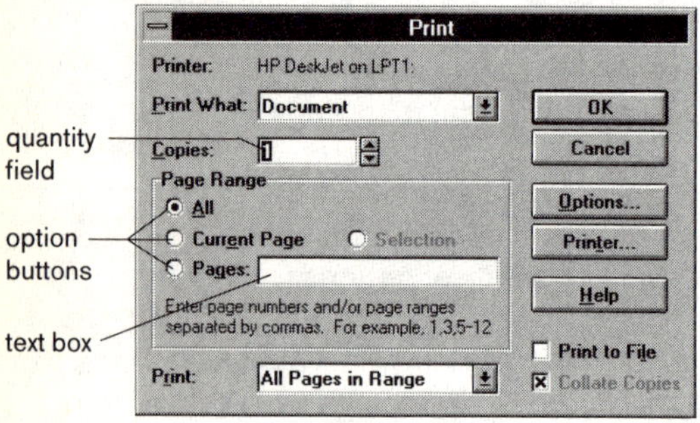

The elements mentioned have the following functions:

- If an options button contains a black dot, the corresponding function is activated. Only one options button may be active in one section at one time. If there is no black dot, the corresponding function is inactive.
- You can type text or numbers in a text box.
- You can specify the required amount in a quantity box by clicking on the arrows (the small triangles).

2.6.1 Making choices in dialog windows

You can specify choices in dialog windows as follows:

using the mouse

- To select the Tab sheet: click on the Tab sheet.
- To select an option from an options list: click on the option.
- To select an option from a drop-down list: click on the arrow to open the list and click on an option.
- To select a check box or options button: click on the box or button.
- To select a command button: click on the button.
- To enter text in a text box: click on the text box and type the text.
- To specify an amount in a quantity box: click on the arrows until the required number appears.

using the keyboard

- To select the Tab sheet: press Ctrl+Tab
- To select an option from an options list: press Tab until an option in the list is marked, use the Cursor Up or Cursor Down key to mark the required option
- To select an option from a drop-down list: press Tab until an option from the required section is highlighted, then press Cursor Down to open the list and move to the required option; press Enter.

- To select a check box or options button: press Tab until the required group is activated, use Cursor Up or Cursor down to mark the option, activate the option by pressing the spacebar.

- To select a command button: press Tab until the button is marked and press Enter.

- To enter text in a text box: press Tab until the box is marked and type the text.

- To specify an amount in a quantity box: press Tab until an amount in the box is marked and then press Cursor Up or Cursor Down until the required amount is shown (you can also type the amount).

If a drop-down list is not fully shown, scroll bars appear next to the list. You can click on these to move through the contents, or press the cursor keys.

If you are working with the keyboard, you can also use the Alt key in combination with the underlined letters to activate the options in the dialog windows.

2.7 Working with the toolbars

In all the Microsoft Office applications, various toolbars are available for various categories of commands. These toolbars enable you to give commands quickly and easily if you have a mouse.

Each toolbar button provides a function. You choose the required command by clicking on the appropriate button. Some toolbars contain lists from which you can make a choice. In order to open a list, click on the arrow at the right-hand side of the list. Subsequently, select the required option by clicking on it.

Most buttons give a clear indication of their function, and if this is not obvious, you can find out a button function by moving the mouse pointer to the toolbar button without clicking on the mouse. The function appears in a small information box, as exemplified by the *Open* button which will open the *Open* dialog window:

In addition, a brief description of the button function is shown on the status line when you move the mouse pointer to the button.

2.7.1 Opening and closing toolbars

Normally, several toolbars are available in each application. You can display any of these, or even completely remove them from the screen if you like.

You can display or hide the toolbars in the following easy way:

- Click on the toolbar using the right mouse button. This produces the toolbar shortcut menu. (Section 2.8 deals with shortcut menus in more detail.)
- Select the toolbar which is to be displayed or hidden from this menu.

If a tick mark is shown in front of the name of the toolbar, this indicates that the toolbar is being displayed. If there is no tick mark, the toolbar is hidden. Clicking on the name displays or hides the toolbar.

The following figure shows the shortcut menu for the toolbars available in Word:

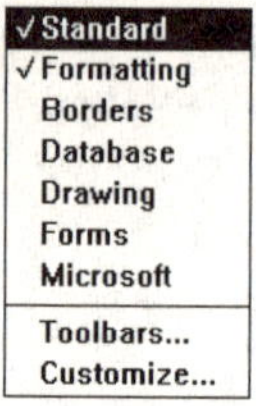

This menu also contains the *Toolbars* and *Customize* options. The *Toolbars* option is presented in the *View* menu of all applications in this package.

The *Toolbars* dialog window, which appears when you activate the *Toolbars* menu option, enables you to display or hide toolbars by placing a cross in the corresponding check boxes. In the Access package, the *Toolbars* window also provides the *Show* or *Hide* buttons for specifying the toolbar display.

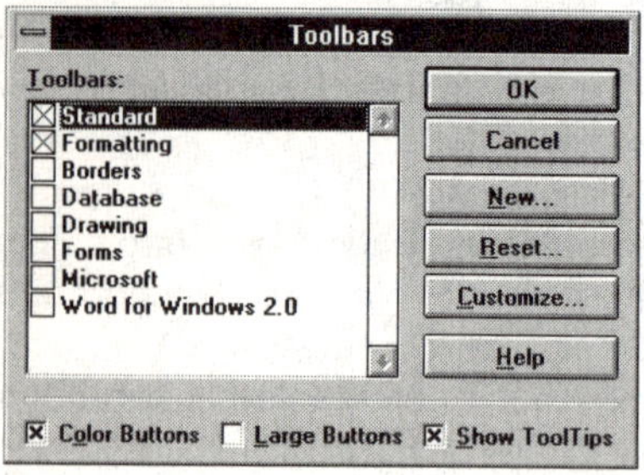

2.7.2 Adjusting the toolbars

The *Toolbars* dialog window not only provides options for switching the toolbar display on and off, it also allows you to modify and create toolbars geared to your own specific requirements.

- The *New* button activates the *New Toolbar* dialog window which enables you to create a new toolbar.
- The *Reset* button restores the marked toolbar to its original state with the buttons in the original order.
- The *Customize* button produces a dialog window which also appears when you select the *Customize* option from the shortcut menu, or the same option from the *Tools* menu (in Word and PowerPoint). This dialog window enables you to adapt the operation and the form of toolbars and menus. The operation of the keyboard can also be regulated in this dialog window. If, for example, you wish to place or remove buttons on the toolbar, open the *Customize* dialog window, ensure that both the dialog window and the toolbar in question are shown, and drag the desired button from the dialog window to the toolbar, or drag the button from the toolbar to an empty position on the screen if you wish to remove it from the toolbar. In addition, you can change the position of buttons on a toolbar by dragging them to the new position while the *Customize* dialog window is open. If you hold down the Ctrl key while dragging, a copy of the button is made. In this way, you can copy a button to another toolbar if this proves to be convenient.
- There are three buttons at the bottom of the *Toolbars* dialog window: *Color Buttons, Large Buttons* and *Show ToolTips*. These ensure that the buttons are shown in colour, in a larger size and with specific information.

Note

The Microsoft Office Manager toolbar is adjusted using a special command from the *Office* menu. Chapter 8 discusses this in greater detail.

2.7.3 Moving the toolbars

Section 2.7.2 outlined how toolbars can be adapted to specific requirements. It is also possible to move them to a different part of the screen. This is done by placing the mouse pointer on an empty part of the toolbar and dragging the toolbar to the chosen position.

If you drag the toolbar frame, the shape of the toolbar will also be altered.

2.8 Shortcut menus

You can make use of shortcut menus in all Microsoft Office applications. We have already had a look at the toolbar shortcut menu in section 2.7.

The shortcut menus appear when you place the mouse pointer at the relevant position on the screen and then click on the right mouse button. They contain menu options which are directly applicable to the current screen element, in other words, they are context-oriented.

The following figure displays the shortcut menu that appears when you click on selected data in a table in Word.

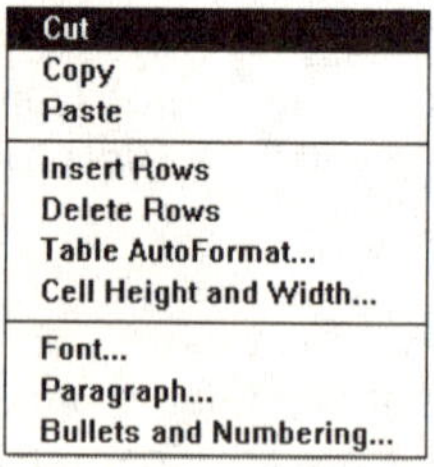

2.9 Altering the default settings

In each Microsoft Office application there are certain default settings that can be altered. This refers, for instance, to the settings for the display of data on the screen, the print settings, the storage of data and the spelling check, to name but a few.

To alter these settings, select *Options* from the *Tools* menu in Word, Excel and PowerPoint, and *Options* from the *View* menu in Access.

The *Options* dialog window, which appears when you select this menu option, provides several categories from which you can choose in order to alter the default settings.

In addition, there are various dialog windows in each application in which an *Options* button is available. Activating this button opens the *Options* dialog window; the Tab sheet relevant to the current task will be displayed.

2.10 Learning to work with the applications

The Microsoft Office applications provide all kinds of functions which facilitate working with the computer, such as the Wizards, the Tip of the Day, the Go To function, the Cue Cards and of course the Help system.

2.10.1 Wizards

The Wizards, which are available in all applications, enable you to create documents, presentations and databases specially geared to your own requirements quickly and easily. Once you have started up a Wizard, you only need to follow the instructions on the screen. How the Wizard is actually started up depends on the applications with which you are working. In Word, for example, a Wizard is started up via the *New* command from the *File* menu, and in Excel, you can start up a Wizard by means of the toolbar buttons. The method of operation depends on the tasks you wish to perform and on the application in which you are working.

You will become familiar with various Wizards in this book. The following figure displays the initial Table Wizard dialog window in Access.

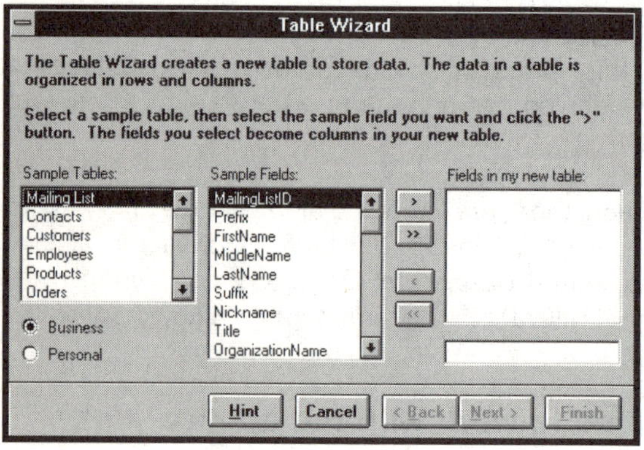

2.10.2 Quick Preview

Word, Excel and PowerPoint provide a brief summary of the most important application features. This overview is activated by selecting the *Quick Preview* option from the *Help* menu.

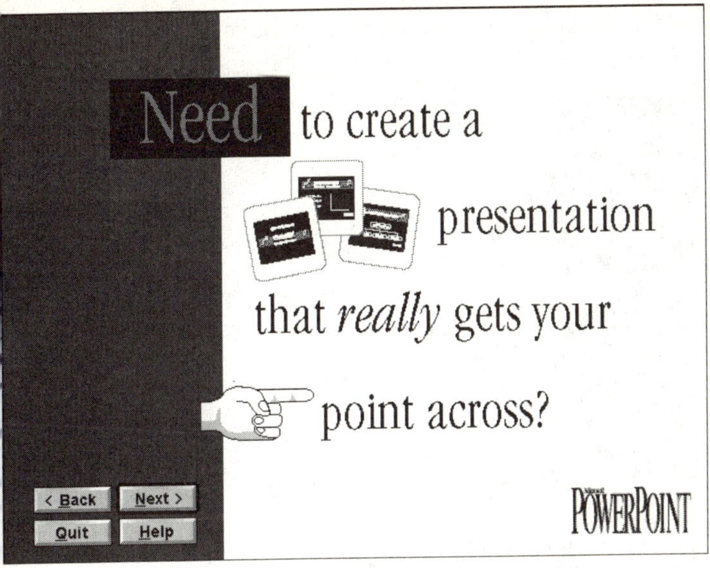

This Preview consists of a demonstration in which you can determine what you want to see by selecting the corresponding buttons.

2.10.3 Cue Cards

PowerPoint, Access and Microsoft Office Manager provide Cue Cards which assist you in carrying out certain tasks. They remain on the screen while you are busy so that you can work and learn at the same time. You can activate the Cue Cards by selecting the option of the same name from the *Help* menu, or the *Office* menu.

The following figure displays one of the Cue Cards from PowerPoint:

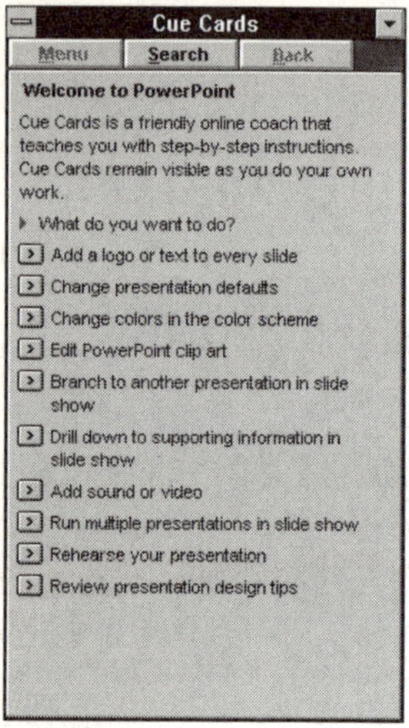

2.10.4 Tip of the Day

When you start up Word or PowerPoint, a small dialog window appears showing the tip of the day, useful snippets of information that help you to work more efficiently with the currently active application. If you wish, you can switch off this function by removing the cross next to the *Show Tips at Startup* check box.

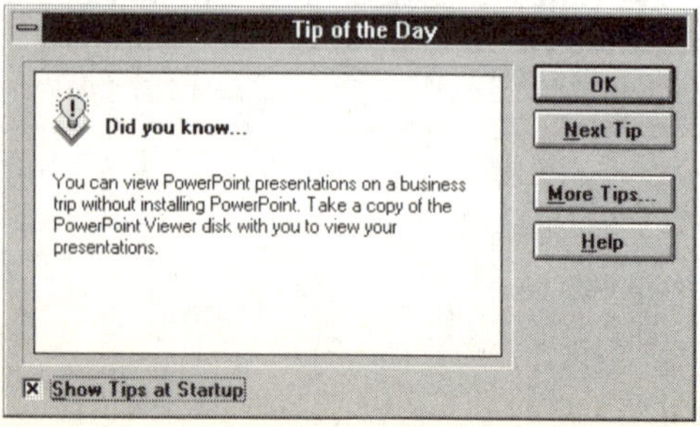

You can always select the *Tip of the Day* option from the *Help* menu later if you want to obtain a tip. You can then activate the *Show Tip at Startup* option again if you like.

Each time you start up the program, a new tip is shown. Click on the *Next Tip* button if you want to see the following tip. If you click on *More Tips*, you can click on an underlined topic to examine all the tips referring to that topic.

2.10.5 Tips in Excel

Tip-Wizard

Excel is also able to supply tips. If you click on the *TipWizard* button on the Standard toolbar, a useful tip appears under the Formatting toolbar. If a tip is available, the lightbulb is yellow.

The tips in Excel refer to the tasks on which you are currently working, and are thus context-oriented. During a session, a tip is only given once; the same tip is only displayed again in a subsequent session if you perform the corresponding action three times.

The tip is switched off when you click on the *TipWizard* button again.

2.10.6 The Help button

Help

If you wish to gain information about a certain element on the screen, click on the *Help* button on the Standard toolbar (or on another toolbar in Access if necessary). The mouse pointer changes into an arrow attached to a large black question mark. Place the mouse pointer on the element that you want to know more about and click on the left mouse button. A help screen then appears.

In this way you can request help about a toolbar button or a menu option by first clicking on the *Help* button and then on the toolbar button or the menu option (you can simply open a menu).

Click on the *Help* button to switch off the function once more.

If you double click on the *Help* button, the Help function search procedure is started up.

2.10.7 More about the Help function

An extensive Help function is available in all applications. It is always possible to consult this function when you are working. Most dialog windows also provide a *Help* button which opens a Help window with information about that specific dialog window. Accordingly, you can always obtain help if any task presents you with problems.

You can also obtain context-oriented help by pressing F1. In this way, you can gain help concerning an opened dialog window or marked menu option.

Microsoft Office

If you choose the *Help* option from the *Office* menu, which you open by clicking on the *Microsoft Office* button on the Microsoft Office Manager toolbar, a window appears containing information about Microsoft Office. (If this toolbar is not shown on your screen, double click on the Microsoft Office icon in the Microsoft Office group window.) You can click on the buttons or on the underlined topics to obtain more information about Microsoft Office or one of the applications.

The Help Contents

If you select the *Contents* option from the *Help* menu in one of the applications, the Contents window appears for that application.

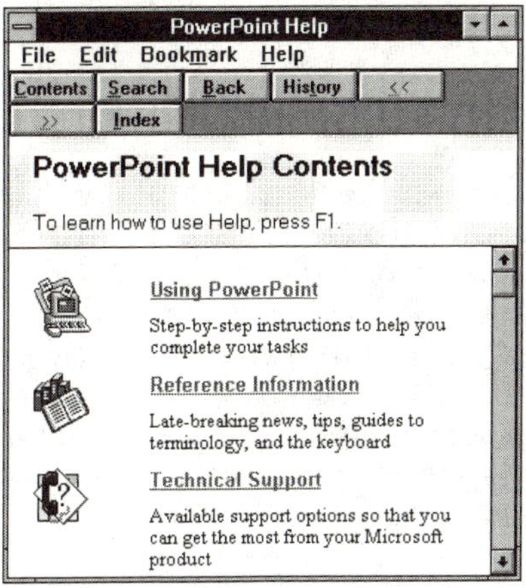

You can scroll down through the list until you encounter the required topic. You can move quickly to topics by clicking on the buttons in the dialog window or by clicking on the underlined references (in green). The mouse pointer changes into a hand when you place it on one of these screen elements. In general, clicking on topics which are fully underlined will lead to a dialog window containing more specific information. Topics underlined with a broken line lead to a window containing a definition of that topic.

Buttons are displayed at the top of each Help window. They provide the following functions:

- *Contents* displays the contents available.
- *Search* starts up the Search function so that you can search for a specific topic. You can also activate the

Search function by selecting the *Search for Help on* option in the *Help* menu of the application itself, or by double clicking on the *Help* button (with the question mark) on the toolbar of the application.
- *Back* returns you to the previously-consulted Help window.
- *History* opens a list of the Help topics you consulted since activating Help. You can select a topic from this list by double clicking on it.
- *Index* opens a list of the topics which are dealt with in the Help function. You can obtain more detailed information by clicking on a chosen topic. The index is ordered alphabetically. Two rows of buttons are displayed at the top of the window. If you click on one of these letter buttons, the Index window moves directly to the list of topics beginning with that letter. You can also open the Index window by selecting *Index* from the application *Help* menu.

If you request information about a specific procedure or topic, the relevant information appears in the Help window. If you want to have this information readily available, you can click on the *On Top* button (in Word and Excel) or otherwise open the *Help* menu in the Help window and select *Always on Top*. In that case, the Help window will be shown on the screen, independent of the currently active window, until you close the Help function. You can move the Help window by dragging the title bar.

Searching for a particular topic
When you wish to search for a particular topic, select *Search for Help on* from the *Help* menu. You can then type the name of the required topic in the upper text box, or select it from the list presented. As soon as you begin to type the name of the topic, a topic beginning with the same letter(s) is marked in the list.

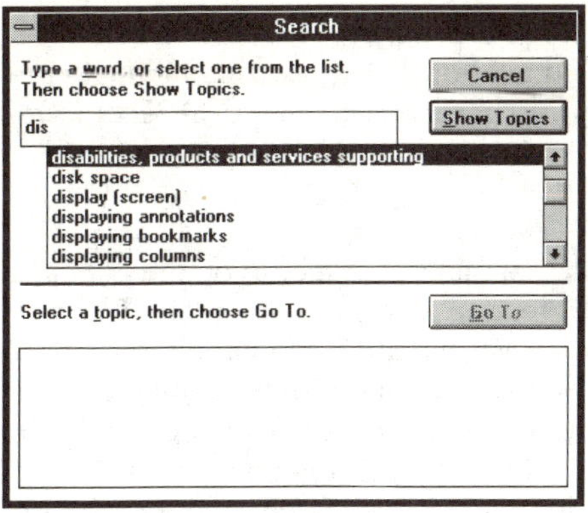

If the appropriate topic has been marked, click on the *Show Topics* button. A list of related topics is displayed in the lower section of the window. You can select one of these. If you type a word that is not included in the list, no related topics will appear.

Subsequently, click on the *Go To* button to obtain the desired information.

Technical Support
The *Technical Support* menu option is available in all Microsoft Office applications. This provides information about the support supplied by Microsoft, and a list of common questions about an application along with the solutions.

Information for users who switch over from another program
The *Help* menus also provide information for users who are used to working with other (similar) programs. Word provides information for those who are familiar with WordPerfect, and Excel provides information about Lotus 1-2-3. You can gain this information by selecting *Quick Preview* from the *Help* menu or by selecting the

option referring to the program in question (such as *WordPerfect Help* in Word). The Access manual contains information for users familiar with dBASE or Paradox for DOS.

About...
Each application contains the menu option *About...* (along with the corresponding program name). This provides information about the application and the licence. Activating the *System Info* button in the subsequent information window will produce data concerning your computer system. The Microsoft Office menu, activated by clicking on the button at the extreme right of the Microsoft Office toolbar, also provides information about your version of Microsoft Office.

2.11 Closing down applications

When you close down an application, all open files are closed. If documents and files which have not yet been saved in the current form are still open, you will be asked if you wish to save them.

All applications can be closed as follows:

- Double click on the Control menu button at the left-hand side of the application title bar
  or
- select the *Exit* command from the *File* menu
  or
- press the Alt+F4 key combination.

3 Working with Microsoft Word 6.0

In this chapter, we shall deal with Word 6.0, the Microsoft Office application for word processing. Word for Windows is, just like the other Microsoft Office applications, a graphic program, which means that the text comes out of the printer in exactly the same way as it appears on the screen. The display mode is referred to as WYSIWYG (What You See Is What You Get). You will discover that Word is very easy to operate and provides a large number of ingenious functions.

If you wish to find out more about the integration of Word documents in files that have been created in other applications, you can always consult the relevant sections in chapters 10 to 13. An overview of the utility programs within Word, such as Graph or ClipArt Gallery (*Insert* menu, *Object*) is presented in chapter 9.

3.1 New in version 6.0

If you are familiar with Word, but not with the most recent version (6.0), the following list will help to give an insight into the functions which are new:

- AutoCorrect: This function will automatically rectify common typing errors.
- AutoText: You can save a great deal of time by having Word automatically insert text that you frequently use.
- AutoFormat: Word automatically formats text by first analysing it and then applying styles to it.
- Shortcut menus: The shortcut menus contain options which are geared to the screen object which you click on using the right mouse button.

- Multiple Undo: You can undo up to 100 of the last commands given.
- Wizards: The Wizards enable you to give your documents a professional layout. Various Wizards are available for diverse types of document.
- New toolbars: There are various new toolbars and toolbar buttons that make it easier to create and modify your documents.
- Advanced cutting and pasting: When you cut and paste text, or drag-and-drop it, the spaces are automatically adjusted.
- Drag-and-drop: You can easily move or copy text or graphics to another window using this method.
- Format Painting: You can now copy a certain format to another object that you wish to format in the same way.
- Drawing: It is now easy to create drawings in your documents.
- Initial: You can format a paragraph by placing a large initial at the beginning.

3.2 Starting up Word

Microsoft Word

There are two ways of starting up Word: either double click on the *Microsoft Word* icon in the Microsoft Office group under Program Manager, or click on the *Microsoft Word* button on the Microsoft Office Manager toolbar at the top right-hand side of the screen.

Microsoft Word

Note
The toolbar in your version may be a little different to the one shown here. This depends on how the package has been installed. We presume that the Microsoft Office

package will be commonly used on offices where the computers are part of a network. In that case, the toolbar shown here will correspond to your network version. For more information about how to customise the toolbars, consult chapter 8.

Exercise

Start up Word if it is not yet running, and click on *OK* in the *Tip of the Day* window once you have read the information.

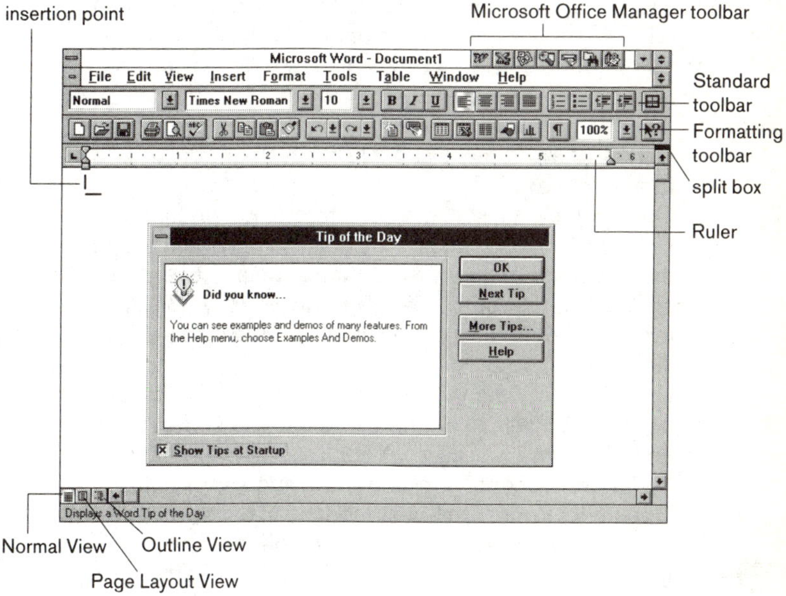

Normally, the Standard toolbar, the Formatting toolbar, the Ruler and the Microsoft Office Manager toolbar are displayed on the screen. Section 2.7 deals with how to display and hide toolbars. Chapter 8 informs you about displaying or hiding the Microsoft Office Manager toolbar. In this book, we shall discuss situations in which these three toolbars and the Ruler are always visible.

3.3 Document displays

A document can be displayed in various forms in Word: in the Normal View, the Page Layout View, the Outline View, the Master Document view and the Print Preview. In addition, it is possible to display the document alone on the screen without toolbars, Ruler and other screen elements (Full Screen).

You select a different type of display from the *View* menu or by clicking on one of the buttons on the horizontal scroll bar. The dot shown in front of the menu option in the *View* menu indicates which display mode is currently active.

- Normal View is most suitable for typing, editing and formatting text.
- Outline View is suitable for structuring documents. For instance, you can specify that you only wish to see the headings so that the document seems to be folded, as it were. You can easily move or copy text, or alter the heading level, from Heading 1 to Heading 2 for instance.
- Page Layout View is very suitable for rearranging the page layout before printing. The page is shown in exactly the same way as it will come out of the printer.
- If you are working with large documents, the Master Document View is the best mode; you can then split a document into several sections and files.

Full Screen

- If you want to use the entire screen for working on your text, select the Full Screen mode. In this mode, the menus and toolbars are not shown, although you can still work with shortcut menus and shortcut keys. When this type of display has been activated, the *Full Screen* button appears in the corner of your screen. Clicking on this button will activate the previous display mode; you can also press Esc to obtain the same result.

- The Print Preview shows the pages reduced in size on the screen. You can then get a good idea of how the layout of the document will be when printed. Switch to one of the other modes to make any changes before printing.

Zoom Control

- In all the display modes except Full Screen, you can activate the *Zoom Control* button to enlarge or reduce the text display on the screen. If you select the *Page Width* option from the drop-down list, the text is adjusted to fit the screen exactly.

It is also possible to display documents in the split-screen mode. This method can be very convenient if you want to refer to different parts of the same document. To activate this mode, open the *Window* menu and select *Split*. Then click on the position where you wish to split the document, or double click on the split box to divide the window into two equal sections. You can also drag the split box to the required splitting position on the screen.

To remove this division, open the *Window* menu again and select *Remove Split*, or double click on the split box.

3.4 Creating documents

New

If you have just started up Word and have not yet begun working, you will have an empty document window on the screen with the temporary working name 'Document1'. It is possible to have several documents open simultaneously in Word. If a document has already been opened and you wish to create a new document, click on the *New* button on the Standard toolbar, or select *New* from the *File* menu.

When you start on a new document, it will be based on the document template NORMAL.DOT. This provides the basic style of the document, with default settings for the font, font size, tabstops etc. If you wish to use a different template or a Wizard to create a document with a special layout (invoices for example), select the *New* option from the *File* menu. In that case, the *New* dialog window is opened in which you can select a template or Wizard to meet your requirements. The new document is based on the chosen style.

Section 3.6 deals with templates in more detail.

A new, empty document which has not yet been saved always has the name 'Document' followed by a number indicating the amount of new documents you have created during the current work session.

3.4.1 Typing text

The insertion point, the flashing vertical stripe, shows the position at which the typed text will appear. While you type, the text will be automatically wrapped to the next line once you have reached the right margin of the page. You should only press Enter when you wish to begin a new paragraph.

Show/ Hide ¶

The *Show/Hide ¶* button determines the display of the so-called nonprinting characters. One of these characters is the paragraph marking (HardReturn) character (¶) which appears when you press Enter. Spaces are indicated by a dot.

Exercise
Ensure that a new empty document window has been activated and type the following text:

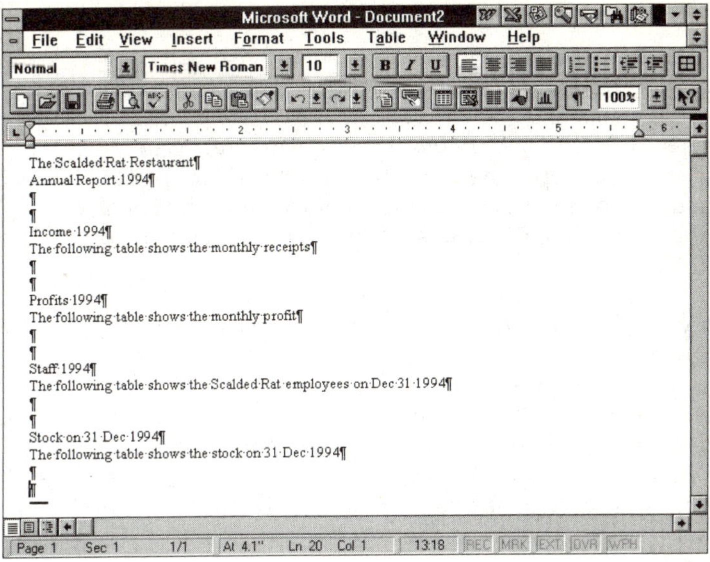

3.4.2 Moving within a document

The insertion point, the flashing vertical stripe, indicates where your text will appear. You can move the position of the text, *in relation to the document window*, by activating the scroll bars. The insertion point, however, remains at the same position.

You can move the insertion point to a new position by placing the mouse pointer at the required position and clicking on the left button. Move the text through the window using the scroll bars to the new position if necessary. In the text area, the mouse pointer assumes the shape of a capital I (sometimes referred to as the I-beam). You can also use the cursor keys on the keyboard to move the insertion point; this is often more convenient if the distance is small.

Tip
It is often quicker and easier to move the insertion point by means of the keyboard. To obtain a list of keys and key combinations you can use, open the *Help* menu and select *Search for Help on*. Type *moving through documents* in the upper text box, click on the *Show Topics* button and select *Using shortcut keys to move through a document* from the lower section. Then click on the *Go To* button.

If you wish to insert text in existing text, place the insertion point at the required position and type the text. The existing text then shifts to the right as you type. You can also activate the overtype mode by pressing the Ins key or by double clicking on the OVR box on the status bar. When you now type, the new text is written over the existing text. Pressing Ins or double clicking on the OVR box will switch you back to the Insert mode in which you were working.

If you wish to remove a character, press the Backspace key if the insertion point is immediately behind (to the right of) the character to be replaced, or on the Del key if the insertion point is immediately in front (to the left of) the character in question.

3.4.3 Marking text and graphics

Prior to moving, removing or formatting existing text or graphics, you have to mark them (also know as 'selecting'). When these kinds of items on the screen have been marked, they are shown in inverse video display. You can cancel a selection by pressing one of the cursor keys or by clicking on the screen anywhere outside the selection.

It is easy to mark text by simply dragging the mouse pointer across the required passage. If you mark a part of a word and extend the marking to cover a part of the next word, both words are automatically marked, along with the space behind the words. This ensures that parts of words are not amputated and thus only partly edited. You can deactivate this function by opening the *Tools* menu, selecting *Options*, clicking on the *Edit* Tab sheet and removing the cross in the *Automatic Word Selection* check box.
If you want to retain this feature but sometimes only wish to mark parts of words, place the insertion point at the required position and mark the letters by pressing and holding down the Shift key and pressing the cursor key(s).

To the left of the text there is an 'invisible' selection area. You can make use of this area to mark text with the mouse. When you move into this selection 'bar', the mouse pointer assumes the shape of an arrow pointing upwards to the right.

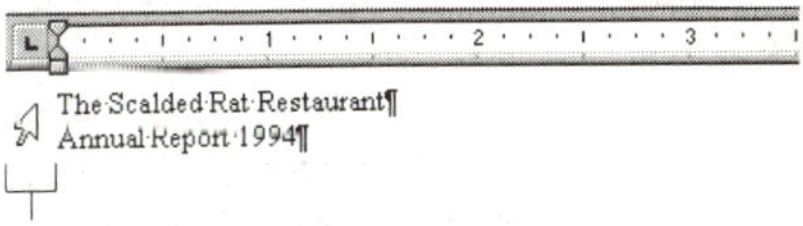

selection bar

When using the mouse to mark text or other screen items, the following actions are possible:

selection	**action**
Text fragment or other item	Drag the mouse pointer across the text or item
Word	Double click on the word
Graphic image	Click on the image

Line of text	Click on the selection bar to the left of the line
Several lines of text	Drag the mouse pointer down over the selection bar
Sentence	Hold down Ctrl and click anywhere in the sentence
Paragraph	Double click on the selection bar or click thrice in the paragraph
Document	Click thrice on the selection bar
Vertical text block	Hold down Alt and drag the mouse pointer down over the block
Passage of text	Place the insertion point at the beginning, hold down Shift and click on the end

Tip

As mentioned, the keyboard is often more convenient for marking text or graphics. If you wish to gain a summary of the key possibilities, open the *Help* menu, choose *Search for Help on*, type **selecting text and graphics** in the upper text box, click on *Show Topics* and click on the *Selecting text and graphics by using the keyboard.* Activate the *Go To* button.

You can also press F8 or double click on the EXT box on the status bar to activate the Extend mode which enables you to increase or decrease the selection by means of the cursor keys. In addition, the F8 key provides the following features:

selection	**key**
Current word	2 x F8
Current sentence	3 x F8
Current paragraph	4 x F8
Entire document	5 x F8

3.4.4 Removing and replacing text

You can remove text or other items by first marking them and then pressing Backspace or Del or by choosing *Clear* from the *Edit* menu. The word to the left of the current insertion point can be removed by pressing Ctrl+ Backspace, and the word to the right of the insertion point can be removed by pressing Ctrl+Del.

Cut

You can also remove marked text by clicking on the *Cut* button on the Standard toolbar or by selecting *Cut* from the *Edit* menu. The selected text is then stored on the Clipboard where it is kept until you add other items to the Clipboard or until you close Windows.

Exercise

Remove the last two sections from our practice text by first marking them and then pressing Backspace.

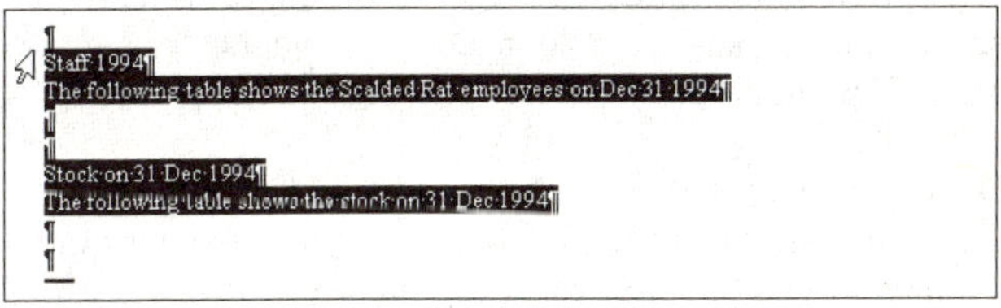

Mark the text

Remove more pieces of text from the example just for practice.

Now undo these actions by clicking on the arrow pointing downwards to the right of the *Undo* button on the Standard toolbar. Then drag the mouse pointer across the deletion commands ('clear').

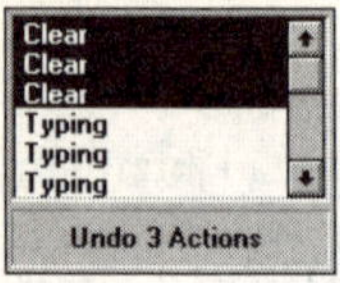

You can replace marked text immediately by typing new text. The marked text disappears directly. You can switch off this function if you wish by opening the *Tools* menu, selecting *Options* and placing a cross in the check box next to *Typing Replaces Selection* on the *Edit* Tab sheet.

3.4.5 Moving and copying text

There are various methods of moving and copying marked text. Moving means that the marked text is moved to a different position and is removed from the original position. Copying means that the text remains at its original position while a copy is placed at a new, specified position.

Drag-and-drop

The drag-and-drop method is a quick and easy method of moving or copying text to a position nearby the original position of the text. It is also possible to make use of this method of you wish to move or copy text or graphics from one document to another. In that case, the best thing to do is to divide the screen window display by selecting *Arrange All* from the *Window* menu when you have opened both documents (*File, Open*).

To move text, mark it, place the mouse pointer on it and drag the small broken frame to the new position.
If you wish to copy text, hold down the Ctrl key while performing the dragging action.

A broken vertical stripe indicates the new insertion point.

Exercise

We shall move the penultimate section of text in our practice document. This is done by marking the text and the two blank lines above it and placing them in the empty space under 'Annual Report'. Use the drag-and-drop method for this.

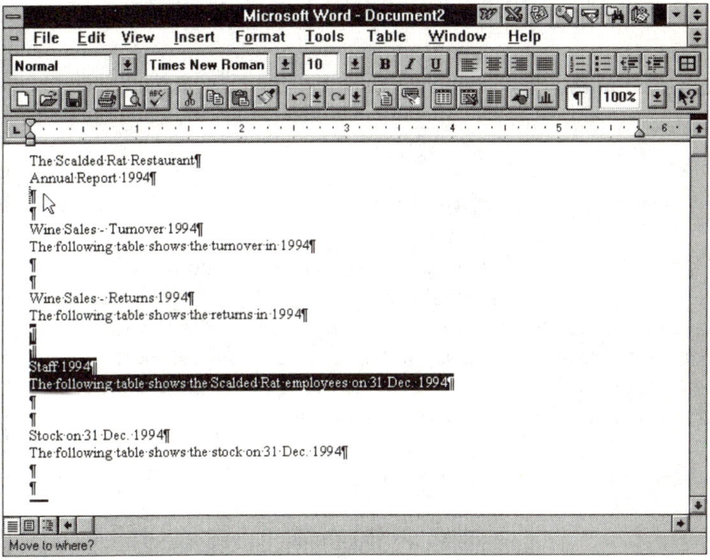

Drag the marked text to the new position

Cutting and pasting

Cut

Another way of moving text is to mark it and then click on the *Cut* button on the Standard toolbar, or select the *Cut* option from the *Edit* menu. You can also use the shortcut keys Ctrl+X or Shift+Del.

Copy

If you wish to copy text, mark it and click on the *Copy* button or select the *Copy* command from the *Edit* menu. You can also press Ctrl+C.

This action stores the selected section on the Clipboard which is a temporary storage area. The contents of the Clipboard are only replaced when you allocate new text or graphics by means of the *Cut* and *Copy* commands.

Paste

Subsequently, place the insertion point at the position where the new text or image is to be situated and click on the *Paste* button, or select the *Paste* command from the *Edit* menu. You can also use the key combinations Ctrl+V or Shift+Ins.

3.4.6 Inserting special characters

When working in Word, you can easily insert letters with accents and other special characters, signs or symbols into your text. To type the **é** for example, press the key for the apostrophe (') and then press the **e**. The following list provides a summary of special characters along with the key combinations used to produce them:

character	**key combination**
à, è, ì, ò, ù	` (accent grave), *letter*
á, é, í, ó, ú, ý	' (apostrophe), *letter*
â, ê, î, ô, û	^, *letter*

You can also use the *Symbol* option from the *Insert* menu to place special symbols in the document. When you select this option, the following dialog window appears:

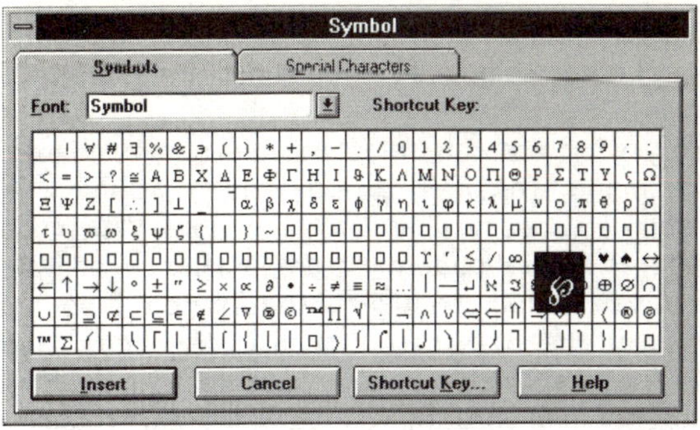

By clicking on the arrow pointing downwards behind the Font box, you can select one of the font types available. Then click on the required character or symbol shown in the grid. The symbol is then displayed a little larger, as shown in the figure above. A list of special characters is shown on the *Special Characters* Tab sheet.

If you click on the *Insert* button in this dialog box, the marked character will be inserted into your document at the current insertion point. Clicking on *Cancel* closes the dialog window.

You can also type special characters by typing their character codes. This is done by switching on the NumLock key, holding down the Alt key, typing a zero on the numeric keypad at the right of the keyboard, followed by the code for the character. A list of the more common letter codes is given in Appendix A at the end of this book (and also in the Word manual).

3.4.7 Find and Replace

The Find and Replace function can prove to be very useful. You can quickly find text, formatting features, special characters and other document components without having to perform a laborious search; you can then replace any of these elements automatically if required.

If you only wish to search, select the *Find* command from the *Edit* menu. The *Find* dialog window appears, in which you can specify what is to be sought. When you have entered the text pattern you are looking for, activate the *Find Next* button. If you want to replace the sought text, click on the *Replace* button. The *Replace* dialog window appears. The text pattern you entered in the Find What text box in the previous dialog window are retained here. You can then specify the characters or other elements which are to replace the sought text pattern. You can also open the *Replace* dialog window by selecting that menu option from the *Edit* menu.

3.5 Saving, closing and opening a document

If you wish to save a document for future use, you will have to store it on disk. When you have done so, you can safely close it if you do not want to continue working with it. You can also leave it open for the time being, since it is possible to have several documents open simultaneously in Word.

3.5.1 Saving a document

Save

If you wish to save a document to disk, click on the *Save* button on the Standard toolbar, or select the *Save* command from the *File* menu. If you have not saved the document previously, the *Save As* dialog window will appear.

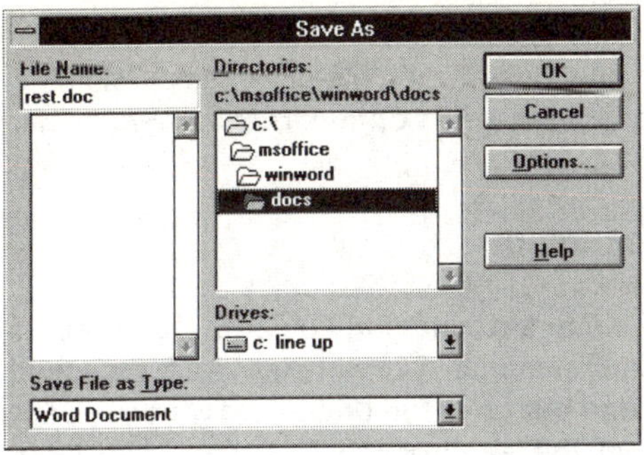

Enter the name of the file in the *File Name* box. Select the directory in which the file is to be saved from the *Directories* list. (We have created the *Docs* directory as a subdirectory of the *Winword* directory for our documents, by switching to the File Manager application in the *Main* window under the Program Manager and selecting *Create Directory* from the *File* menu there. You can specify your own preferred storage location.)
Select the appropriate drive from the *Drives* section, and if you wish to save the file as a normal Word document, select this option from the *Save File as Type* section. The file name is then automatically allocated the .DOC extension.

The *Summary Info* box appears when you click on *OK*. Here you can specify a description of the contents of the file. Click on *OK* to quit this window.

Exercise
Save the Word document that you created in this chapter. Assign it the name REST.DOC and store it in a directory of your choice.

If you have saved a file previously, you can save the most recent version by clicking on the *Save* button. It is saved directly, under the same name in the same directory. In this case, the *Save As* dialog box does not appear. If you wish to save a previously saved file under a new name or directory, select the *Save As* option from the *File* menu.

3.5.2 Closing a document

If you wish to close a document, select the *Close* command from the *File* menu. You can also double click on the Control menu button of the document window, or select *Close* from the Control menu. If you have made modifications to the document since you last saved it, you will be asked if you want to save the changes.

3.5.3 Opening a document

Open

To open a document, click on the *Open* button on the Standard toolbar, or select *Open* from the *File* menu. The *Open* dialog window then appears.

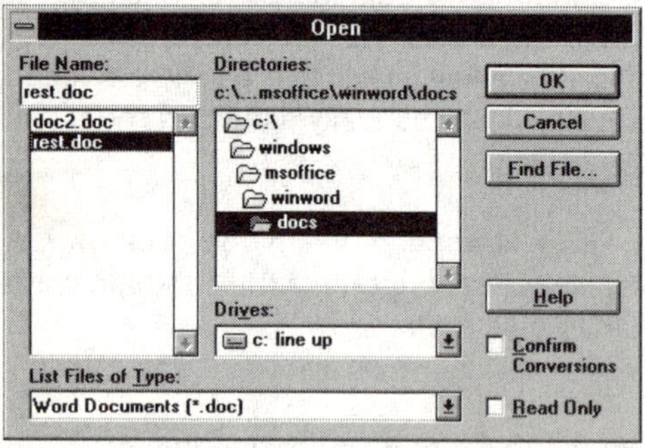

Click on the *Directories* list until you have opened the directory in which the required file is stored. The file will then appear in the *File* list. If it is not already shown in the *File Name* box, click on it and then on *OK*. You can also use the *Find File* button to find a file if you are no longer sure where it is stored. In this dialog window, you can specify various search criteria such as *Include Subdirectories* if you no longer know exactly in which directory the file is to be found. You can also make use of the so-called ‘wildcards’, * and **?** to represent letters if you cannot remember the precise file name.

3.6 Document templates

New

A document is always based on a document template or a Wizard. Normally, each new document in Word is based on the NORMAL.DOT template, and this is also the case if you create a new document by clicking on the *New* button on the Standard toolbar.

As mentioned, a template is the basis of the document. Each template provides default settings for the font, font size, tabstops etc. There are templates available for invoices, address lists, letters and so on. If you want to base a new document on a special template or if you want to use a Wizard to create a special type of document, select *New* from the *File* menu to open the *New* dialog window.

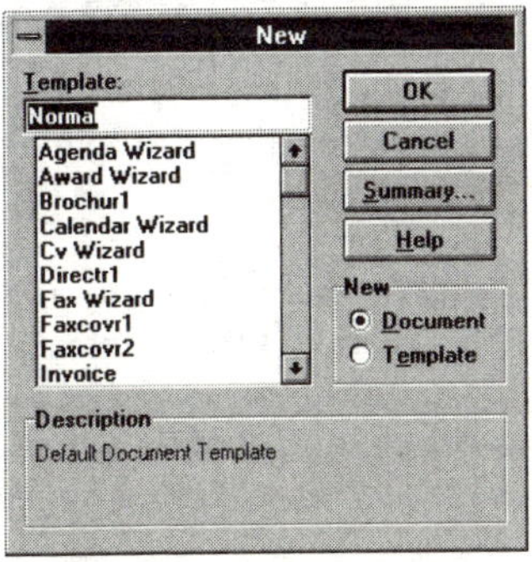

You can select a template or Wizard from the *Template* list. The *Description* section at the bottom of the window provides a description of the marked template or Wizard. If you wish to create a new document based on the marked template or Wizard, select *Document* from the *New* section in the window; if you wish to create a new template, click on the appropriate option button.

In addition to text, graphics and formatting features, a template can also contain styles, macros and text fragments. If you create or alter styles, macros or text fragments, these modifications are always saved in the template on which the document is based. If you wish to copy elements from one template to another, select *Templates* from the *File* menu and activate the *Organiser* button in the *Templates and Add-Ins* dialog window. In the subsequent *Organiser* window, you can copy elements from one template to another and also remove elements from a template.

3.7 Styles

If you begin a new document based on the NORMAL.DOT template, the text you type is formed according to the settings of the Normal style. In fact, a style is a collection of formatting features which have been saved under a certain name in a template. New text is automatically allocated the Normal style.

In Word, there are a number of character and paragraph styles which can be applied to a marked text. Automatic formatting can be imposed on a text in this way. For instance, you can format headings by means of the Heading 1 to Heading 9 styles.

You can adapt styles to your own requirements and you can also create your own styles. The modifications are stored in the template on which the currently active document is based.

You can select a style from the *Style* list on the Standard toolbar and apply it to a text. If you want to apply a paragraph style (shown in boldface in the list) to one paragraph, place the insertion point at the beginning of that paragraph and then select the style from the list. If you wish to apply a character style (not in boldface) select the text to which the style is to apply and then select the style from the list.

Style

When you open this list, a number of standard, frequently-used styles appear, along with the styles which have been used, created or modified in the currently active document. If you hold down the Shift key when you open the list, all available styles are displayed.

3.8 Character formatting

If you wish to assign certain formatting features to characters, first select the characters and then select the required features. You can use the Formatting toolbar, the shortcut keys or the *Font* option from the *Format* menu to do this. You can also choose a character style from the *Style* list on the Formatting toolbar.

Tip
To obtain a list of shortcut keys for character formatting, select *Search for Help on* from the *Help* menu. Type **character formatting** in the upper text box in the *Search* dialog window, click on *Show Topics*, select *Using shortcut keys to format characters* from the lower box and click on the *Go To* button.

If you select a formatting command without first selecting text, formatting features are applied to all subsequently typed text. This formatting will apply until you specify otherwise.

Help

Tip
You can always request a brief description of the formatting features which have been applied or still apply to the text. This is done by clicking on the *Help* button on the Standard toolbar and then on the text you wish to check.

3.8.1 The Formatting toolbar

You can use the buttons on the Formatting toolbar to format characters as well as complete paragraphs (see section 3.9). The buttons on this toolbar have the following functions:

button/name	**function**
 Style	Opens the *Style* list from which you can select a style for application or modification
 Font	Opens the *Font* list from which you can select a font for new text or for selected text to be modified
 Font Size	Opens the *Font Size* list to specify the size of new text of selected text to be modified
 Bold	Places new and selected text in boldface
 Italic	Places new and selected text in italics
 Underline	Underlines new or selected text
 Align Left	Left-aligns a paragraph

Center	Centres a paragraph
Align Right	Right-aligns a paragraph
Justify	Justifies text in a paragraph
Numbering	Creates a list with numbering (to emphasise items)
Bullets	Creates a list with bullets (to emphasise items)
Decrease Indent	Decreases the indent distance by one tabstop
Increase Indent	Increases the indent distance by one tabstop
Borders	Displays the Borders toolbar

Exercise

We shall format the REST.DOC document by applying special character formatting features.

Procedure:

1 Select the first line 'The Scalded Rat Restaurant' by clicking on the selection area to the left of it.

2 Open the *Font* list on the Formatting toolbar and select the Arial font from the list. The selected text is then displayed in this font.

Times New Roman

Font

10

Font Size

3 If the first line is still selected, open the *Font Size* list and select size 14. The first line is then displayed in this size.

Bold

4 Select the words 'The Scalded Rat' and click on the *Bold* button on the Formatting toolbar to place these words in boldface.

Italic

5 While the words 'The Scalded Rat' are still selected, click on the *Italic* button on the Formatting toolbar to place these words in italics.

3.8.2 Copying the format

Word provides the *Format Painter* function which makes it possible to copy formatting features quickly and easily from one section of text to another.

Exercise

We shall now copy the formatting features we applied to the word 'Restaurant' on the first line, to the words 'Annual Report 1994' on the second line.

Procedure:

1 Select the word 'Restaurant'.

Format Painter

2 Click on the *Format Painter* button on the Standard toolbar.

When you move the mouse pointer to the text area, it takes on the shape of a paintbrush.

3 Select the text 'Annual Report 1994'. This text is now formatted in the Arial font with font size 14.

3.8.3 The Font dialog window

The *Font* dialog window, which you open by selecting *Font* from the *Format* menu, provides many character formatting features.

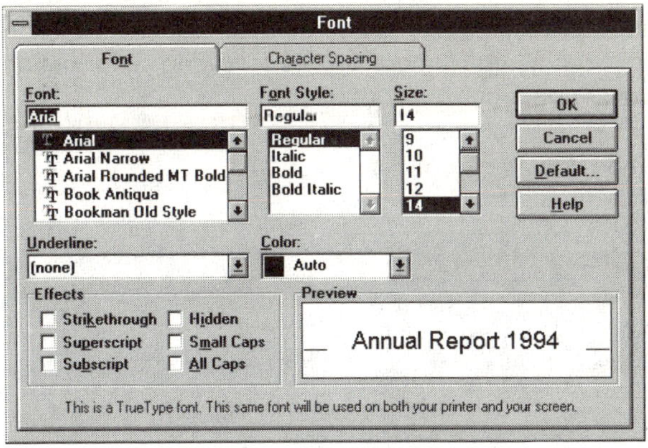

Exercise

We shall now alter the format of the text 'Annual Report 1994' by means of options in the *Font* dialog window.

Procedure:

1 Select the text 'Annual Report 1994'.
2 Open the *Format* menu and select *Font*.
3 Select *Century Schoolbook* from the Font list.
4 Select *12* from the *Size* list.
5 Open the *Underline* list and select *Words Only*.
6 Click on *OK*.

The document now looks like this (when the nonprinting characters are not displayed):

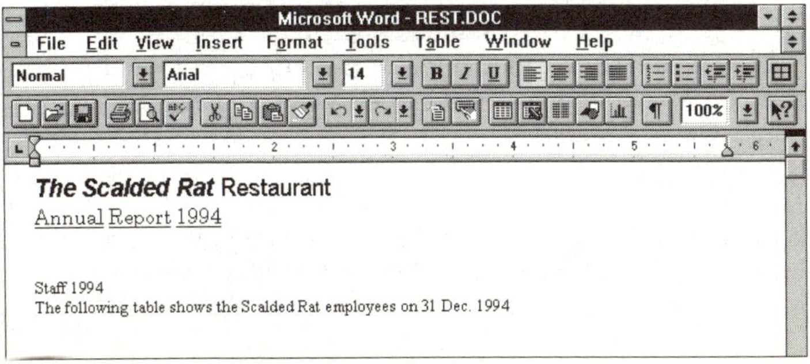

If you use the *Help* indicator button to examine the character formatting features, the following information should appear on your screen:

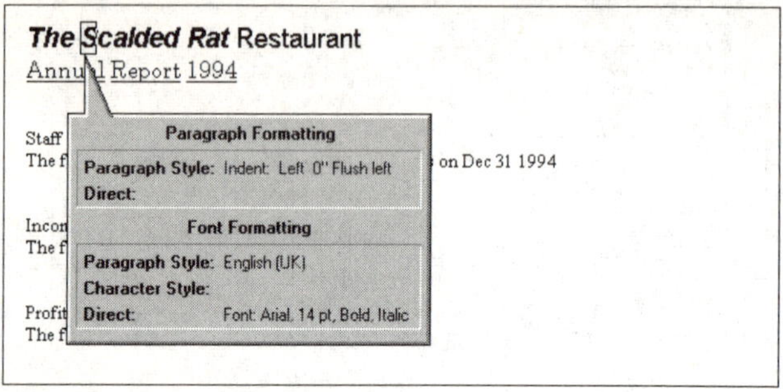

3.9 Paragraph formatting

You can format paragraphs by selecting them and then making use of the facilities available on the Formatting toolbar, the shortcut keys for formatting, the Ruler or the *Paragraph* option from the *Format* menu. If you alter the paragraph formatting, the modifications apply to the entire paragraph and not just to words or characters. If you wish to alter the format of only one paragraph, you do not need to select it first, you only need to place the insertion point in the appropriate paragraph.

Paragraph formatting can apply to text alignment, line spacing, tabstops, the distance between paragraphs, indentation, bullets or numbering or placing borders and shading around the text. You can also have a paragraph begin with a large capital.

Tip
If you wish to obtain a list of shortcut keys for paragraph formatting, select *Search for Help on* from the *Help* menu, type **paragraph formatting** in the upper text box, ac-

tivate the *Show Topics* button and select **Using short-cut keys to format paragraphs** from the lower section and then click on *Go To*.

Note

A paragraph mark not only indicates the end of a paragraph, it also contains all the formatting features you applied to the paragraph. When you delete a paragraph mark, you also delete all the formatting features you applied to the paragraph. The paragraph is then assigned the formatting features of the previous paragraph.

Exercise

Centre the title of the document and the text immediately underneath. Apply the Heading 3 style to the texts 'Staff 1994', 'Wine Sales - Turnover 1994', 'Wine Sales - Returns 1994' and 'Stock on 31 Dec. 1994'.

Procedure:

Center

1 Select the first two lines and click on the *Center* button on the Formatting toolbar to place them in the middle of the line

Align Left

Normally the text is left-aligned in Word. This is indicated by the fact that if you place the insertion point on a text which has not been altered, the *Align Left* button on the Formatting toolbar is shown as 'active' (light grey).

2 Select the text 'Staff 1994'.
3 Open the *Style* list on the Formatting toolbar and select Heading 3.
4 The text is still selected. Double click on the *Format Painter* button on the Standard toolbar and then select the headings 'Wine Sales - Turnover 1994', 'Wine Sales - Returns 1994' and 'Stock on 31 Dec. 1994'.
5 Click on the *Format Painter* button to deactivate it.

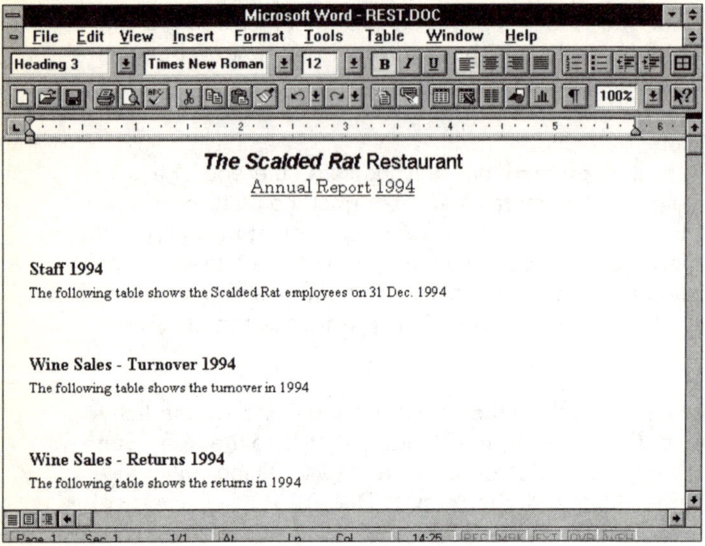

Exercise

Create a new list with items in a numbered list.

Procedure:

1 Move the insertion point to the beginning of the empty line under 'The following table shows the Scalded Rat employees...'.

2 Press Enter twice to create a blank line and type the text as shown in the figure overleaf:

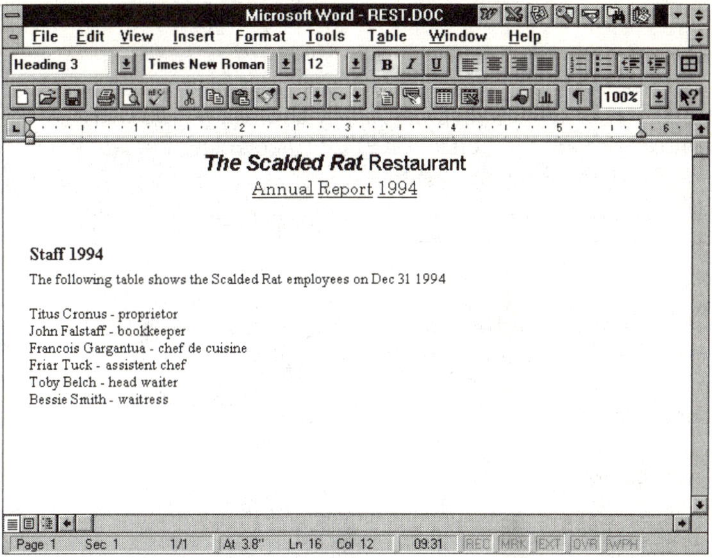

Numbering

3 Format the text as a numbered list by selecting the entire list and then clicking on the *Numbering* button on the Formatting toolbar.

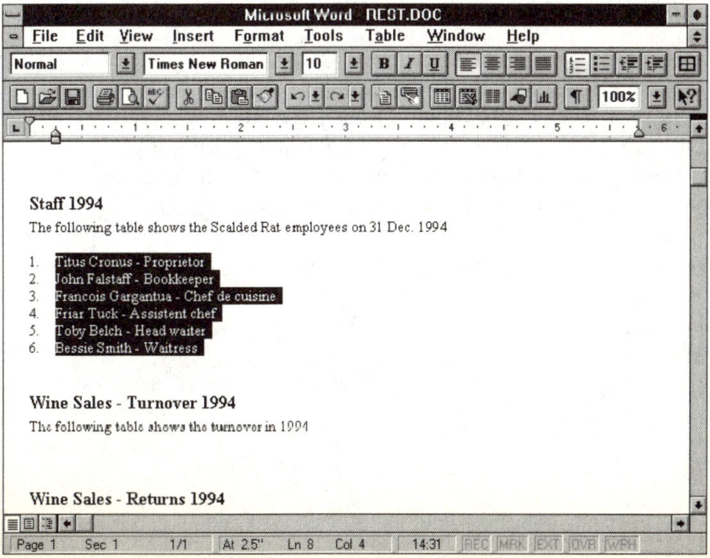

3.9.1 The Ruler

You can use the Ruler to alter the paragraph indentation and to specify the tabstops quickly and easily. You can display or hide the horizontal Ruler by selecting the *Ruler* command from the *View* menu.

To indent selected paragraphs, drag the following elements on the Ruler to the required position:

indentation	**element**
indent the first line	
indent from the left margin	
indent first line from the left margin	
indent from right margin	

Tab Alignment

The *Tab Alignment* button is situated at the left left-hand side of the Ruler. If you wish to use the Ruler to place a tabstop, click on the *Tab Alignment* button until the required alignment appears. Then click on the position on the Ruler where you wish the tabstop to be placed.

type of tab alignment	**symbol**
left alignment	
centred	
right alignment	
decimal tab	

To remove a tabstop, simply drag it from the Ruler.

You can also select the *Tabs* option from the *Format* menu to specify tabstops.

3.10 Page setup

In general, it is advisable to activate the settings for the page layout when you begin a new document. Then you can specify the paper size, the print orientation, headers, footers etc. straight away. These settings can also be modified later if required. They can apply to the entire document or to a specific section if you divide the document into sections.

The page layout can be specified in the *Page Setup* dialog window which is opened by selecting the option of the same name from the *File* menu. You can specify the section of the document to which the settings are to apply (*Apply To*). This dialog window provides Tab sheets for determining the margins, the paper size, paper source and the page layout.

3.10.1 Specifying the margins using the Rulers

You can also alter the page margins by means of the Rulers. To do this, activate the Page Layout View or the Print Preview and drag the margin boundaries on the horizontal and/or vertical Ruler.

Page Layout

Print Preview

You can activate the Page Layout View by clicking on the *Page Layout View* button on the horizontal scroll bar, or by selecting the *Page Layout* option from the *View* menu. The Print Preview is activated by clicking on the *Print Preview* button on the Standard toolbar, or by selecting *Print Preview* from the *File* menu.

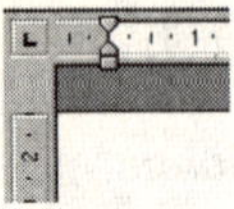

Drag the margin boundaries

The margin boundaries are represented by the small stripes between the existing margins (the grey area on the Ruler) and the actual text area of the page (the white part of the Ruler). When you place the mouse pointer on these stripes, a two-headed arrow appears. You can then drag the margin in the desired direction.

3.10.2 Headers and footers

Headers and footers are printed at the top and bottom, respectively, of each page. Page numbers can also be included in the header or footer. If you wish to place a header or footer in your document, select *Header and Footer* from the *View* menu.

Note
You can also insert page numbers in a document by means of the *Page Numbers* option from the *Insert* menu.

Exercise
We shall create a header in the REST.DOC document.

Procedure:

1 Open the *View* menu and select *Header and Footer*.

A header window appears, the Page Layout View is automatically activated, and the Header and Footer toolbar is opened.

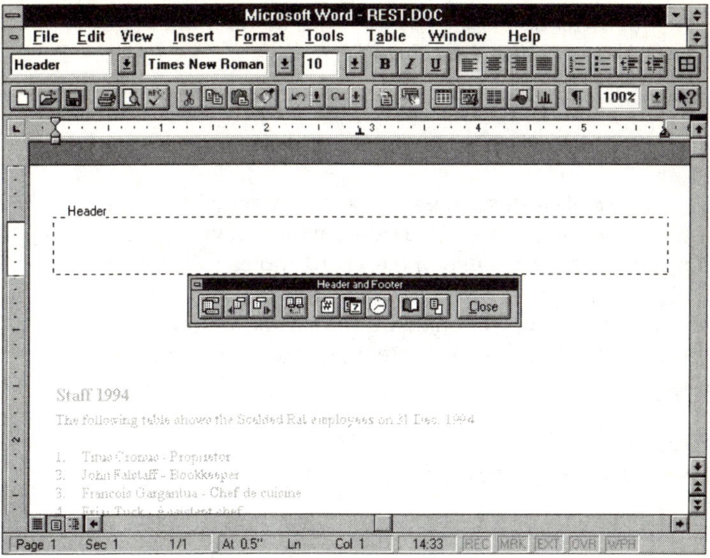

Switch Between Header and Footer

2 Click on the *Switch Between Header and Footer* button on the Header and Footer toolbar in order to activate the footer.

3 Ensure that the insertion point is flashing in the upper left hand corner of the footer box and type **Annual Report 1994 - Page** and type a space behind the word 'Page'.

Page Numbers

4 Click on the *Page Numbers* button on the Header and Footer toolbar to insert the current page number.

Align Right

5 Click on the *Align Right* button on the Formatting toolbar to right-align the text.

6 Mark the entire footer including the page number and click on the *Bold* button on the Formatting toolbar.

Bold

7 Click on the *Close* button on the Header and Footer toolbar to close the toolbar.

The footer will be displayed when you activate the Page Layout View and the Print Preview.

3.11 Working with tables

You can easily insert tables into a document when working in Word. If you wish to divide data into rows and columns, you can make use of the Word Tables function. In that case, you do not need to press the Tab key to divide text into columns; you can type the text and modify it in the cells displayed on the screen, just as you would normally do.

Exercise
Create a table in a new document.

Procedure:
1 Click on the *New* button on the Standard toolbar to open a new document.
2 Type the text **Plans for 1995**, press Enter twice and type the text: **In 1995 we shall provide the following facilities:**
3 Select the text 'Plans for 1995' and open the list of Styles by clicking on the drop-down list arrow on the Formatting toolbar. Select *Heading 3* from the list to format the text in this style.
4 Press Enter twice.
5 Click on the *Insert Table* button on the Standard toolbar.

This opens a grid over which you can drag the mouse to specify the number of rows and columns in the table to be inserted.

6 Drag the mouse across the grid until '5 x 6 Table' is shown under the grid.

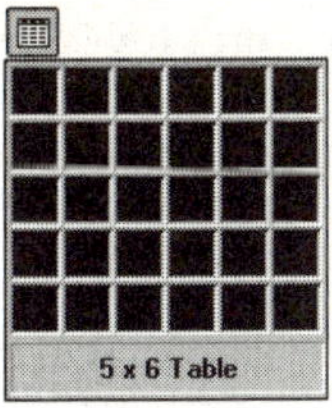

A new empty table will appear on the screen.

7 Type the following data in the table; you can move from cell to cell by pressing Tab. When you reach the last cell with the last name, press Tab to create a new line with the same layout. If you press Tab at the end of this line, you can create a seventh line.

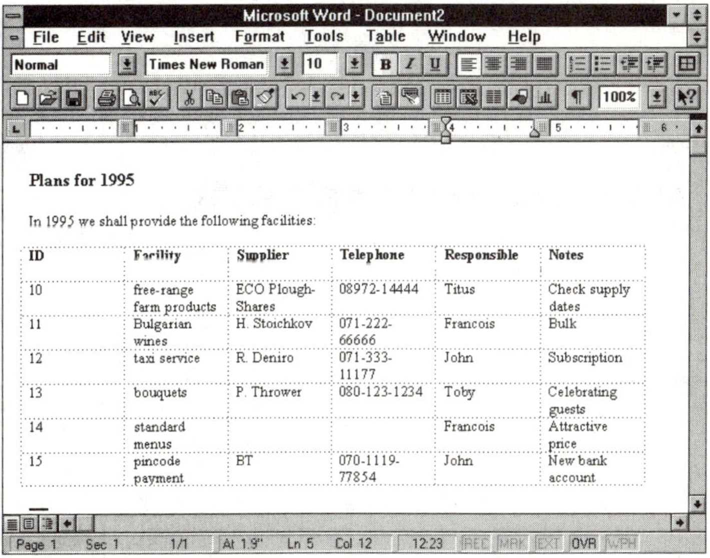

8 Select the first row, the headings, by placing the mouse pointer in the selection area to the left of the text and clicking.

9 Click on the *Bold* button on the Formatting toolbar to convert the marked text to bold.

10 Click on the *Save* button on the Standard toolbar to save the new document as NEWFAC.DOC.

3.12 Checking the documents

Word provides functions to check various aspects of your documents, such as the spelling check.

3.12.1 Spelling check

Spelling

To check the spelling in your document, click on the *Spelling* button on the Standard toolbar, or select *Spelling* from the *Tools* menu.

If Word encounters a word which does not exist in its own internal dictionary, the *Spelling* dialog window will appear.

The *Suggestions* section provides a number of suggestions for the highlighted word. You can accept one of these if the original word is misspelled and the correct version is shown. You can click on the relevant word and then activate the *Change* button. You can also type the correct word in the *Change To* box yourself.

Sometimes the word is correct even although it is not contained in the Word dictionary. In that case, you should click on the *Ignore* button. If the same word occurs several times in the text, it will be highlighted each time. If you wish to ignore the word during the rest of the spelling check, click on the *Ignore All* button.

If you wish to add a word to the your personal dictionary consisting of the words in the Word dictionary and your own additions, select the *Add* button. They are added to the CUSTOM.DIC file. If you wish to add a word and then correction to the AutoCorrect list click on the *AutoCorrect* button.

The *Undo Last* button will undo the last change.

3.12.2 AutoCorrect

The AutoCorrect function is one of the new functions provided by Word 6. This function automatically replaces misspelled or abbreviated words with the correct versions.

Exercise
We shall add a number of common typing errors to the AutoCorrect list so that they can be rectified automatically while we are working.

Procedure:

1 Open the REST.DOC if necessary and select *AutoCorrect* from the *Tools* menu. You will see that a number of common typing errors have already been included in the list.
2 Activate the *Replace Text as You Type* check box if necessary.
3 Type the word **empl** in the *Replace* text box and type the word **employee** in the *With* box.

This means that if you now wish to enter the word 'employee' you only have to type the first four letters ('empl'). This will help alleviate the typework. You can of course specify other words or abbreviations which refer more closely to your own situation. It is easy, for example, to type PVC as an abbreviation of Polyvinylchloride or ManU for Manchester United.

4 Select the *Add* button.
5 Type other abbreviations and words which you tend to misspell, along with the rectified versions; click on *Add*.
6 Click on *OK*.

Just to try this out, type the word **empl**. You will see that the word is immediately changed to 'employee'. Remove it from the text again.

Tip
You can also use the AutoCorrect function to insert large sections of text or complete graphics. To do so, first select the passage of text or the image in the document prior to selecting *AutoCorrect*. The text or image is then placed in the *With* section. Ensure that the *Formatted Text* option button has been activated if you wish to insert formatting elements along with the text and/or graphics.

If you are asked if you want to save the modifications in the current template when you close down Word, reply Yes. Fragments of text in AutoCorrect are saved in the currently active template.

3.13 Printing documents

Print

If you wish to print a document using the default settings, click on the *Print* button on the Standard formatting toolbar.

However, if you wish to make other print specifications, select the *Print* option from the *File* menu. The *Print* dialog window appears in which you can change many of the print settings.

3.13.1 Print Preview

Before printing a document, it is advisable to examine the Print Preview. This indicates how the document will appear when printed. You can then make changes, in the Print Preview, if required.

Exercise
Display a Print Preview of the REST.DOC document.

Print Preview

Procedure:
Click on the *Print Preview* button on the Standard toolbar, or select *Print Preview* from the *File* menu.

The document is then displayed in the Print Preview mode.

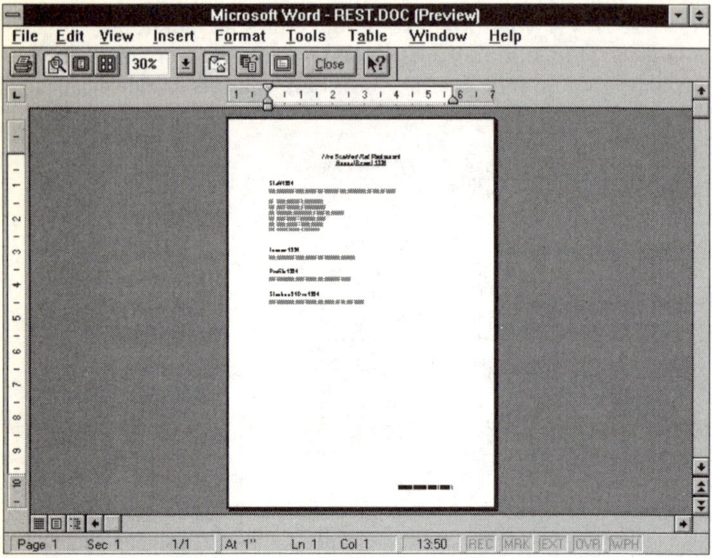

The Print Preview toolbar appears under the menu bar on the screen. The buttons have the following functions:

button/name	function
 Print	Prints the document with the current default settings.
 Magnifier	Activates or deactivates the zoom mode. If this is activated, the mouse pointer assumes the shape of a magnifying glass. You can zoom in on the page by clicking on the print preview at the required position. You switch off the zoom function by clicking on a random position on the screen.
 One Page	Scales the editing view to see the whole page in Page Layout View.
 Multiple Pages	Shows multiple pages on the screen.

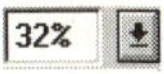	Zoom Control	Enlarges or reduces the section of document shown.
	View Ruler	Shows or hides the Ruler
	Shrink to Fit	Attempts to fit the document to one less page
	Full Screen	Activates or deactivates the Full Screen mode.
	Close	Close the Print Preview.
	Help	Activates the Help function. Click on the screen element, command or text feature you want to find out more about.

Exercise

We shall now close the Print Preview, save the REST.DOC document and close down Word.

Procedure:

1. Click on the *Normal View* button on the horizontal scroll bar.
2. Open the *File* menu and click on *Save*.
3. Open the *File* menu and select *Exit*.

4 Working with Microsoft Excel 5.0

This chapter gives an introduction to working with Microsoft Excel 5.0, the Microsoft Office spreadsheet program. This extensive program is ideal for managing, analysing and providing a graphical representation of your data.

If you wish to know more about the integration of Excel documents with files that have been created in other applications, you can consult the relevant sections in chapters 10 to 13. You can find an overview of utility programs within Excel, such as the Comparison Editor or the ClipArt Gallery, in chapter 9.

4.1 New in version 5.0

If you are already familiar with working with Excel, but are not yet acquainted with version 5.0, you can consult the following summary of some of the new functions:

- Workbooks: a Microsoft Excel file is now referred to as a workbook. All worksheets in one file are stored in a workbook.
- Entering data and formulas: you can now edit the cell contents in the cell itself instead of only on the formula bar.
- Function Wizard: the Function Wizard enables you to define function arguments quickly and easily.
- List management: working with lists has become very straightforward in Excel 5.0.
- The Tip Wizard gives context-oriented suggestions while you are performing tasks.

- Drag-and-drop: the Drag-and-drop method provides many possibilities. For example, to add data to a chart, simply drag the data to the chart.
- PivotTable Wizard: the PivotTable Wizard enables you to create a pivot table to analyse data in a list or database.

4.2 Starting up Excel

Microsoft Excel

You can start up Excel by opening the Microsoft Office group in the *Window* menu of the Program Manager and then double clicking on the *Microsoft Excel* icon in the group window. You can also start up the program by clicking on the *Microsoft Excel* button on the Microsoft Office toolbar.

Microsoft Excel

Exercise
Start up Excel in one of the ways mentioned above. An empty worksheet is opened on the screen.

There are many toolbar buttons available in Excel 5.0, so many in fact that they cannot all be displayed because the screen would be too cluttered. You can use the *Toolbars* option from the *View* menu to add buttons to the toolbar. This is done by clicking on the *Customize* button in the *Toolbars* dialog window and then opening the categories of toolbars. You can then drag any of the buttons shown onto a toolbar in the Excel screen.

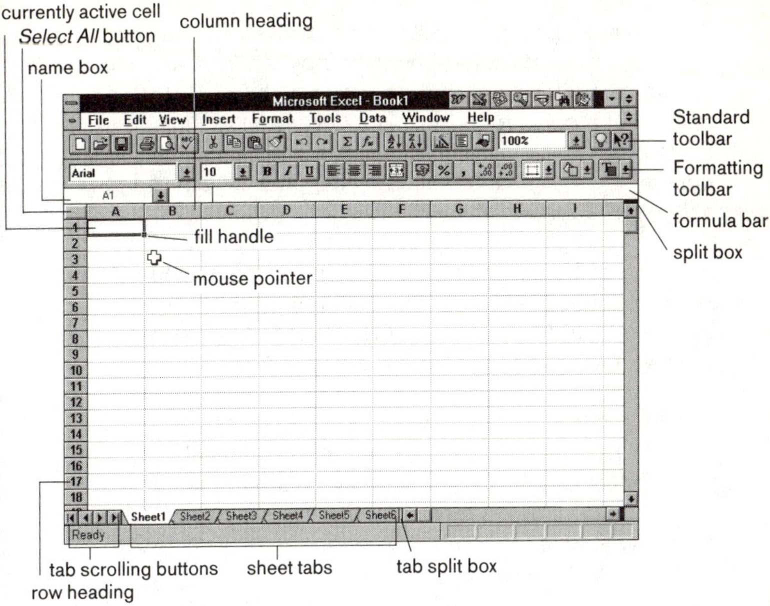

4.3 Creating workbooks

When you start up Excel a new empty workbook appears. A workbook is another name for an Excel file and consists of various worksheets. This subdivision into worksheets makes the management of data much more orderly.

New

You can create another new workbook by clicking on the *New* button on the Standard toolbar or by selecting the *New* command from the *File* menu.

A new empty workbook which has not yet been saved begins with the name Book, followed by a number. New workbooks that you have created during a session are assigned consecutive numbers. The worksheets are always given the name Sheet, followed by the number of the worksheet.

A worksheet consists of columns and rows. The columns are vertical and are indicated by letters; the rows are horizontal and are indicated by numbers. The intersection of a column and row is a cell. A cell is indicated by its position on the worksheet, the intersection of column and row, A1 for instance or G8. This is referred to as the cell address.

A series of adjacent cells is referred to as a range. A range is always indicated by naming the first cell in the upper left-hand part of the range and then the last cell in the lower right-hand corner, for example A2:C18.

The cell that is currently active, in other words, the cell activated by the mouse or cursor keys, is indicated by a black border. In the previous figure, cell A1 is the active cell. The active cell is also shown in the name box at the left-hand side of the formula bar. You can only enter data in the currently active cell.

4.3.1 Moving within workbooks and worksheets

The data you type appear in the active cell. You can shift the contents of a worksheet relative to the screen by clicking on the scroll bars. However, the active cell remains the same.

If you want to activate another cell, simply click on it. To activate another worksheet, click on the sheet tab. The name of the active worksheet is shown in boldface. To name a worksheet, double click on it. The *Rename Sheet* dialog window appears in which you should type the name. This can be very convenient for remembering which data are stored on which worksheet.
If the name of a worksheet is not shown, you can use the tab scroll buttons to move through the tabs. This action does not select any tabs, it only makes them visible.

button	**result**
	Moves back to the first tab
	Moves to the last tab
	Moves to the previous tab
	Moves to the next tab

If you hold down the Shift button while clicking on one of the last two buttons, you can move several tabs at once.

You can also use the cursor keys on the keyboard to activate another cell. This is only really convenient if the distance between the cells is not too large.

Tip
There are many key combinations in Excel for moving to another cell. To obtain a list of these, open the *Help* menu, select *Search for Help on*, type **moving, active cell** in the upper text box, activate the *Show Topics* button, select *Keys for Moving and Selecting in Worksheets and Workbooks* and click on the *Go To* button.

If you want to move quickly to a certain cell or range, activate the name box by clicking on it and type the cell address. The specified cell or range of cells is immediately activated.

4.3.2 Selecting cells

If you wish to move, copy, format or delete cells, you have to select (mark) them first. Marked cells are shown in inverse video display on the screen. A selection can be undone by pressing one of the cursor keys or by clicking outside the selection.

You can select one cell by clicking on it or by moving to it by means of the cursor keys. You can select a range of adjacent cells by dragging the mouse across them. This can also be done by selecting the first cell in the range, pressing and holding down the Shift key and extending the selection range by pressing the cursor keys.

As mentioned, a series of cells in a worksheet is called a range. A range may consist of adjacent or non-adjacent cells. To select non-adjacent cells, hold down the Ctrl key while clicking on the cells you wish to select, or drag the mouse across the ranges of cells to be selected.

Tip
You can also use a number of key combinations to select cells in Excel. To obtain an overview of these, open the *Help* menu, select *Search for Help on*, type **moving, active cell** in the upper text box, click on the *Show Topics* button, select *Keys for Moving and Selecting in Workbooks and Worksheets* from the lower section and click on *Go To*.

If you want to select an entire row, click on the row heading; to select an entire column, click on the column heading. If you want to select all the cells in the worksheet, click on the *Select All* button in the upper left-hand corner or the worksheet at the intersection of the row and column headings.

It is also possible to select several worksheets at one time. To do so, click on the tab of the first sheet to be selected, hold down the Shift key and click on the tab of the last sheet to be selected. All intervening worksheets will be selected. To select worksheets which are not adjacent, hold down the Ctrl key while clicking on the appropriate tabs.

In the tab shortcut menu (click on the right mouse button when the mouse pointer is on a tab), you can choose the *Select All Sheets* option to select all worksheets.

4.3.3 Data input

Entering data in a cell

You can enter data in an active cell by simply typing. What you type is shown both in the active cell and on the formula bar. The buttons on the formula bar become visible as soon as you begin typing data in a cell. The data are only actually placed in the cell when you have confirmed the input by clicking on the *Enter* box (with the tick) or by pressing Enter. When you press Enter, the cell immediately below becomes the active cell. If you wish to activate another cell once you have entered data, do not press Enter, press one of the cursor keys or click on the appropriate cell.

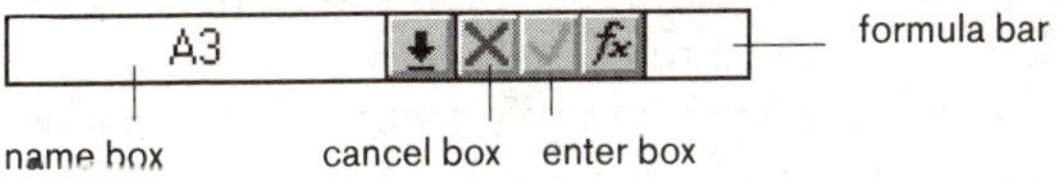

The formula bar shows the value or the formula in the currently active cell. The address of the active cell is shown in the name box. You can also use the name box to assign a name to a cell or cell range or to move quickly to a specified cell or range.

Entering data in a selection

You can also enter data in a range of selected cells. If you wish to enter the same data in all the selected cells, type the data in the first cell and then press Ctrl+Enter.

Undoing the data input

You can cancel the values you have typed by pressing Esc or by clicking on the *Cancel* button on the formula bar. If you wish to correct an error while typing, you can press the Backspace key. You can also move the insertion point in the cell by clicking on the required position in the cell if you have not yet finished entering the data. The Edit mode is then activated (see the status bar).

Editing existing data

If you wish to edit existing data, double click on the relevant cell or press F2. The insertion point will begin flashing in the cell. You can then edit the data. You can also modify the data on the formula bar. Use the mouse or the cursor keys to move to the required position. You can also use the mouse to select part of the data by dragging the mouse pointer across the required section and then delete that section by pressing Del or Backspace. You can also replace it directly by typing new data.

To delete the contents of a cell, activate the cell and press Del. If you wish to delete values in a range, select the range first and then press Del. If you want to delete the contents, format or notes, select the cell or range of cells and select *Clear* from the *Edit* menu. Subsequently choose *All, Formats, Contents* or *Notes.*

If you only want to delete the contents of a cell, you can drag the fill handle of the cell into the cell so that the cell becomes grey. Then release the mouse button. If you want to delete the contents, format and notes, hold down Ctrl while dragging the fill handle. Release the mouse button and then the Ctrl key.

Exercise

Type the following data in the range A1:G18

	A	B	C	D	E	F	G
1	The Scalded Rat Restaurant						
2	Wine sales 1994 (bottles)						
3							
4	White		1st quarter				Total
5	South Afr.		72	55	81	94	
6	Californian		58	48	64	67	
7	Bordeaux		45	36	47	52	
8	Chablis		32	20	33	37	
9	Riesling		37	32	33	48	
10	Total						
11							
12	Red						
13	Algerian		35	19	26	50	
14	Rioja		41	28	36	56	
15	Bordeaux		415	379	406	537	
16	Cotes du Rhone		209	189	188	246	
17	Chianti		29	14	21	36	
18	Total						

You can enter numbers, text and formulas in a cell. Normally Excel right-aligns numbers and left-aligns text. If an entry consists of both text and numbers such as a house address, Excel will align the entry as text since it is quite logical that the numbers are not going to be used for calculation.

If the text is longer than the cell is wide, the text is nevertheless shown in its entirety on the screen unless there are data in the adjacent right cell. In that case, the text is not completely shown.
You can change the column width by opening the *Format* menu, selecting *Columns* and then *Width*. You can also place the mouse pointer on the dividing line between the columns so that it changes into a black two-headed arrow, and then drag the line to the required width. This is dealt with in more detail in section 4.6.4.

If a number is too wide for a cell, it is shown in scientific display, such as 3.33E+14 for example. If a lengthy number has a format other than General, a series of number symbols is shown in the cell (#######).

4.3.4 AutoFill

You can use the AutoFill function to extend a series of values. This is done by dragging the fill handle. The contents of the first cell in the row or column is taken as the source of the values to be placed.

Exercise
To illustrate this, we shall place the text '2nd quarter', '3rd quarter' and '4th quarter' in the cells D4 to F4.

Procedure:
1 Activate cell B4.
2 Drag the fill handle to the right so that the grey selection area fills the cells D4 to F4.

You will see that the proper text is placed in the cells when you release the mouse button.

When you select months, dates and sequential terms (1st, 2nd etc.), Excel recognises these as being parts of a series. Therefore it is sufficient to select one cell; Excel does the rest. In other cases, you should select two cells with sequential terms (specify these if necessary) and then select them before dragging the fill handle.

You can also use menu options to do this. Select the range to be filled. Open the *Edit* menu and select *Fill* and then *Series* from the subsequent submenu, ensure that *Rows* is activated, the *Step Value* is 1 and the *AutoFill* option button is activated. Click on *OK*.

4.4 Saving a workbook, closing it and opening it again

4.4.1 Saving a workbook

Save

To save a workbook on disk, click on the *Save* button on the Standard toolbar, or select *Save* from the *File* menu. If you have not saved the workbook previously, the *Save As* dialog window is opened.

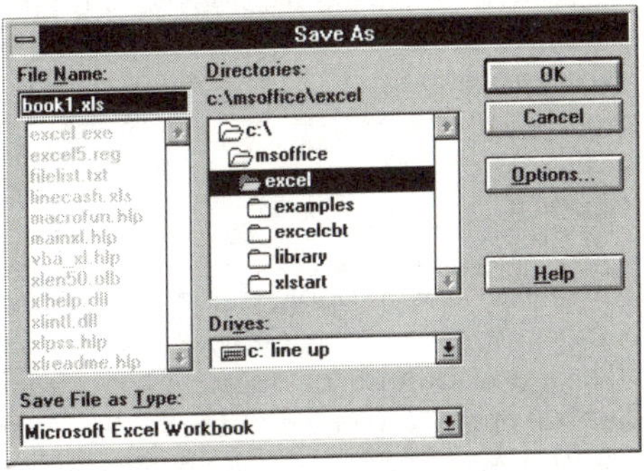

Enter the name of the file in the *File Name* text box. Select the directory in which you wish to store the file. You can always create a new directory for your file by switching to the Program Manager (Alt+Tab), activating the File Manager (Main window), open the *File* menu, select the *Create Directory* option.
Choose the appropriate drives from the *Drives* list and specify the type of file in the *Save File as Type* box. If you wish to save the file as a normal Excel workbook, accept the default setting *Microsoft Excel Workbook*. The file is automatically assigned the XLS extension.

If you wish, you can specify further description of the file in the *Summary Info* dialog window which subsequently appears. Click on *OK*.

Exercise

Save the Excel workbook, which we have just created, under the name BOTTLES.XLS in a directory of your own choice.

If you have saved the file previously, the *Save* command from the *File* menu will save the file under the same name in the same directory as on the previous occasion. In that case, no dialog window will appear for further specifications. If you wish to save a previously-saved file under a new name or in a new directory, select the *Save As* command from the *File* menu.

4.4.2 Closing a workbook

When you want to close a workbook, select the *Close* command from the *File* menu, or double click on the document Control menu button, or select *Close* from the workbook Control menu. If you did not save the most recent changes to the workbook, you will now be asked if you want to do so.

4.4.3 Opening a workbook

Open

To open a workbook, click on the *Open* button on the Standard toolbar or select the *Open* file from the *File* menu. The *Open* dialog window appears.

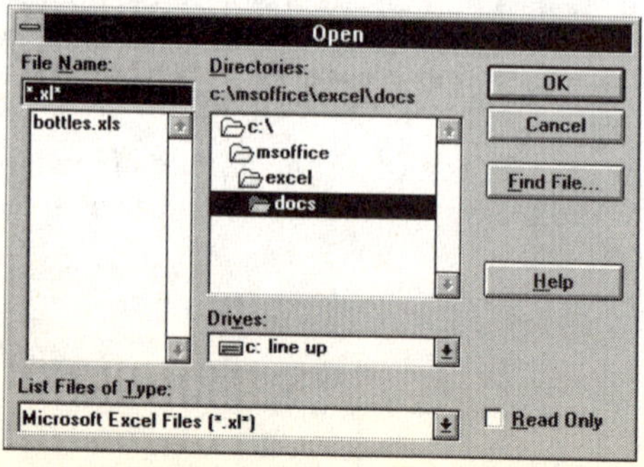

Select the required workbook from the appropriate directory and click on *OK*. If you are no longer sure where you stored the file, you can make use of the *Find File* button to help you.

4.5 Working with worksheets

A workbook can consist of a number of worksheets. You can also assign names to each of these worksheets to assist you in remembering which data are stored where. If you do not allocate a name, the sheets retain their default names Sheet1, Sheet2 etc. There are 16 worksheets in a newly opened workbook. You can reduce this amount to one if you wish, or increase it to 255. Thus, you can remove or add worksheets. You can also change the names of the worksheets as you go, and also copy or move worksheets within a workbook or copy or move them to another workbook.

You can also include graphic sheets, Visual Basic module sheets, dialog sheets, Microsoft Excel 4.0 macro sheets and Microsoft Excel 4.0 international macro sheets in workbooks.

4.5.1 Naming worksheets

If you wish to assign a name to a worksheet in a workbook, activate the worksheet, open the *Format* menu, select *Sheet* and then *Rename*. You can also simply double click on the tab to open the *Rename Sheet* dialog window. Type the new name and then click on *OK*.

Exercise
Assign the name 'quantity 1994' to Sheet1 in the BOTTLES.XLS workbook.

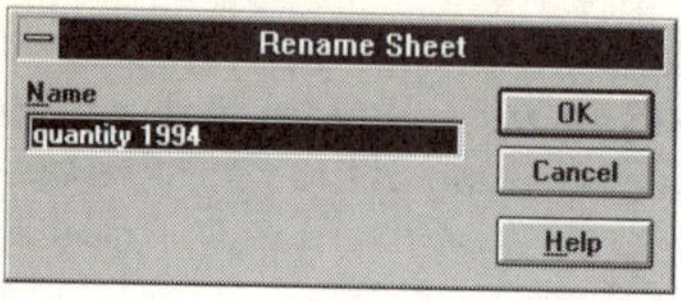

4.5.2 Copying worksheets

As mentioned, you can copy worksheets within a workbook and also from one workbook to another.

If you wish to copy a worksheet within a workbook, hold down the Ctrl key while dragging the selected tab across the row of tabs. A small triangle appears which will indicate where the copy will be placed. Release the mouse button at the required tab sheet, then the Ctrl key.

You can also open the *Edit* menu and select *Move or Copy Sheet* if you want to copy one or more sheets within a workbook or to another opened workbook or to a new workbook.

Exercise
We shall now copy the first sheet twice to the next position.

Procedure:

1 Click on the Sheet1 tab and hold down the mouse button. A small sheet symbol appears along with a small black triangle.
2 Press and hold down the Ctrl key. A plus appears in the sheet symbol.
3 Drag the mouse pointer until the small triangle moves from above the first sheet to above the second one.
4 Release the mouse button, then the Ctrl key.
5 Repeat steps 1-4 to make a second copy.

You will see that the names of the sheets are automatically adjusted (with consecutive numbers). The new sheets are inserted in front of Sheet2.

Exercise
Assign the names 'returns 1994' and 'purchase 1994' to the new sheets.

Procedure:
1 Double click on the tab of the copied sheet. The *Rename Sheet* box appears.
2 Type the name 'returns 1994' in the *Name* text box.
3 Click on *OK*.
4 Do the same for the second copy and assign it the name 'purchase 1994'.

4.5.3 Removing sheets

If you wish to remove a sheet from a workbook, first select the sheet to be removed. Open the *Edit* menu and select *Delete Sheet*. Confirm your decision in the subsequent dialog box.

4.5.4 Moving sheets

You can move sheets within a workbook and you can also move them to another opened workbook. To move a sheet within a workbook, select the sheet and drag its tab along the row of tabs until you come to the required position. The small black triangle indicates where the sheet will be inserted. You can also perform the same action by opening the *Edit* menu and selecting *Move or Copy Sheet*. A dialog window then opens in which you can specify where the selected sheet is to be inserted. You can also move several sheets at once.

If you want to move one or more sheets to another workbook, select the sheet(s) to be moved and select *Move or Copy Sheet* from the *Edit* menu. Choose the destination workbook from the subsequent *Move or Copy* dialog window. If you want to move the sheet(s) to a new workbook, open the *To Book* drop-down list and select *(new book)*. The *Create a Copy* option at the bottom of the dialog window will make a copy of the activated sheet at the new position.

4.5.5 Inserting sheets

If you want to insert one or more sheets, first activate one of the existing worksheets. The new sheets will be inserted in front of this sheet. Open the *Insert* menu and select *Worksheet*.
You can perform the same action more quickly by pressing the shortcut key combination Shift+F11, or by clicking on the *New Worksheet* button which you can add to your toolbar by opening the *View* menu, selecting *Toolbars* and then activating the *Customize* button. Activate the *File* category in this window, and drag the *New Worksheet* button (2nd row, 2nd from the left) onto the document toolbar.

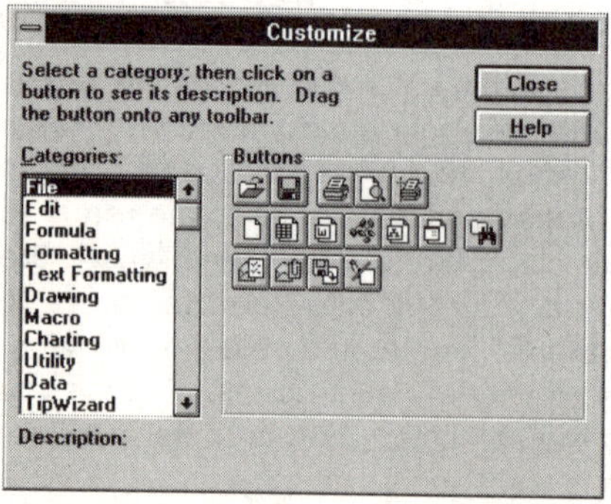

4.6 Working with rows and columns

You will inevitably have to adapt worksheets to your own personal requirements. Columns may have to be widened or narrowed and the height of the rows may have to be adjusted to present the data in an orderly way.

Tip
In addition to the methods mentioned, you can also make use of the shortcut menus for rows and columns by clicking on the row or column headings with the right mouse button.

4.6.1 Removing rows and columns

If you remove a row or column from a worksheet, the other rows and columns shift up so that no vacuum exists. You can also delete rows and columns in such a way that only the cell contents, format or notes are deleted while the rows and columns themselves remain intact.

If you wish to remove one or more rows or columns, select the rows or columns and then choose *Delete* from the *Edit* menu. You can also press the key combination Ctrl+hyphen.

If you want to remove only the contents of rows or columns, select the row(s) or column(s) and choose *Clear* from the *Edit* menu. Then you can choose one of the options *All, Formats, Contents* or *Notes*. If you wish to clear only the contents of selected rows or columns, you can simply press the Del key.

4.6.2 Inserting rows and columns

Rows and columns can be inserted into a worksheet quickly and easily. To do so, first select the row or column before which the row or column is to be inserted. A new row is inserted above the selected row, a new column is inserted to the left of the selected column. If you want to insert several rows or columns, first select a number of rows or columns **equal to** the number of rows or columns you want to insert. Then select *Rows* or *Columns* from the *Insert* menu. You can also press the shortcut key combination Ctrl+Shift+Plus sign (numeric keypad, NumLock on).

Exercise
We shall add a new row above row 11 on the first 3 (named) worksheets in our BOTTLES document.

Procedure:
1 Activate the first tab in the BOTTLES workbook if it is not already active.
2 Click on the 11 in the row headings at the left-hand side of the screen. The entire row is selected.
3 Open the *Insert* menu and select *Rows*. A row is inserted.
4 Repeat steps 1-3 for the other worksheets.

4.6.3 Inserting cells

If you want to insert a cell or cells in a worksheet, first select a range that is exactly **equal** in size to the range you want to insert. Then open the *Insert* menu and select *Cells*. The *Insert* dialog window appears. Here you must specify whether the existing cells are to be shifted to the right or downwards, or whether an entire row or entire column is to be inserted above or to the left, respectively, of the selected range.

4.6.4 Adjusting column width and row height

There are default settings for the column width and row height. These apply to all new worksheets. This can lead to numbers or text being incompletely shown due to the lack of space, although the computer does keep track of the specified values in its internal memory.

If you want to adjust the column width, first select the column(s) by clicking on the column headings. Then move the mouse pointer to the dividing line between the column headings so that it changes into a black two-headed arrow. Drag the column width to the required size. You can also adjust the column width so that it will exactly accommodate the contents. This is done by double clicking on the dividing line to the right of the corresponding column heading.

You can also select the column(s) or cells in the column(s) and then choose *Column* from the *Format* menu. A submenu appears. Choose *Width* and type the required width in the subsequent text box. If you choose *AutoFit* selection from this submenu, the column width is adapted in such a way that all the data in the column can be displayed.

If you want to adjust the width of all the columns in the worksheet, first click on the *Select All* button (at the intersection of the row and column headings) before giving the command to alter the column width.

Exercise
We shall alter the width of all columns in the BOTTLES.XLS worksheets so that they can accommodate all the data.

Procedure:

1 Activate the first worksheet, 'quantity 1994'.

2 Click on the *Select All* button in the upper left-hand of the worksheet.
3 Open the *Format* menu and select *Column*.
4 Select *AutoFit Selection*.

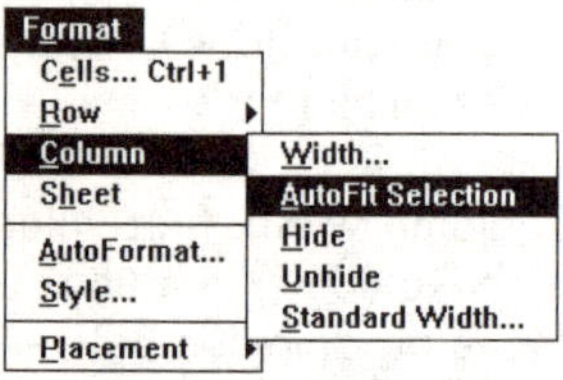

5 The worksheet is adjusted. Now do the same for the other two named worksheets.

Altering the row height takes place in a similar way. Using the mouse, you can drag the dividing line above or below a row heading to the required position. If you want this to apply to several rows, select them first. If you open the *Format* menu and select *Row*, followed by *Height*, you can specify the new height in the subsequent values box. To automatically adjust the row height quickly and easily, double click on the dividing line between the row headings.
If you wish to change the column widths or row heights back to the original select the *Standard Width* or *Standard Height* from the appropriate submenu in the *Format* menu.

4.6.5 Moving or copying a range of cells

Cut

Paste

To move a cell or range of cells, select the cell or cells to be moved, place the mouse pointer on the edge of the selection so that it turns into an arrow, and drag the cell or cells to the new location. If the selected area contains formulas, they will remain unchanged.

You can also move cells by selecting them first, activating the *Cut* button on the Standard toolbar, activating the destination cells (or only the top left cell in the range) and then choosing the *Paste* button from the Standard toolbar or pressing Enter. This can also be done by selecting the *Cut* and *Paste* options from the *Edit* menu.

Copy

Paste

Copying a cell or cells is done in much the same way. Select the cell or range, click on the *Copy* button on the Standard toolbar, move to the top left cell of the destination range and click on the *Paste* button on the Standard toolbar. This can also be done by selecting the *Copy* and *Paste* options from the *Edit* menu.
You can also place the copied data at several positions in the worksheet by selecting the *Paste* button or menu option once you have activated the desired destination cell(s). If you only wish to copy the data to one place, you can press the Enter key instead.

You can also insert copied cells, shifting the existing cells up to make room for them. This is done by choosing the *Copied Cells* option from the *Insert* menu. You can cancel the copy command (and the activated cells) by pressing Esc or by selecting a different command.

You can also use the mouse to copy cells quickly and easily. First select the cell(s), move the mouse pointer to the edge of the selection area so that it changes into an arrow, press and hold down the Ctrl key, and drag the selection to the required position. Release the mouse button and then the Ctrl key.

When you copy cells without formulas, the contents remain unchanged in the destination area. However, if you copy cells containing formulas and references, the formulas will be changed to conform to the new position.

Exercise

We shall copy the range C4:G4 to the range C13:G13 on all three named worksheets in our BOTTLES workbook.

Procedure:

1 Select the range C4:G4.
2 Open the *Edit* menu and select *Copy*.
3 Activate cell C13.
4 Open the *Edit* menu and select *Paste*.
5 The selected cells are copied.
6 Open the second worksheet, 'returns 1994'.
7 Activate cell C13 and select *Paste* from the *Edit* menu. The data on the Clipboard in the computer memory are copied to the selected area.
8 Do the same for the third worksheet, 'purchase 1994'.

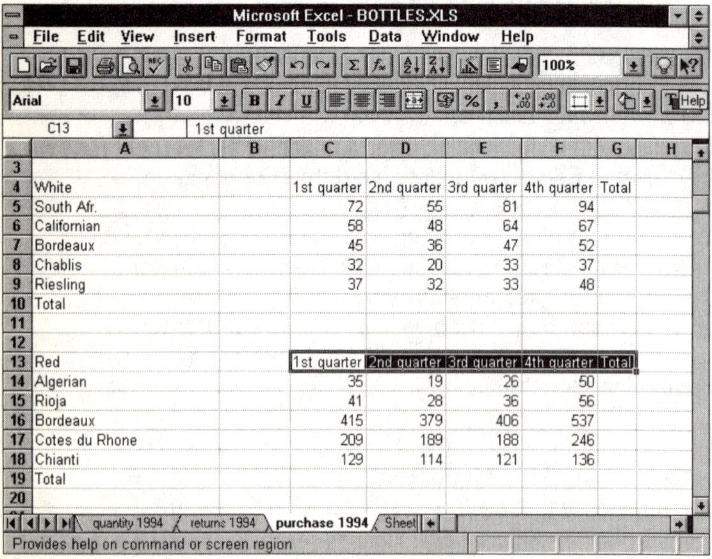

Cell references

Cell references (also know as 'addresses') are used to identify cells in a worksheet. When formulas are used in a worksheet, the cell references tell Excel where to find the required values; for example, the formula =C5+D5+E5+F5, which you will shortly enter in cell G5 for the Total, instructs Excel to add up the values in these cells.

There are three kinds of cell references: relative, absolute and mixed.

- A relative reference is one in which values in cells are taken in relation to the cell containing the formula. This sounds complicated but it is not. If you enter the formula =C5+D5+E5+F5 in G5 (the Total of South African wines in our example), the sum will be given when you press Enter. If you then copy this formula to the cells below, you will not want to arrive at an identical sum for the figures in row 6 (Californian wines). You will want the sum of the cells C6+D6+E6+F6. Excel recognises this and adapts the formula accordingly. The cell references are changed to relate to the location of the cell containing the formula. Try this out. Type the formula =C5+D5+E5+F5 in cell G5. Press Enter. The sum is shown. Now activate the same cell, G5. The formula is displayed on the formula bar. Open the *Edit* menu and select *Copy*. Activate cell G6. Open the *Edit* menu and choose *Paste*. The formula on the formula bar has been adapted to relate to the currently active cell. (Section 4.7 deals with this in more detail.)

- An absolute reference in a formula will ensure that the specified cell **and no other cell** will be used in a calculation. The cell reference will not be adapted to suit the location of the cell in which the copied formula has been placed. This is sometimes necessary, for example, in cases where percentages of an overall total have to be worked out. The dollar sign is used to indicate that a cell reference is absolute (thus $G$19 for example).

- A mixed reference is a combination of a relative and an absolute reference. A dollar sign is placed in front of either the column letter or row number.

If you wish to change the type of cell reference in a formula, select the cell containing the formula and then the relevant cell reference on the formula bar. Then press F4 to switch to a different kind of reference until the required type is displayed. Press Enter.

4.6.6 Range names

If you are working with formulas or if you want to move quickly to a certain range of cells, it can be convenient to use names to represent these cells.

You can switch to a cell by simply typing its reference in the name box and then pressing Enter. But if you are not sure about exactly which cell you want to activate, you will have to make a guess. Alternatively, if you assign a name to a cell or range of cells, you can always move to the required position by selecting the name. This is very convenient with extensive worksheets.

To assign a name to a cell or range of cells, activate the cell or select the range and click on the name box at the extreme left of the formula bar. Type the name and press Enter. When you want to switch to the cell or cell range later, click on the arrow pointing downwards to the right of the name box. A list of assigned names appears. Select the appropriate name.

You can also apply range names in calculations.

Exercise
To put this into practice, we shall assign the name 'total_white' to cell G10 on the *quantity 1994* worksheet. Cell G19 will subsequently receive the name 'total_red'.

Procedure:

1 Activate cell G10 and then click on this reference in the name box. It turns blue.
2 Type the name 'total_white'. Press Enter.
3 Follow similar steps to assign the name 'total_red' to cell G19.

Note
Excel only accepts letters, numbers and underlining in allocated names. Names must not be longer than 255 characters.

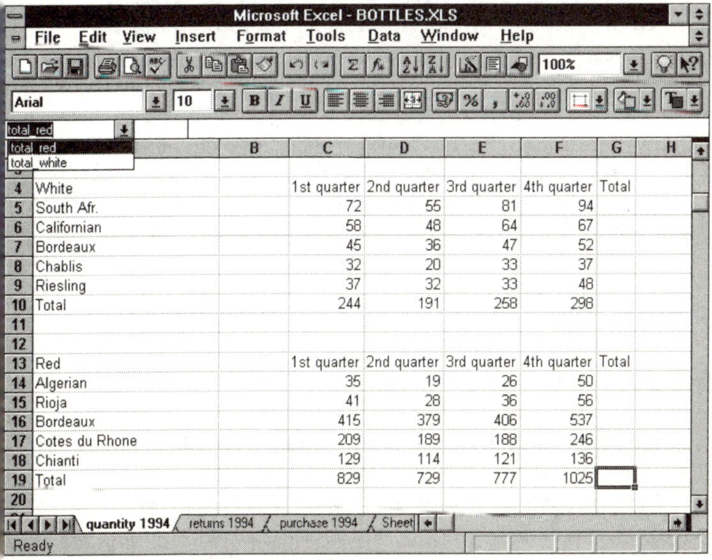

4.7 Calculating values by means of formulas and functions

A good spreadsheet program provides the possibility of working with functions and formulas.

A formula consists of a mathematical calculation containing so-called **operators**, such as + and -. A formula may contain cell references, values, worksheet functions and names. A function is a ready-made formula.

Excel provides a large number of functions. To obtain an overview of these, open the *Help* menu and select *Search for Help on*. Type **functions, worksheet** and click on *Show Topics*. Select *Alphabetical List of Worksheet Functions* or *Worksheet Functions Listed by Category* from the lower window.

When you want to enter a formula in a cell, you first have to activate the cell in which the formula is to be placed. The formula is then entered as follows:

- Type an equals sign (=) to activate the formula bar.
- Type the formula. You can enter cell references in the formula by selecting the cells from the worksheet (clicking on them is the easiest way of doing this). This will automatically enter relative references in the formula. Enter the required operators between the values or the cell references.

4.7.1 The SUM function

Imagine that you wish to add up the figures in cells C5 to C9 and enter the result in cell C10. You can do this quite simply by typing the formula: =C5+C6+C7+C8+C9. However, if you are working with longer series of cells, it is more convenient to make use of the SUM function.

In that case, the formula in cell C10 would be: =SUM(C5:C9).

AutoSum

Microsoft Excel provides the ingenious AutoSum function which examines which values you might want to add up. It then enters the SUM function and the range of cells automatically on the formula bar. If you want to make use of this function, activate the cell next to the cell or column containing the values you wish to add up. Then click on the *AutoSum* button on the standard toolbar. You can also press the key combination Alt+Equals sign.

Exercise
We shall now calculate the totals according to quarterly sales and in terms of wine category.

AutoSum

Procedure:

1 Select cell B10 in the *quantity 1994* worksheet. Click on the *AutoSum* button. The function =SUM(C5:C9) appears in the cell. A light frame is active around the range C5:C9. This is indeed the range you wish to add up, so press Enter to confirm the formula. If this were not the correct range, you can alter the formula by dragging the mouse pointer across the proper range of cells which then becomes active.
2 Repeat this for cells D10, E10 and F10.
3 Select cell G5 and click on *AutoSum*. The formula =SUM(C5:F5) is shown. This is what we need so press Enter.
4 Repeat these steps for cells G6, G7, G8 and G9. You will notice that the function will want to add up the 'wrong' cells in G7. This is because the function is designed to add up values in columns unless otherwise specified. Drag the mouse pointer across the appropriate cells, in this case C7:F7.

You can also enter several SUM formulas simultaneously when working with AutoSum. The following exercise illustrates this.

Exercise
Calculate the totals for the amount of bottles sold.

Procedure:
1 Select the range B14:G19.
2 Click on the *AutoSum* button.

AutoSum

3 The totals of the rows and columns are automatically entered in the empty cells next to and under the numbers.

If you want to calculate a final total based on rows and columns containing subtotals, first select the range containing the subtotals and the row or column in which you wish to place the final total. Then click on the *AutoSum* button. You can also simultaneously add up rows at columns containing subtotals.

You worksheet should now look something like this:

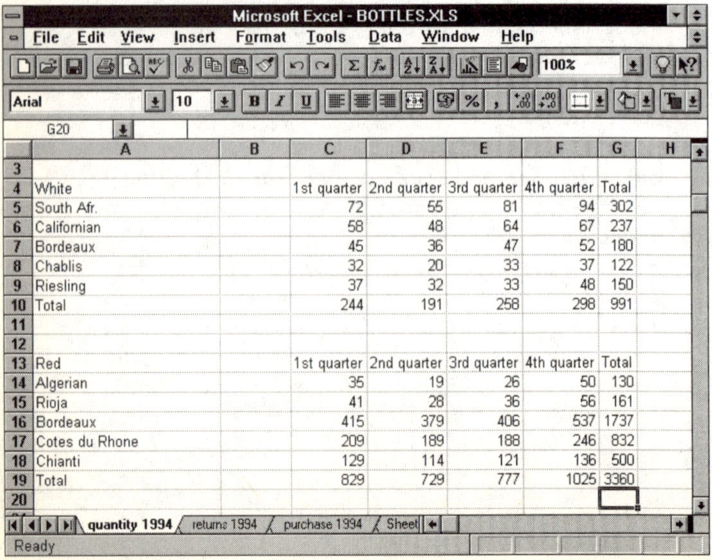

	A	B	C	D	E	F	G	H
3								
4	White		1st quarter	2nd quarter	3rd quarter	4th quarter	Total	
5	South Afr.		72	55	81	94	302	
6	Californian		58	48	64	67	237	
7	Bordeaux		45	36	47	52	180	
8	Chablis		32	20	33	37	122	
9	Riesling		37	32	33	48	150	
10	Total		244	191	258	298	991	
11								
12								
13	Red		1st quarter	2nd quarter	3rd quarter	4th quarter	Total	
14	Algerian		35	19	26	50	130	
15	Rioja		41	28	36	56	161	
16	Bordeaux		415	379	406	537	1737	
17	Cotes du Rhone		209	189	188	246	832	
18	Chianti		129	114	121	136	500	
19	Total		829	729	777	1025	3360	
20								

4.7.2 The Function Wizard

Function Wizard

Excel provides so many functions that you may be confused as to which function you should use for a certain calculation, or how you should actually apply the function. The Function Wizard is there to assist you. You activate this Wizard by clicking on the *Function Wizard* button on the Standard toolbar after selecting the cell in which you want to enter the function.

Exercise

We shall calculate the returns for 1994 on the corresponding worksheet.

Procedure:

1 Activate the *returns 1994* worksheet.

2 This sheet contains the quantitative data we copied from the first worksheet. You can simply type over the existing data when entering new data, but to approach things in a neat orderly way, we shall clear the data first. Select cells C5:F9 by dragging the mouse pointer across them. Press Del. The data are cleared.

3 Activate the now empty cell C5 and click on the *Function Wizard* button on the Standard toolbar.

The *Function Wizard* dialog window is opened.

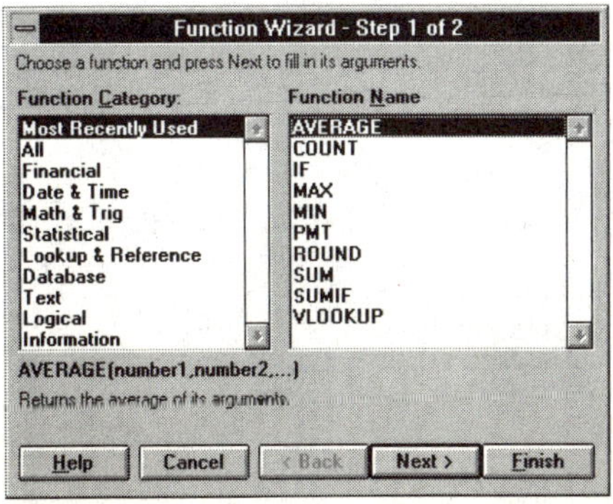

Cell C5 is to show the figure produced by multiplying the amount of bottles of South African wine by the selling price in the restaurant, £8.75. This price is a so-called 'absolute value'.

4 Select the *Math& Trig* function from the *Function Category* list.
5 Select *Product* from the *Function Name* list.
6 Click on the *Next* button.

You now have to enter a value in the *number1* text box. The easiest way of entering function arguments is to click on them. Ensure that the *Function Wizard* window does not obstruct your view; drag it to another part of the screen by clicking on the title bar.

7 Click on the *quantity 1994* tab. The text 'quantity 1994'! is automatically entered in the text box.
8 Click on cell C5. This cell reference is also automatically entered in the text box.
9 Click on the *number2* text box in the dialog window. Type **8.75**, which is the selling price of the wine.

Note
If you enter a decimal value lower than 1, you do not need to enter the 0. For instance 0.9 can simply be entered as .9.

10 Click on the *Finish* button in the dialog window.

The formula on the formula bar is now as follows:

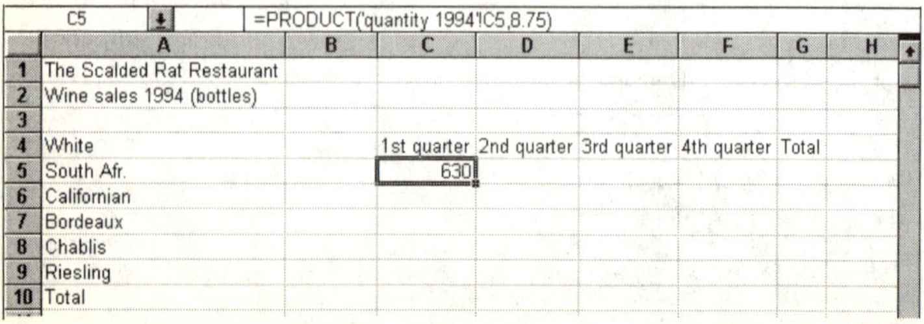

You can now copy the formula to cells D5 to F5. The cell references will be automatically adjusted because they are relative..

Copy

Paste

11 Activate cell C5.
12 Click on the *Copy* button on the Standard toolbar. A moving dotted line appears around the cell.
13 Click on cell D5.
14 Click on the *Paste* button on the Standard toolbar.
15 Click on cells E5.
16 Click on the *Paste* button again.
17 Click on cell F5.
18 Click on the *Paste* button.

If you examine the formulas shown on the formula bar for each cell, you will see that the cell references have indeed been adjusted to suit each column. The value 8.75 remains the same in all formulas.

You can now apply the same procedure to enter the values in cells D6 to F9, activating the *Function Wizard* for each category in each new row. The price of Californian wine is £9.65, Bordeaux £8.30, Chablis £16.55 and Riesling £5.90.

Tip

An easy way of entering these data is to copy the formula from the first cell, C5 to the other cells C6 to C9. The cell reference will change to suit the new position, but the selling price is not correct. Press F2 to activate the Edit mode. Press Backspace to delete the incorrect value and enter the selling price of the new category (Californian, Bordeaux etc.). The appropriate formula is thus entered in each row. You can now copy the formula to each column, as in steps 11 to 18 above.

Exercise

Clear the values in the cells C14:F18. Follow the same procedure as above to enter the relevant values in these cells. The selling price per wine category is:

Algerian	£8.95
Rioja	£9.85
Bordeaux	£9.25
Cotes du Rhone	£9.10
Chianti	£8.65

Your worksheet will now look like this:

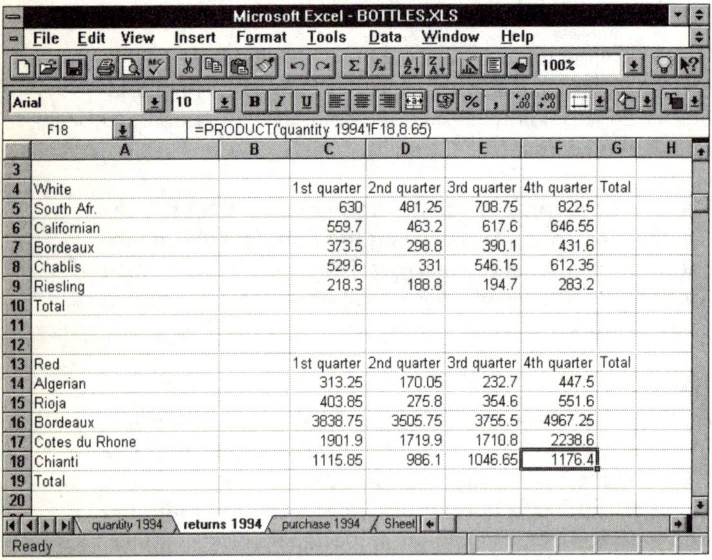

	A	B	C	D	E	F	G	H
3								
4	White		1st quarter	2nd quarter	3rd quarter	4th quarter	Total	
5	South Afr.		630	481.25	708.75	822.5		
6	Californian		559.7	463.2	617.6	646.55		
7	Bordeaux		373.5	298.8	390.1	431.6		
8	Chablis		529.6	331	546.15	612.35		
9	Riesling		218.3	188.8	194.7	283.2		
10	Total							
11								
12								
13	Red		1st quarter	2nd quarter	3rd quarter	4th quarter	Total	
14	Algerian		313.25	170.05	232.7	447.5		
15	Rioja		403.85	275.8	354.6	551.6		
16	Bordeaux		3838.75	3505.75	3755.5	4967.25		
17	Cotes du Rhone		1901.9	1719.9	1710.8	2238.6		
18	Chianti		1115.85	986.1	1046.65	1176.4		
19	Total							
20								

Exercise

We shall now calculate the totals in the appropriate cells of the *returns 1994* worksheet.

AutoSum

Procedure:

1. Mark the range C5:G10 and click on the *AutoSum* button.
2. Mark the range C14:G19 and click on the *AutoSum* button.

The worksheet now looks like this:

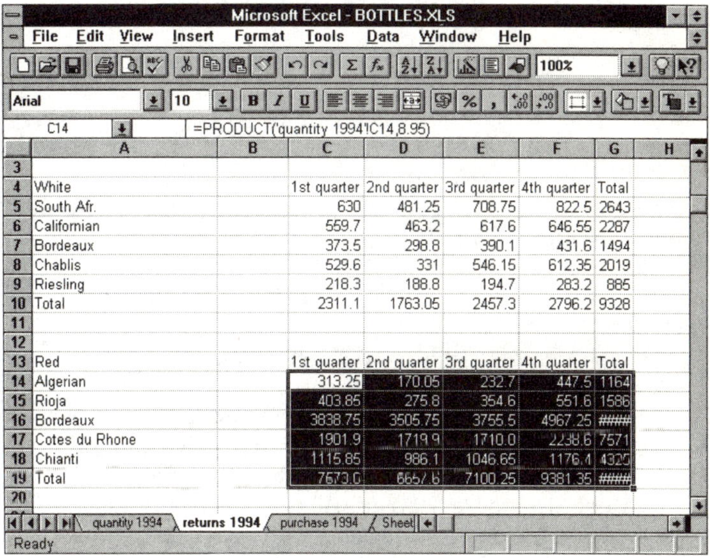

You notice that column G is now too narrow to display all the totals. Mark the range C13:G19, open the *Format* menu, select *Column* and then *AutoFit Selection*. The data are now fully displayed.

Change the subtitle of the worksheet in cell A2 to 'Returns per sort'.

Exercise

Fill in the *purchase 1994* worksheet in the same way as you did with the *returns 1994* worksheet. This time you will have to enter the purchase price of each category:

White	
South African	£3.15
Californian	£3.45
Bordeaux	£3.10
Chablis	£5.35
Riesling	£2.05
Red	
Algerian	£2.95
Rioja	£3.45
Bordeaux	£3.20
Cotes du Rhone	£3.15
Chianti	£2.80

Procedure:

1 On the *returns 1994* worksheet, mark the cells C5:G9.

2 Click on the *Copy* button on the Standard toolbar.

3 Move to the *purchase 1994* and activate cell C5.

4 Click on the *Paste* button on the Standard toolbar. The entire range is copied. All the values in this range are based on formulas which are displayed on the formula bar. We shall adjust these.

5 Activate cell C5 and press F2 to edit the formula.

6 Delete the absolute value in cell C5 (8.75) and replace it with the appropriate value, in this case 3.15. Press Enter. We shall now copy this formula containing the proper purchase price to the cells in columns D, E and F.

7 Activate cell C5 again and click on the *Copy* button on the Standard toolbar.

8 Click on cell D5 and then on the *Paste* button. The proper formula, in which the relative cell reference is changed, is copied to cell D5.

9 Click on cell E5 and then on the *Paste* button.

10 Click on cell F5 and then on the *Paste* button. You will see that the Totals in column G are automatically adjusted because the formulas in that column refer to the sum of the values in columns C, D, E and F.

11 Activate cell C6 (Californian) and press F2 to edit the formula. Enter the appropriate purchase price (3.45). Press Enter to confirm.

12 Copy this formula to the other columns in the same way as described above in steps 8 to 10.

13 Enter the other values for the entire worksheet.

14 Change the subtitle for the worksheet (A2) to 'Purchase price per sort'.

When you have completed the worksheet as described, it will look like this:

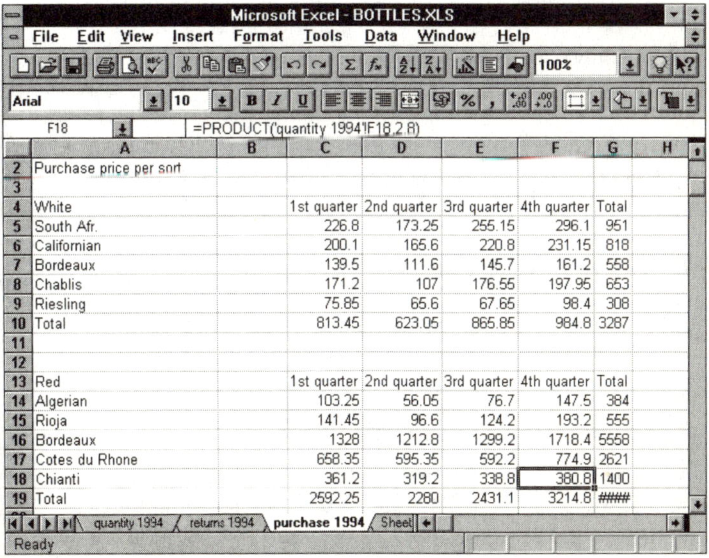

	A	B	C	D	E	F	G	H
2	Purchase price per sort							
3								
4	White		1st quarter	2nd quarter	3rd quarter	4th quarter	Total	
5	South Afr.		226.8	173.25	255.15	296.1	951	
6	Californian		200.1	165.6	220.8	231.15	818	
7	Bordeaux		139.5	111.6	145.7	161.2	558	
8	Chablis		171.2	107	176.55	197.95	653	
9	Riesling		75.85	65.6	67.65	98.4	308	
10	Total		813.45	623.05	865.85	984.8	3287	
11								
12								
13	Red		1st quarter	2nd quarter	3rd quarter	4th quarter	Total	
14	Algerian		103.25	56.05	76.7	147.5	384	
15	Rioja		141.45	96.6	124.2	193.2	555	
16	Bordeaux		1328	1212.8	1299.2	1718.4	5558	
17	Cotes du Rhone		658.35	595.35	592.2	774.9	2621	
18	Chianti		361.2	319.2	338.8	380.8	1400	
19	Total		2592.25	2280	2431.1	3214.8	####	

You will notice that the totals in column G are not completely shown because the column is too narrow. Select the range G4:G19 and open the *Format* menu. Select *Column* and *AutoFit Selection*. The width of the column is automatically adjusted to accommodate the totals.

4.8 Formatting worksheets

Just like Word, Excel also provides all kinds of possibilities for formatting text and numbers. The Formatting toolbar plays an important role in this.

4.8.1 Formatting numbers

The standard settings in Excel are referred to as the Normal style settings. When you are working with numbers, you might wish to give them a different format, perhaps with currency symbols or with a fixed number of numbers (or none) behind the decimal point.

The Formatting toolbar provides a number of buttons which enable you to display numbers in a certain format, quickly and easily.

button/name	**significance**
 Currency Style	Applies the currency style to the selected cells
 Percent Style	Displays the values in selected cells as percentages
 Comma Style	Applies the currently defined comma style to the values in the selected cells with a (specified) number, usually 2, of figures behind the decimal point.
 Increase Decimal	Displays more decimals behind the point.

Decrease Decimal — Displays less decimals behind the point.

Exercise

We shall select the ranges C5:G10 and C14:G19 on the *returns 1994* and *purchase 1994* worksheets and apply the currency style to them.

Procedure:

Currency Style

➢ Select the specified ranges and click on the *Currency Style* button on the Formatting toolbar.

You will see that many of the cells are now too narrow to accommodate the new currency notation. We shall alter the widths so that all the values are displayed.

Procedure:

1 Activate the first worksheet, *returns 1994*.
2 Click on the *Select All* button.
3 Open the *Format* menu and select *Column*.
4 Click on *AutoFit Selection*.

If you wish to apply a different numeric format, you can make use of the *Format Cells* function which is opened by selecting *Cells* from the *Format* menu. You should select the cells you wish to format first.
The *Number* tabsheet in this dialog box enables you to choose a format from all kinds of categories and codes. You can also specify your own particular code by typing it in the *Code* text box.

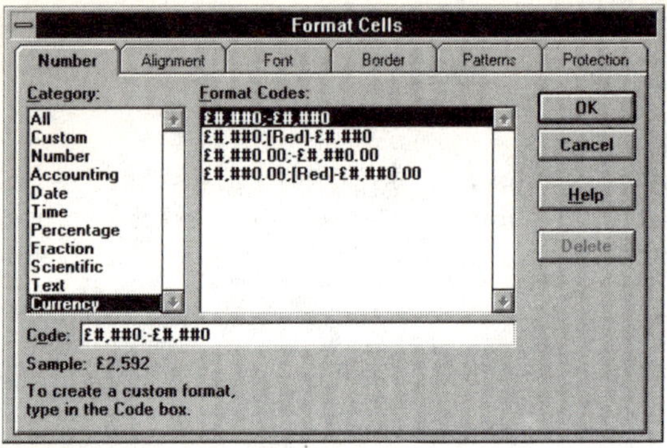

4.8.2 Formatting text

As mentioned, you can also format text when working in Excel.

Exercise
We shall format the titles of each worksheet.

Procedure:

1 Activate the *quantity 1994* worksheet.
2 Select cells A1 and A2.
3 Open the *Font* list on the Formatting toolbar and select the *Monotype Corsiva* font from the list.

Font

4 The cells are still marked. Open the *Font Size* list and select size *12*.

Font Size

Bold

5 The cells are still marked. Click on the *Bold* button on the Formatting toolbar.

Format Painter

6 The cells are still marked. Click on the *Format Painter* button on the Standard toolbar.

7 Click on the *returns 1994* worksheet and drag the mouse pointer (now in the shape of a paintbrush) across cells A1:A2 to copy the text format.

8 Ensure that cells A1:A2 are marked and click on the *Format Painter* button again. Click on the *purchase 1994* worksheet and drag the mouse pointer across cells A1:A2.

The *returns 1994* worksheet now looks like this:

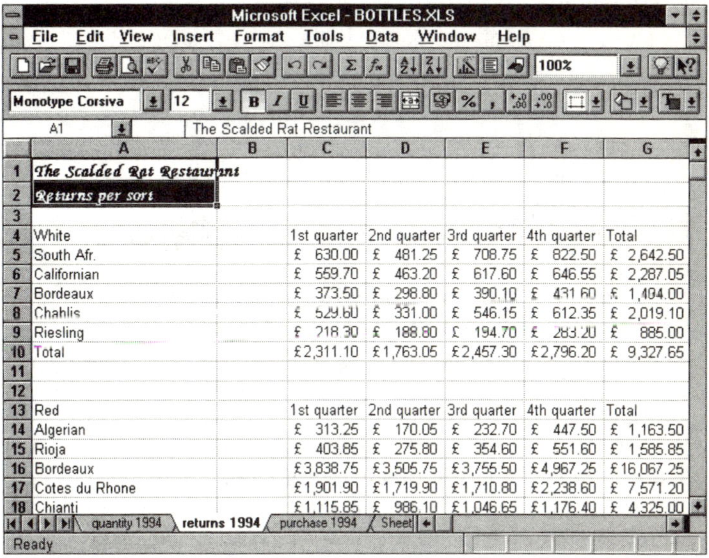

	A	B	C	D	E	F	G
1	The Scalded Rat Restaurant						
2	Returns per sort						
3							
4	White		1st quarter	2nd quarter	3rd quarter	4th quarter	Total
5	South Afr.		£ 630.00	£ 481.25	£ 708.75	£ 822.50	£ 2,642.50
6	Californian		£ 559.70	£ 463.20	£ 617.60	£ 646.55	£ 2,287.05
7	Bordeaux		£ 373.50	£ 298.80	£ 390.10	£ 431.60	£ 1,494.00
8	Chablis		£ 529.60	£ 331.00	£ 546.15	£ 612.35	£ 2,019.10
9	Riesling		£ 218.30	£ 188.80	£ 194.70	£ 283.20	£ 885.00
10	Total		£2,311.10	£1,763.05	£2,457.30	£2,796.20	£ 9,327.65
11							
12							
13	Red		1st quarter	2nd quarter	3rd quarter	4th quarter	Total
14	Algerian		£ 313.25	£ 170.05	£ 232.70	£ 447.50	£ 1,163.50
15	Rioja		£ 403.85	£ 275.80	£ 354.60	£ 551.60	£ 1,585.85
16	Bordeaux		£3,838.75	£3,505.75	£3,755.50	£4,967.25	£16,067.25
17	Cotes du Rhone		£1,901.90	£1,719.90	£1,710.80	£2,238.60	£ 7,571.20
18	Chianti		£1,115.85	£ 986.10	£1,046.65	£1,176.40	£ 4,325.00

Tip

Excel also provides the *AutoFormat* function (*Format* menu) which applies ready-made formats to selected sections of your worksheets. Shading and underlining help emphasise certain categories.

4.9 Creating charts

A chart is an excellent means of presenting certain trends (or absence of these!) in a collection of data, particularly in cases where the figures illustrate a development over a period of time.

When you create a chart based on worksheet data, the values in the chart are displayed as data points in the form of bars, lines etc. These are grouped together in ranges which are distinguished from one another by colours or patterns.

4.9.1 Creating an embedded chart

An embedded chart is a chart which is situated in the same worksheet as its associated data.

The Chart Wizard is an ideal tool for creating this type of chart.
First select the data that you wish to display in chart form, including the cells containing category or range names.

Exercise
To illustrate this, we shall create an embedded chart based on the data in the *quantity 1994* worksheet. We must first adjust this worksheet a little. Because we wish to retain a version of this worksheet as it now is, we shall first make a copy of it; we can then make adjustments to this copy.

Procedure:
1 Activate the *quantity 1994* worksheet.
2 Open the *Edit* menu and select *Move or Copy Sheet*.
3 Click on *returns 1994* in the *Before Sheet* section

to ensure that the copy will be made just behind the original. Click on the *Create a Copy* check box. Click on *OK*.

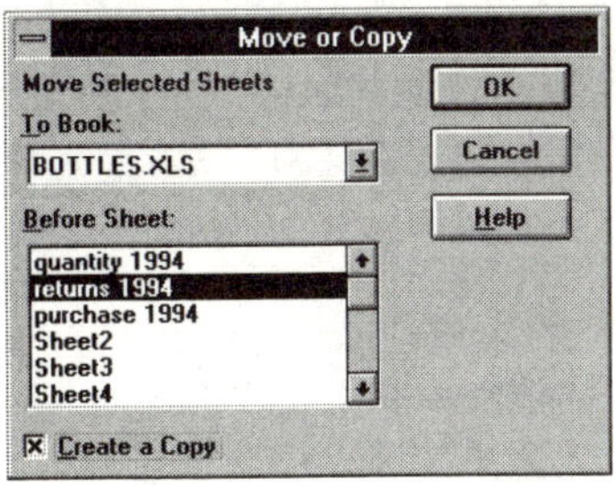

4 Double click on the *quantity 1994 (2)* tab and change the name to *quantity 1994 (chart)*.

5 Because the data to be used in a chart have to be right next to their category headings, we must now remove column B from the worksheet. Click on the column heading and open the *Edit* menu. Click on *Delete*. The entire column is deleted and all the data shift to the left.

6 Now we must remove the categories 'White' and 'Red' since, being collective names, they cannot be shown as data at the same level as the individual types of wine. Activate cells A4 and A13 and press Del.

7 Now join the data in one long list by removing rows 10, 11, 12 and 13. This is done by clicking on the row headings and selecting *Delete* from the *Edit* menu.

8 To avoid confusion between different data with the same name change the name 'Bordeaux' in the current row 12 to 'Bordeaux (Red)'. This is done by activating the cell and simply typing the new name.

AutoSum

9 Select the range B5 to F15 and click on the *AutoSum* button to calculate the new totals.

Your screen should now look like this:

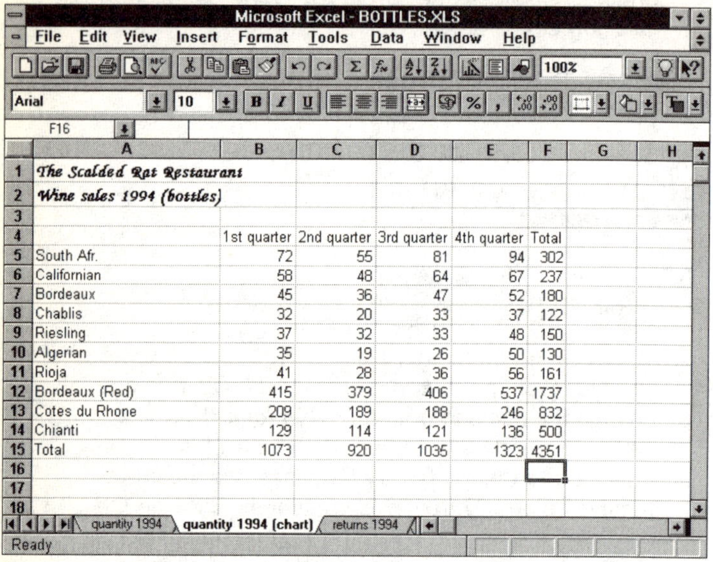

	A	B	C	D	E	F
1	*The Scalded Rat Restaurant*					
2	*Wine sales 1994 (bottles)*					
3						
4		1st quarter	2nd quarter	3rd quarter	4th quarter	Total
5	South Afr.	72	55	81	94	302
6	Californian	58	48	64	67	237
7	Bordeaux	45	36	47	52	180
8	Chablis	32	20	33	37	122
9	Riesling	37	32	33	48	150
10	Algerian	35	19	26	50	130
11	Rioja	41	28	36	56	161
12	Bordeaux (Red)	415	379	406	537	1737
13	Cotes du Rhone	209	189	188	246	832
14	Chianti	129	114	121	136	500
15	Total	1073	920	1035	1323	4351
16						
17						
18						

10 Select cells A4:E14.

Chart Wizard

11 Click on the *Chart Wizard* button.

12 Click on the worksheet if you wish to have the chart automatically placed in the worksheet. You can also specify the position and the size of the chart by dragging the mouse across the required area.

13 The *ChartWizard - Step 1 of 5* dialog box appears. If the range is correctly specified here ($A$4:$E$14), click on the *Next* button, otherwise enter the correct range.

14 *Step 2* appears. Click on the *Column* option if it is not already active, and then on *Next*.

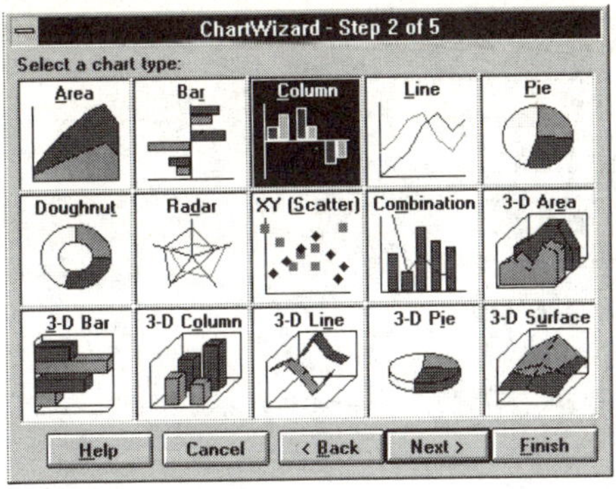

15 Select option 6 in the subsequent window if it is not already active, and then click on *Next*.

16 The following dialog window will appear. Make sure that the settings correspond to those shown in the figure, and press *Next*.

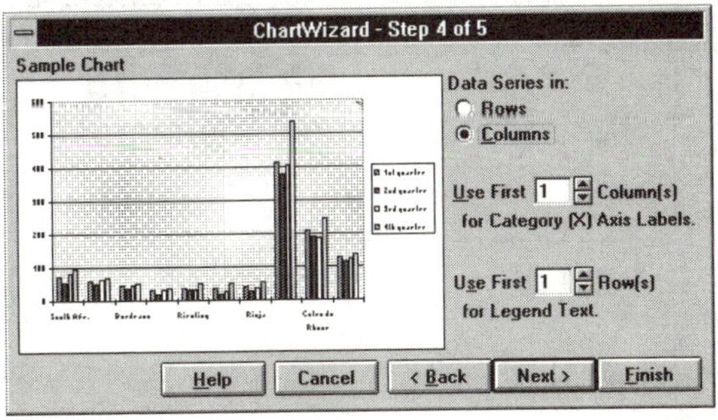

17 Complete the *Step 5* dialog box as shown, by typing the text 'Quantity sold' in the *Chart Title* box and 'Number of bottles' in the *Value (Y)* box in the *Axis Titles* section. Click on *Finish*.

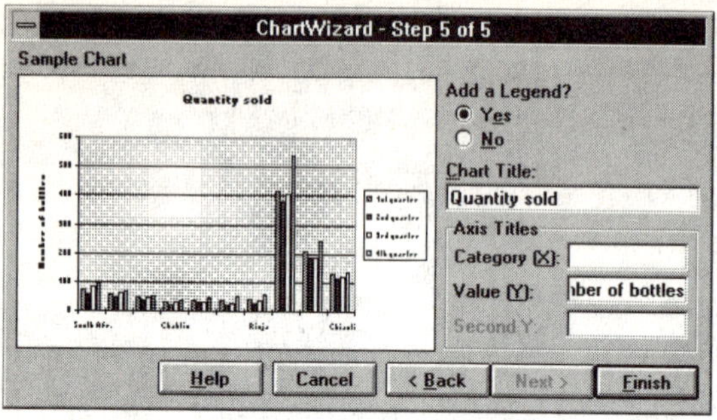

The chart appears in the worksheet, along with the Chart toolbar, at the position where you clicked.

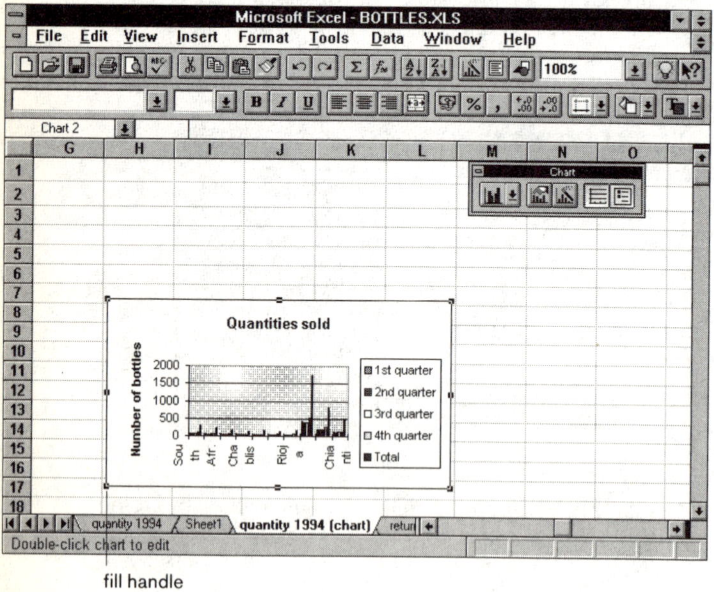

You can enlarge or reduce the chart by dragging the fill handles. If you click on the worksheet the Chart toolbar and the handles disappear; clicking on the chart will restore them. If you double click on the chart, a dialog window appears in which you can edit the chart.

As you see, even when we enlarge our chart, not all the names are shown. We shall alter this. Double click on the chart to switch to the Edit mode. Then double click on the horizontal (X) axis. The *Format Axis* dialog box opens. Click on the *Alignment* tabsheet. Click on the type of text alignment you wish to have. We prefer the middle one.

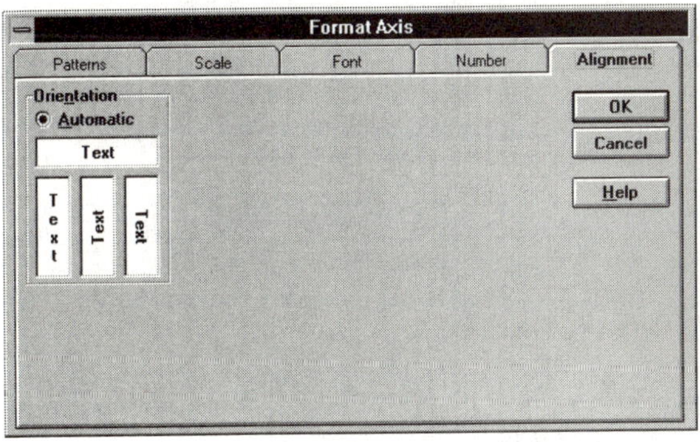

Click on the *Font* tabsheet and select *Size* 8. This should ensure that the text is small enough to be displayed. Click on *OK* and enlarge the box. All the names should now be shown.

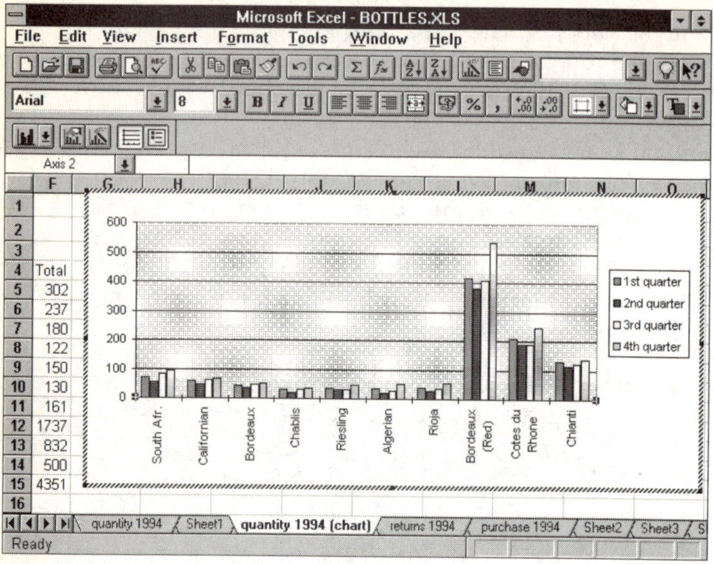

4.10 Printing worksheets

Print

If you wish to print a workbook in accordance with the settings you made in the *Page Setup* dialog window, simply click on the *Print* button on the Standard toolbar.

However, if you wish to specify other print options, open the *File* menu and select *Print*. The *Print* dialog window appears in which you can modify all kinds of settings.

The settings you have specified in the *Page Setup* dialog window always apply to any print job.
If you wish to print an embedded chart without the rest of the worksheet, first double click on the chart so that the chart window is activated. Then select *Print* from the *File* menu. You will see that **Selected Sheet(s)** is replaced by **Selected Chart**. Click on *OK*.

4.10.1 Print Preview

Prior to printing a chart, worksheet or whole workbook, it is advisable to have a look at the Print Preview first. This shows how the document will be printed. You can make alterations if necessary before the printing process begins.

Exercise
We shall look at the Print Preview for our newly-made *quantity 1994 (chart)*.

Procedure:

Print Preview

1 Click on the *Print Preview* button on the Standard toolbar, or select *Print Preview* from the *File* menu.

The document as it will be printed under the current settings is shown on the screen.

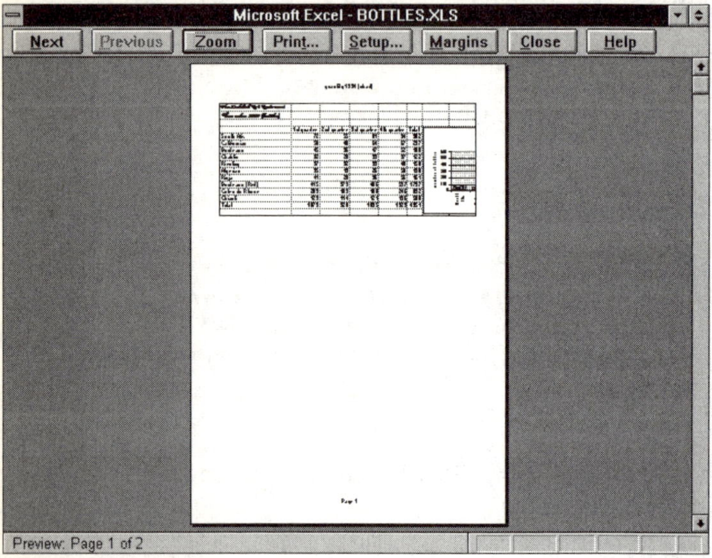

As you see, not all the chart is shown. We shall return to the worksheet and move the chart to a position under the numerical data.

2 Click on the *Close* button. The worksheet is shown on the screen.
3 Open the *View* menu and select *Zoom*. Specify *50%*. Now you have a good overview of both the worksheet and the chart.
4 Use the fill handles at the lower left-hand corner and upper right-hand corner to move the chart to a position under the data.

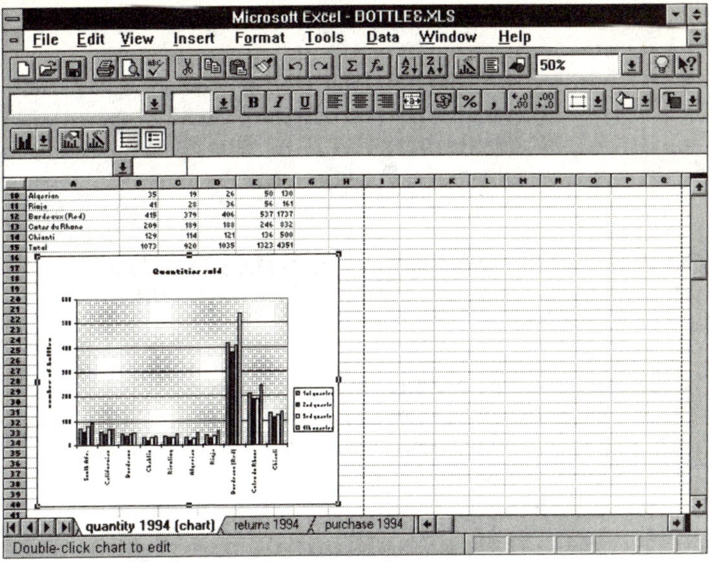

When you are satisfied with the result, you can try the *Print Preview* once more.

The *Print Preview* window provides a number of buttons. They have the following functions:

button	**function**
Next	Displays the next page.
Previous	Displays the previous page.
Zoom	Switches between enlarged and reduced display.
Print	Produces the *Print* dialog window. If you had opened the Print Preview from the *Print* window, the selected pages will be printed when you activate this button.
Setup	Produces the *Page Setup* dialog window.

Margins	Activates/deactivates the page margins, the header and footer margins and column widths so that you can easily adjust the margins and widths of the printed page.
Close	Closes the Print Preview.

Exercise

Close the Print Preview, save the BOTTLES.XLS document and close Excel.

Procedure:

1 Click on the *Close* button in the Print Preview.
2 Open the *File* menu and select *Save*.
3 Open the *File* menu again and select *Exit*.

5 Working with Microsoft PowerPoint 4.0

This chapter discusses working with PowerPoint, the Microsoft Office package for making presentations. Its sophisticated functions for compiling data, allied to its designing and timing qualities, enable you to create professional presentations for your material. You can make presentations using overhead transparencies, paper or 35 mm slides, or for electronic display. In addition, you can make notes for the speaker and summaries and handouts for the public at large. You can also insert into your presentation documents and sections of documents which have been created in other applications.

PowerPoint will guide you throughout the entire process of creating a presentation. PowerPoint, just like Word and Excel, also provides shortcut menus, toolbars and button info.

5.1 New in version 4.0

PowerPoint 4.0 is equipped with a number of new features which considerably facilitate working with this presentation program:

- AutoContent Wizard: This Wizard assists you in shaping your ideas into a presentation. Even if you have no ideas at all, you can create a presentation using the AutoContent Wizard!
- Pick a Look Wizard: This Wizard helps in applying a professional design to your presentation.
- Free Rotate: You can now turn text and other screen objects up to 360 degrees without any problem.
- Freeform Drawing: You can now draw on slides while showing a presentation on screen.

5.2 Starting up PowerPoint

Microsoft Power-Point

You can start up PowerPoint by double clicking on the *Microsoft PowerPoint* icon in the Microsoft Office group under the Program Manager or by clicking on the *Microsoft PowerPoint* button on the Office Manager toolbar.

Microsoft PowerPoint

If other applications are active (such as Excel or Word) and your computer is not functioning optimally, you can close down these applications; we shall not be making use of them in this chapter.

When PowerPoint is started up, the *Tip of the Day* box appears with a small tip about working with the program. Acknowledge this by clicking on *OK* and the box is closed again.

The opening screen in PowerPoint is not an empty screen in which you can directly enter data as in Word or Excel. Instead, a dialog window appears providing a choice between opening an existing presentation or creating a new one.

The options in this window are as follows:

- The *AutoContent Wizard* activates a Wizard which guides you through the process of creating and structuring a new presentation.
- The *Pick a Look Wizard* helps you choose of one of the professional designs for your presentation.
- *Template* produces a dialog window from which you can select a template for the layout of your new presentation.

- *Blank Presentation* begins with a blank presentation with all values for colour, fonts and design features set to the default values.
- The *Open an Existing Presentation* option produces a dialog window from which you can choose an existing presentation.

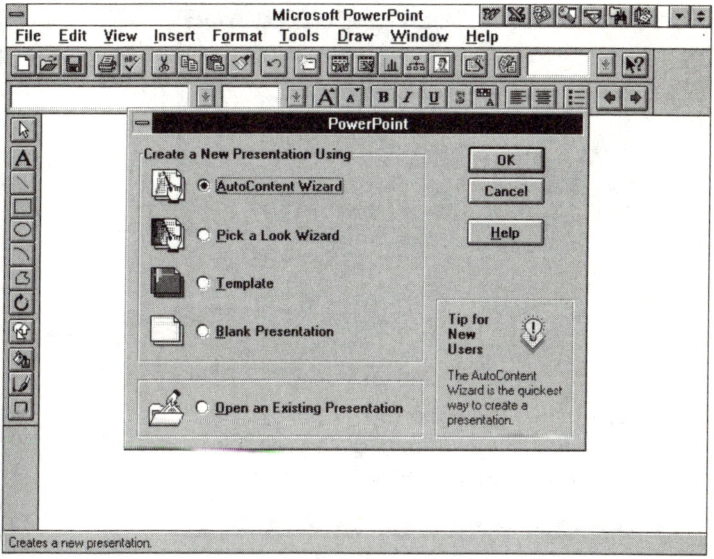

5.3 Creating a presentation

If you wish to have PowerPoint help you in determining the structure of a new presentation, the best option to choose is *AutoContent Wizard*.

Exercise
We shall create a new presentation to demonstrate how PowerPoint goes to work. We shall make use of the Auto-Content Wizard to guide us through the unknown.

Procedure:

1 Activate the *AutoContent Wizard* in the *PowerPoint* opening dialog window.
2 Click on *OK*.

The first window of the *AutoContent Wizard* appears:

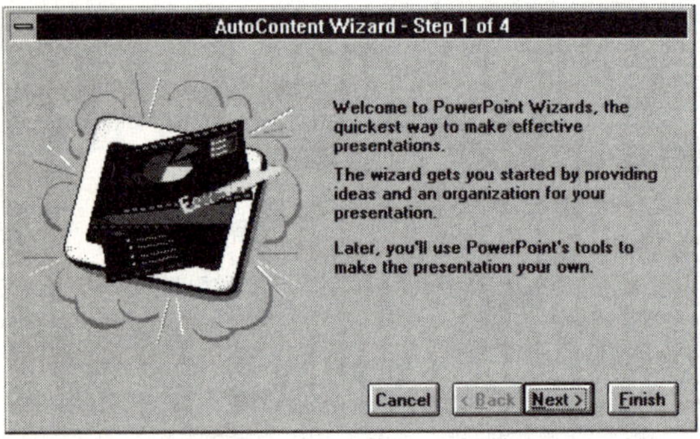

3 Click on the *Next* button.
4 Complete the subsequent dialog window which will create the title slide, and click on *Next*.

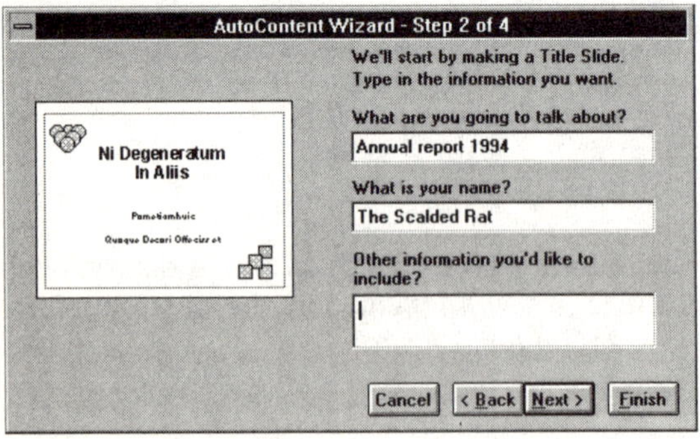

5 In the following dialog window, click on the *General* option and then on *Next*.

6 Click on *Finish* in the last window.

The *Cue Cards* window will probably now appear on your screen (depending on the settings in your program). These *Cue Cards* provide useful tips for working with PowerPoint. There is a check box at the bottom of this window, *Show cue cards with AutoContent Wizard*. Placing a cross here specifies that cue cards will be displayed when you make use of the *AutoContent Wizard*. You can close this window by double clicking on the Control menu symbol (button in the upper left-hand corner), or by opening this menu and selecting *Close*; you could also press the shortcut key combination Alt+F4.

7 Ensure that the *Show cue cards with AutoContent Wizard* option is active and close the *Cue Cards* window.

Your screen now displays a summary of the new presentation. You can make all kinds of modifications to this. We shall discuss this in section 5.6.

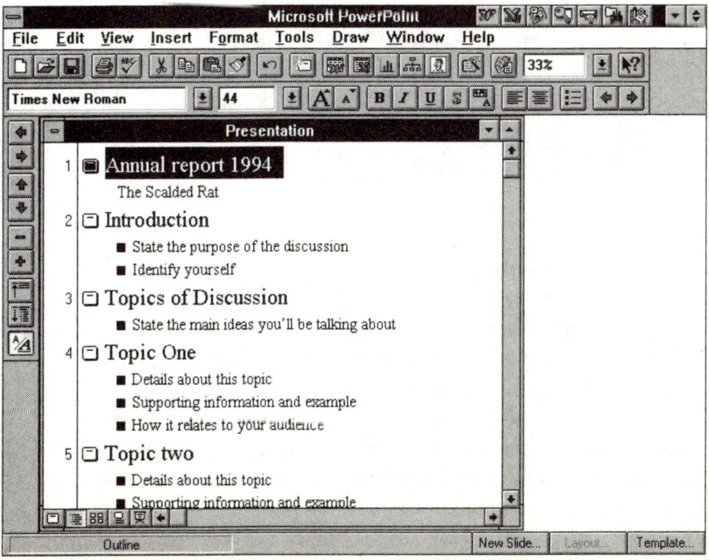

5.4 Saving, closing and opening a presentation

If you wish to save a presentation, you have to store it on disk. You do not have to close one presentation in order to begin another, since it is possible to have several presentations open in PowerPoint simultaneously.

5.4.1 Saving a presentation

Save

To save a new presentation on disk, click on the *Save* button on the Standard toolbar, or select the *Save* option from the *File* menu. If you have not saved it previously, the *Save As* dialog window will appear:

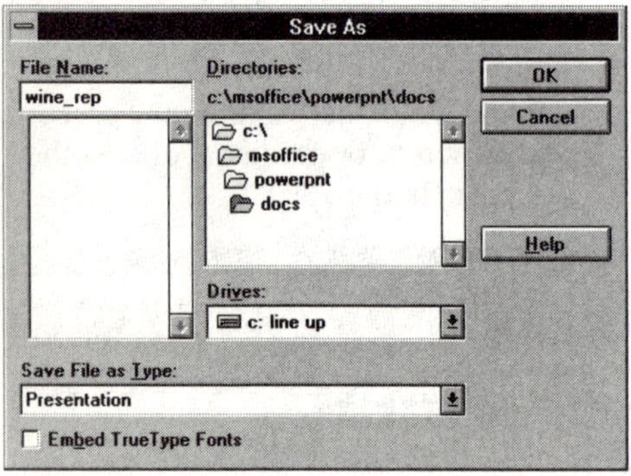

The file name is entered in the upper text box. Select the directory in which you want to save the presentation from the *Directories* list. Check that the proper drive is displayed in the *Drives* section (you might want to store the file on diskette in A: for instance). If you want to save the file as a PowerPoint presentation, ensure that *Presentation* is shown in the *Save File as Type* box. The file is then automatically assigned the extension PPT, which you do not have to type.

Exercise
Save the newly-created presentation under the name WINE_REP.PPT in the directory of your choice. (We have created a subdirectory of *powerpnt* called *docs* in which to save our documents.)

The *Summary Info* dialog window appears when you click on *OK* in the *Save As* dialog window. You can enter additional information about the file, for your own reference. Click on *OK*.

Note
If you have already saved the file, it will be saved again in the most recent version when you give the *Save* command. It is thus saved under the same name in the same directory. No dialog window appears in which you can specify additional parameters or description. If you want to save a previously-saved file with new parameters (under a new name or in another directory for example), use the *Save As* command from the *File* menu. You can specify the new settings in the subsequent dialog window.

5.4.2 Closing a presentation

When you want to close a presentation, select *Close* from the *File* menu or double click on the Control menu button or select *Close* from the Control menu. If you have not saved the presentation since the previous modifications, you will be asked whether or not you want to save these.

5.4.3 Opening a presentation

Open

To open a presentation, click on the *Open* button on the Standard toolbar or select the *Open* command from the *File* menu. The *Open* dialog window appears:

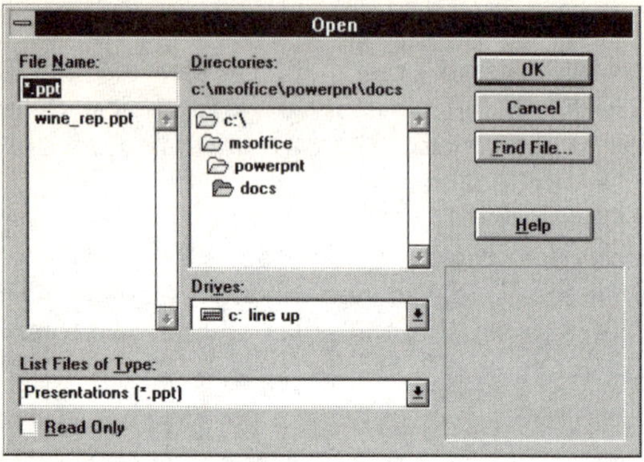

Select the appropriate presentation in the dialog window and click on *OK*. Clicking on the *Find File* button opens a dialog window in which you can specify search criteria to search for a file which you cannot directly locate. You may have forgotten its full name or the directory in which it is stored. You can also make use of the wildcards, ? and *, to represent one or a random number of characters respectively.

5.5 Various modes of display

You can view your presentations in various ways. Word provides three display modes (Normal, Page Layout and Outline); PowerPoint provides five:

- slide view
- outline view
- slide sorter view
- notes pages view
- slide show.

You can activate these types of display by selecting them from the *View* menu. You can also make use of the buttons at the bottom of the presentation window:

button	**display**
	Slide View
	Outline View
	Slide Sorter View
	Notes Pages View
	Slide Show

The presentation you created in this chapter will be initially displayed in the Outline View. The Outline toolbar is then shown.

The various display modes work as follows:

- In the Slide View, one slide at a time is shown. All the graphic features are available.
- In the Outline View, only the titles and the main head ings of the slide are visible. This display is convenient when you are organising the presentation and wish to insert text quickly.
- In the Slide Sorter View, all the slides are shown. You can change the order of sequence of the slides and you can determine how they are to be displayed in the presentation. You cannot edit the slides directly in this display mode.
- In the Notes Pages View, you can make and display the speaker's notes which correspond to the sides being shown. Each page corresponds to one slide.
- In the Slide Show View, you can display the slides as a slide show. They occupy the entire screen.

5.6 The Outline View

The Outline View enables you to work quickly and easily with text. Other graphic elements are not displayed. In the example presentation you will create in this chapter, you will initially work with text. Accordingly, the Outline View mode should be active. This is shown in the status box at the bottom of the screen.

The presentation window shows the initial structure of the presentation. There are various headings and subheadings, which you will alter to conform to your own requirements.

The icon in the form of a slide indicates that the text behind the icon is the slide title. If only a horizontal line is displayed in the icon, this means that the slide contains only text, with no graphic elements. If graphic elements are present on a slide, symbols are shown on the icon. The number of the slide is shown in front of the icon.

The buttons on the Outline View toolbar, flanking the left-hand side of the screen, enable you to make adjustments to the existing layout. These buttons have the following significance:

button/name	**function**
 Promote (Indent less)	Moves selected paragraphs in an outline one place to the left, in other words, to a higher level
 Demote (Indent more)	Moves selected paragraphs in an outline one place to the right, in other words, to a lower level
 Move Up	Moves selected paragraphs upwards in the outline
 Move Down	Moves selected paragraphs downwards in the outline

	Collapse Selection	Conceals all summarised items on the selected slide so that only the title is displayed
	Expand Selection	Displays all summarised items under the title on the selected slide
	Show Titles	Displays only the slide titles
	Show All	Shows all levels within the slide
	Show Formatting	Displays/hides all character formatting.

5.6.1 Altering and inserting text

When working in the Outline View, it is possible to replace the existing text with your own text by dragging the mouse across the text to mark it and then typing the required text. To select the whole slide, click on its icon. If you press Enter when working in an outline, you insert a new paragraph at the same level as the previous one.

Tip
If you want to obtain an overview of the shortcut keys which you can use to select text when working in the Outline View, open the *Help* menu and choose *Search for Help on*. Type **outline** in the upper text box, click on the *Show Topics* button, choose *About Working with Text in the Outline View* from the lower box. Click on *Go To*. Then click on *Selecting text in an outline* from the subsequent dialog window.

Exercise
We shall now make some alterations to the presentation in the Outline View.

Procedure:

1 Ensure that the new presentation is displayed in the Outline View. Click on the *Maximize* button to make the presentation window screen filling.

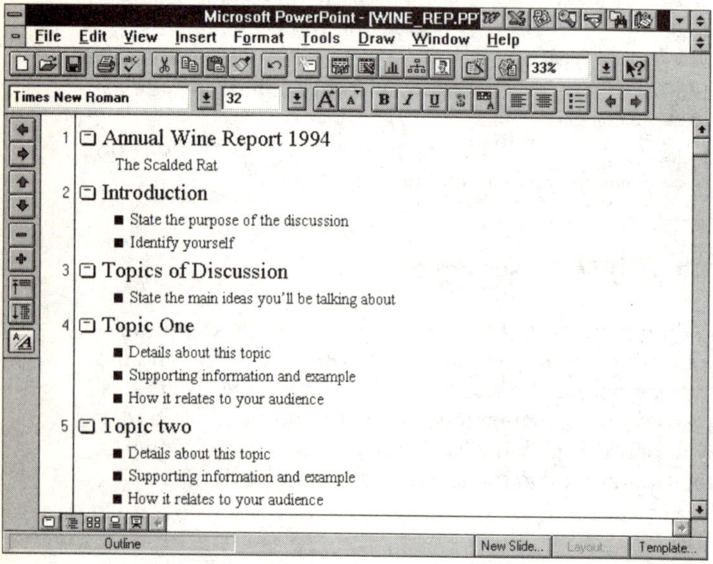

2 Change the existing text as shown in the figure below. A new subheading is added by pressing Enter when the cursor is at the same level. A subheading is deleted by marking the appropriate section of text and pressing Del. Delete existing superfluous headings in the same way.

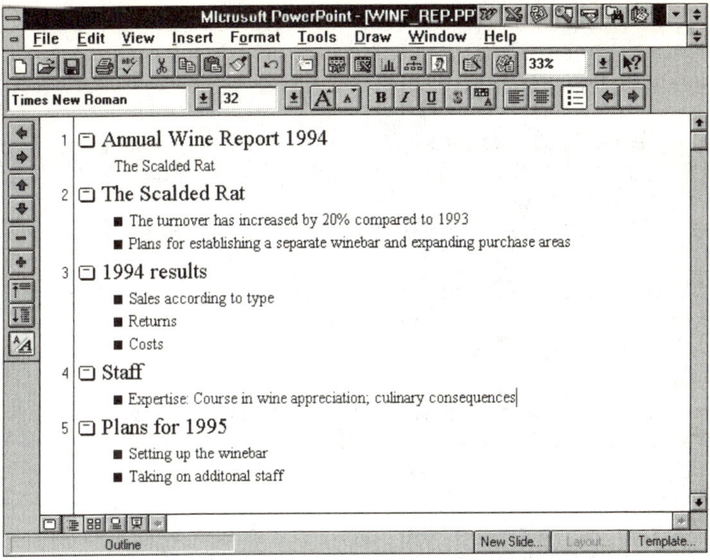

5.6.2 Raising or lowering the paragraph levels

The following exercise deals with copying a slide and changing the level of the paragraphs.

Exercise

We shall copy slide number 3 and make alterations to the copied version.

Procedure:

1. Click on the slide icon next to the number 3 at the left-hand side of the presentation. The entire slide is selected.
2. Click on the *Copy* button on the Standard toolbar.
3. Move the insertion point to just behind the word 'Costs' at the end of slide number 3.
4. Click on the *Paste* button on the Standard toolbar.

Copy

Paste

A copy of slide number 3 is inserted directly underneath. All subsequent slides are shifted up one position and are allocated a higher, successive number.

5 Select 'Sales according to type' in the present slide number 4. This is done by clicking on the bullet in front of the text.

Promote

6 Click on the *Promote* button on the Outline toolbar.

The selected text is promoted from the subheading level to the heading level. This means that it automatically becomes a new slide.

7 Do the same to the other subheadings in this (now number 5) list, 'Returns' and 'Costs'.

Tip
You can also promote or demote a paragraph by dragging a paragraph to the left or to the right. First place the mouse pointer to the left of the paragraph so that it acquires the shape of a four-headed arrow. Then drag the paragraph.

5.6.3 Removing and inserting slides

Just for practice, we shall now remove a slide from the list and then add a new one.

Exercise
Remove slide 4 and then add a new one between 'Staff' and 'Plans for 1995'.

Procedure:

1 Select slide 4, '1994 Results', and open the *Edit* menu. Select *Delete Slide*. You can also select the slide and simply press Backspace or Del.
2 Place the insertion point behind the text in slide number 7, the slide entitled 'Staff'.

New Slide

Click on the *New Slide* button on the status bar at the bottom of the screen, or open the *Insert* menu and choose *New Slide*.

3 Add the text, 'Organization Chart' to slide 8:

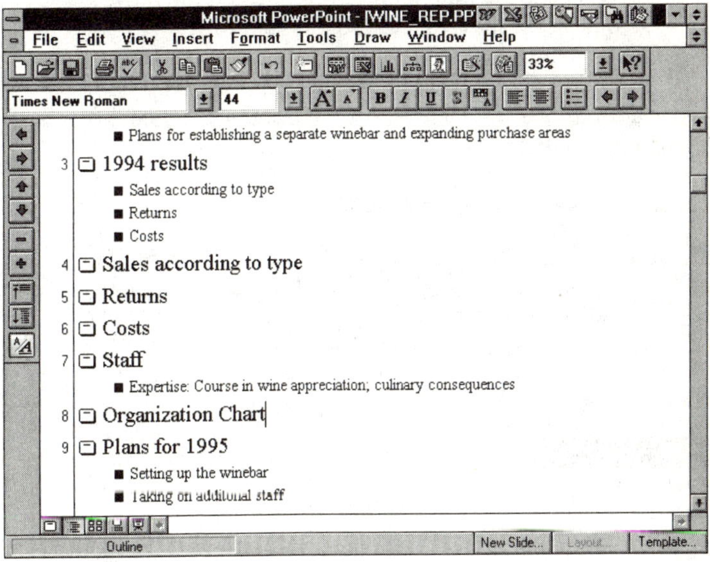

5.6.4 Moving slides

We shall continue our practice by moving two slides.

Exercise

Move slides 7 and 8 upwards.

Procedure:

1 Click on and drag the slide 7 icon upwards to just under slide 2.

While you are dragging the slide, a horizontal line appears indicating where the slide will be positioned when you release the mouse button.

Move Up

2 Now move the slide 8 icon upwards using the *Move Up* button on the Outline toolbar, just for practice. Click on the icon to activate it and click on the *Move Up* button. Each click moves the icon one step upwards. Move the slide so that it occupies position number 4 in the list.

The list will now look something like this:

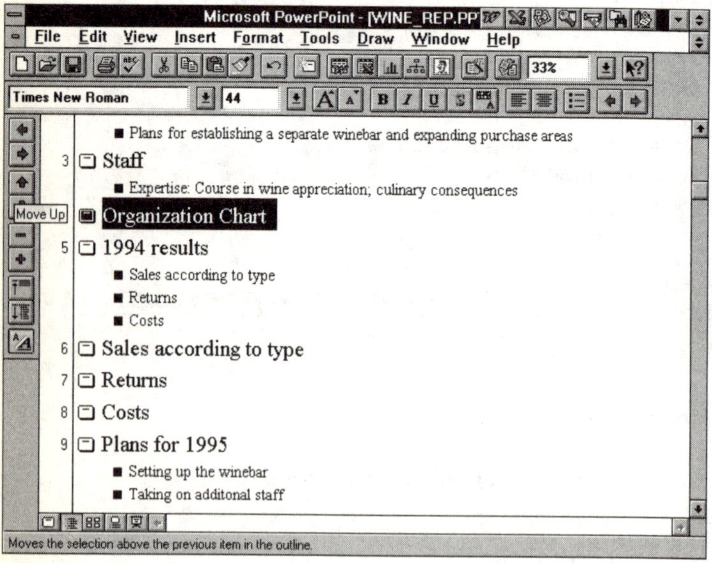

5.6.5 Showing only the titles

If the list should become rather lengthy and you want to have a quick view of the slides you have included in the list, you can activate the Show Titles display so that only the titles are shown.

Exercise

We shall activate the Show Titles mode to produce a summary of points.

Procedure:

Show Titles

Click on the *Show Titles* display.

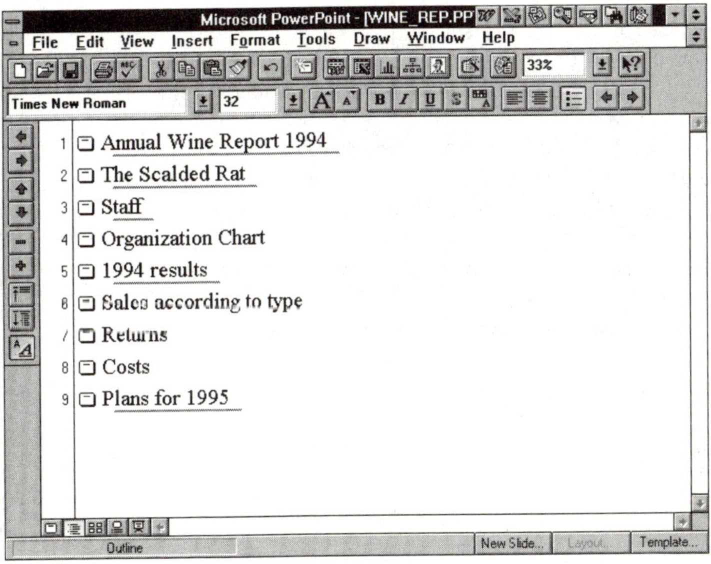

Only the titles are shown. If there are subheadings under any specific title, the title is underlined.

Show All

To show all the text on the screen once more, click on the *Show All* button on the Outline toolbar.

5.7 The Slide View

In the Slide View, only one slide at a time is shown on the screen. Graphic elements, if present, are shown. There are no graphic elements as yet in the presentation you have created up to now (these will be added in chapter 9).

Exercise
We shall now activate the Slide View.

Procedure:

Slide View

You can either click on the *Slide View* button at the bottom of the screen or select *Slides* from the *View* menu.

The currently active slide is shown. It occupies the major part of the window. The Outline toolbar has been replaced by the Drawing toolbar.

To switch to a different slide, press the PgUp or PgDn key, or click on the *Previous Slide* or *Next Slide* button in the vertical scroll bar. You can also use the scroll bar to browse forwards and backwards through the presentation.

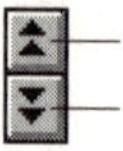

You can edit the text and other elements by placing the insertion point at the required position and by selecting the text. Existing text is replaced by typing new text.

Text or other elements is always displayed in a frame when you select the text or click on the elements to be edited. You can then drag the frame to a new position if desired. If you click on the edge of the frame, eight sizing handles appear. You can click on these to drag the frame to a larger or smaller format.

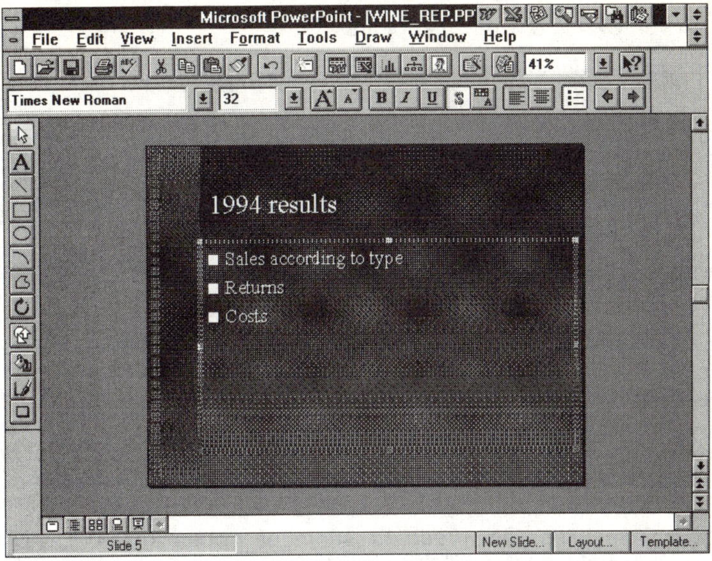

5.7.1 Designing the presentation using the Pick a Look Wizard

You can apply all kinds of formatting features directly when working in the Slide View, in much the same way as you format text in Word. However, it is often much more convenient to use the Pick a Look Wizard to alter various aspects of the layout.

Exercise
We shall change the presentation design by means of the Pick a Look Wizard.

Procedure:

Pick a Look Wizard

1 Click on the *Pick a Look Wizard* button on the Standard toolbar.

The first Wizard window appears.

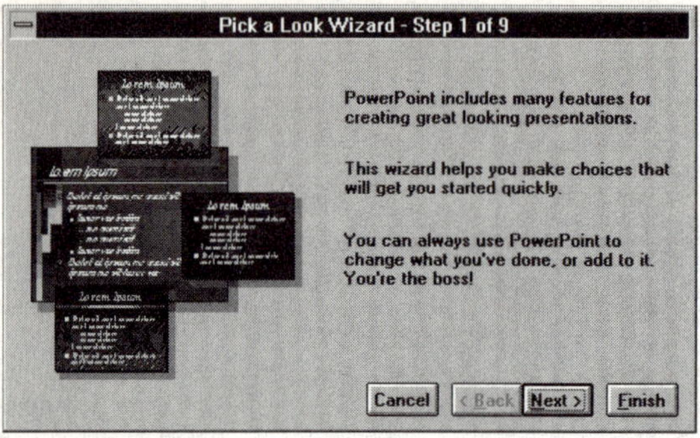

2 Read the text in the window and click on the *Next* button.
3 Select the *On-Screen Presentation* option in the next window and click on the *Next* button.
4 In the next window, *Step 3 of 9*, click on the *More* button in order to open the *Presentation Template* dialog window. You can choose a design for the presentation here.

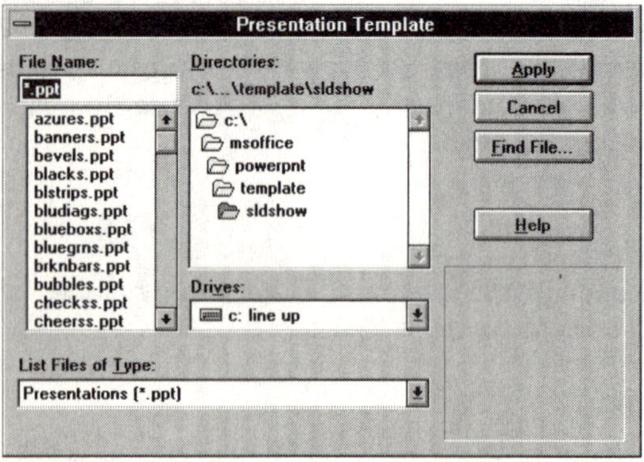

When you click on a template name in the list, a sample appears in the box in the lower right-hand section of the window. Try this out to get an idea of the possibilities.

5 Select *brknbars.ppt* or another template of your own choice and click on *Apply*. The *Step 3 of 9* window appears again.
6 Click on the *Next* button.
7 The next window deals with how you would wish your presentation to be printed. All the options are crossed. We shall accept this and move onto the next window by clicking on *Next*.
8 In the subsequent window, you have to specify which data you want to have displayed on your slides. In our current example, we shall not include any of these optional data on our slides. Remove any data shown and click on *Next*.

The following three windows appear if you specified that you wished to have Speaker's Notes, Audience Handout Pages and Outline Pages in *Step 4 of 9* (as we did in point 7 above).

9 In the *Notes Options* box, specify any data you would want to have on the Speaker's Notes. We decide to activate all the options and to enter the name of the firm, *The Scalded Rat*, in the corresponding text box. Then click on *Next*.
10 Specify the same information in the following dialog window, *Handout Options* and click on *Next*.
11 In the following dialog window, *Outline Options*, specify only the date, since this version only provides a summary of the topics being dealt with. Click on *Next*.
12 Click on *Finish* in the last dialog window.

The presentation will now be compiled according to the specifications just made. The last slide, for example, will look like this:

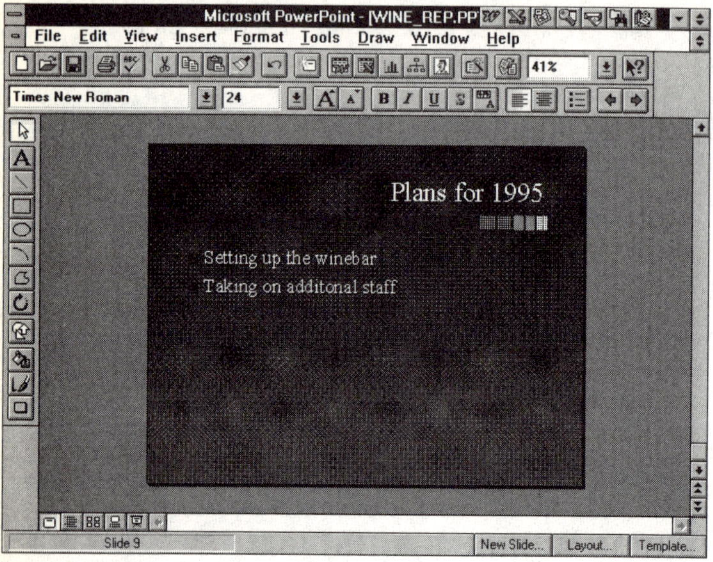

5.7.2 Adding a slide

If you wish to add a new slide to a slide display, you can make a choice out of a number of different possibilities.

To add a new slide, click on the *New Slide* at the lower right-hand part of the screen.

A dialog window appears in which you can select a lay-out style for the new slide. The box at the bottom right of the dialog window gives a concise description of the currently activated layout; you activate a layout by click-ing on it.

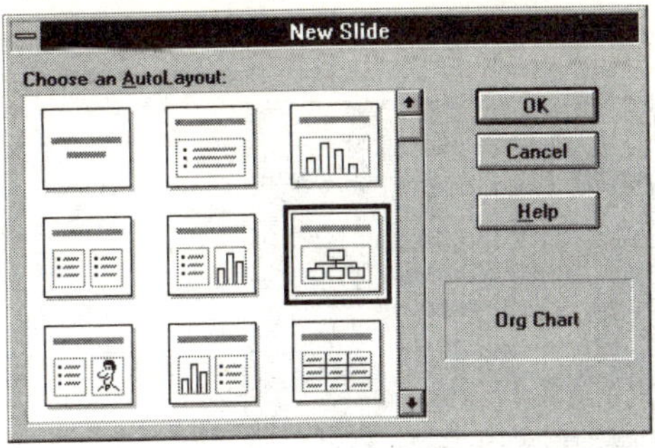

If you add a new slide in this way, this slide appears on the screen with all kinds of frames which provide information about inserting text or other elements.

Layout

Tip
You can open a similar window by clicking on the *Layout* button. You can then select a new layout for the currently active slide.

Exercise
We shall now add a new slide displaying an organizational chart. This organizational chart shows the structure of the firm.

Procedure:

1 Activate Slide 3.

New Slide

2 Click on the *New Slide* button.

3 Select *Org Chart* (the sixth button) in the dialog window.

4 Click on *OK*.

A new slide appears on the screen.

5 Click in the upper section.

The text disappears and a flashing insertion point cursor is shown.

6 Type **The Scalded Rat Organisation**.
7 Double click in the lower section.

The Microsoft Organization Chart Help program is activated.

8 Replace the text in the boxes with the following names and functions. You can select existing text by dragging the mouse across it. Then type the new text which is written over the old, or press Backspace or Del to delete the text.

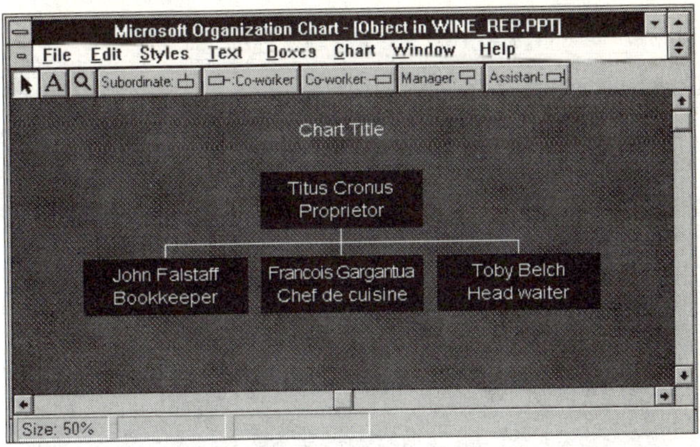

Tip
To adapt the background colour of the boxes to your taste, or to make them more legible, select a box and then open the *Boxes* menu in the *Organization Chart* window. Select *Box Color* and click on a suitable colour.

9 Click on the *Subordinate* button along the top of the dialog window.

Subordinate

10 Click on the box containing the name Francois Gargantua. A new box appears in which you can enter the name of a subordinate.
11 Click on the new box and enter the name **Friar Tuck** and the function **Assistant chef**.
12 Enter the name **Bessie Smith** as a subordinate of Toby Belch in the same way.
13 Open the *File* menu in the dialog window and select *Update WINE_REP.PPT*.
14 Open the *File* menu in the dialog window once more, and select *Exit and Return to WINE_REP.PPT*.
15 The slide is shown in the Slide Show display.

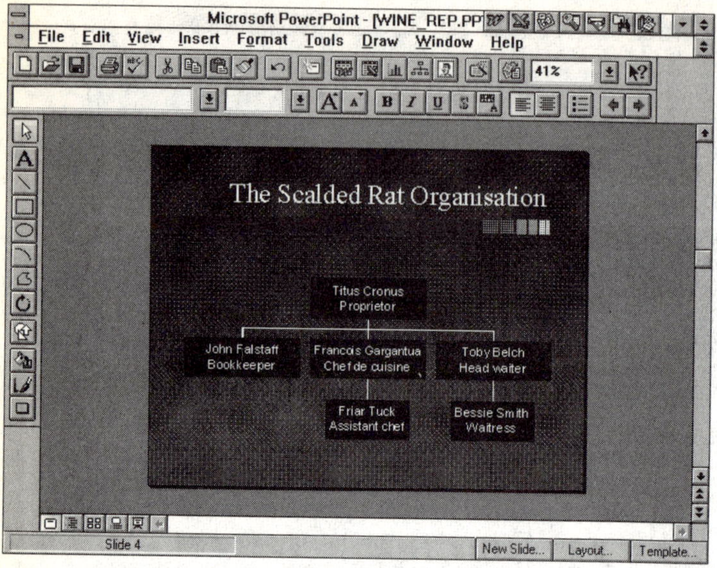

5.8 The Slide Sorter View

The slides are shown next to one another in the Slide Sorter View, just as if they were lying on a light box. You can the easily place them in a certain order but you cannot edit them. If you wish to see a slide in the Slide View, double click on it. To move it to a new position, simply click on it and drag it to the new position.

Exercise
We shall now display the slides in the Slide Sorter View and also remove one of the slides.

Procedure:

Slide Sorter View

1 Activate the Slide Sorter View by selecting *Slide Sorter* from the *View* menu, or by clicking on the *Slide Sorter View* button at the bottom of the screen.

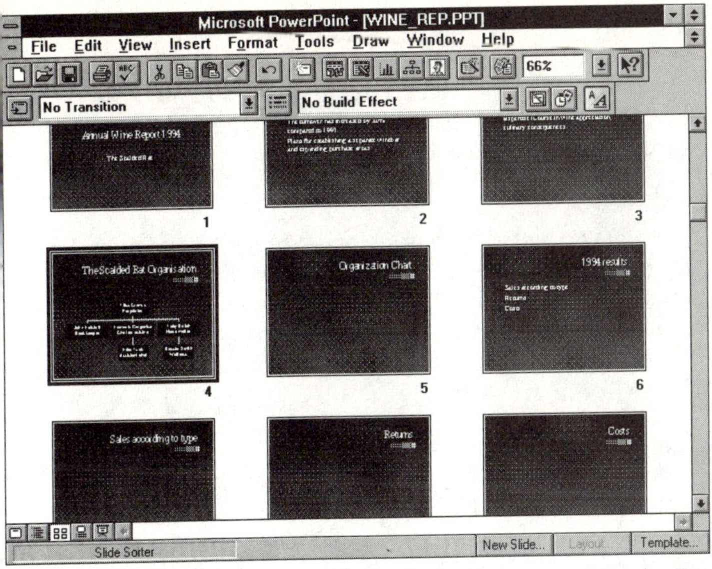

2 Because we have just created slide number 4 with the Organization Chart, slide number 5 has become superfluous. Wo shall remove it. Click on slide number 5, with tho text 'Organization Chart', and press Del or Backspace. You can also choose *Delete Slide* from the *Edit* menu.

If you want to select several slides at once, hold down the Shift key while clicking on the slides. You can undo the selection by following the same procedure.

5.9 Drawing

You can draw on the slides by means of the Drawing toolbar. This is only possible in the Slide View or the Notes Pages View.

This Drawing toolbar closely resembles those in Word and Excel.

5.9.1 Rotating objects

Free Rotate

In the Slide View or Notes Pages View, you can make use of the Drawing toolbar to rotate objects. This does not only apply to objects you have created using the Drawing toolbar.

You rotate an object by clicking on it to select it and then clicking on the *Free Rotate* tool. Move the (circular) mouse pointer to one of the sizing handles so that the mouse pointer assumes the shape of a four-headed arrow. Drag the mouse in the required direction.

5.9.2 AutoShapes

Auto-Shapes

In addition to the lines, circles, freehand drawings etc. you can make using the Drawing toolbar, you can also select a number of ready-made shapes. These are activated by clicking on the *AutoShapes* button and then selecting one of the shapes which appears on the subsequent palette. When you have selected the required shape, drag the mouse pointer across the slide to determine the size of the shape to be created.

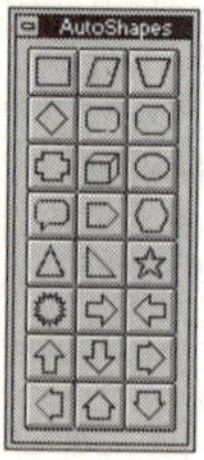

5.10 Printing

You can choose whether you want to print the slides, notes pages, handouts or the outline. You probably made this choice when you applied the Pick a Look Wizard (see section 5.7.1).

If you want to check that the slides have the proper layout before printing them, open the *File* menu and select *Slide Setup*. This opens the dialog window of the same name, in which you can specify the sizes, numeration and orientation. You can also determine the orientation of any handouts, Notes and Outlines.

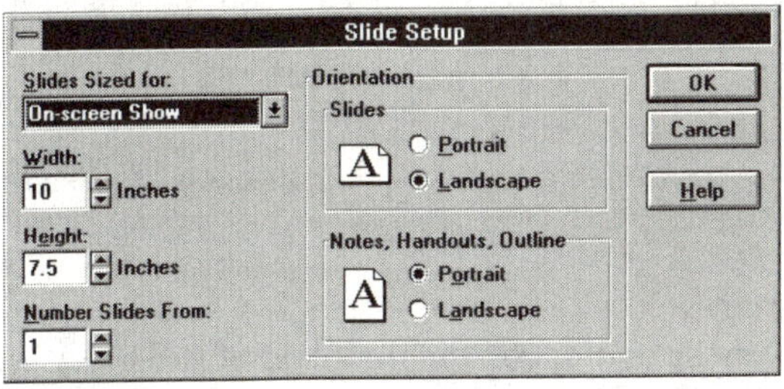

When you are ready to start printing, open the *File* menu and select *Print*. The *Print* dialog window appears in which you can select what you want to print from the *Print What* section.

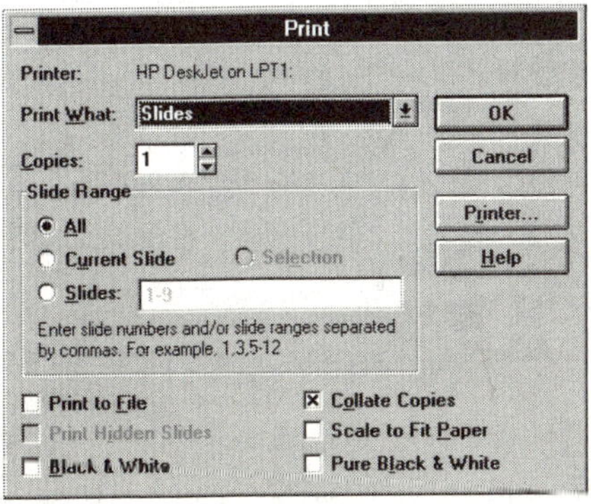

5.11 Giving a presentation

If you wish to show the presentation on the screen, you can also apply all kinds of effects. You can specify special Transition effects for the transition from one slide to another. By means of the Build effect function, you can produce a slide on the screen piece by piece.

The Slide Sorter View is the best mode for applying these types of effects because you can view all the slides simultaneously.

Exercise
We shall add Transition and Build effects to the slide show.

Procedure:

Slide Sorter View

1 Activate slide number 1 in the Slide Sorter View.
2 Click on the *Transition* button or open the *Tools* menu and select *Transition*.

Transition

The *Transition* dialog window appears.

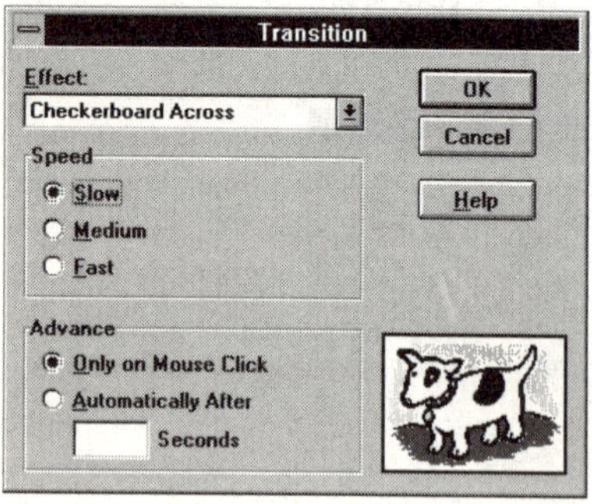

You can select one of the effects provided in the *Effects* list. The sample box in the lower right-hand corner displays what the transition will look like when chosen. You can also specify the speed with which the transition will take place. You can also determine whether the next slide is to appear automatically after a specified number of seconds or whether it is to be activated by a mouse click.

Opening the drop-down list next to the *Transition* button on the Slide Sorter toolbar will provide the same list of effects from which you can choose.

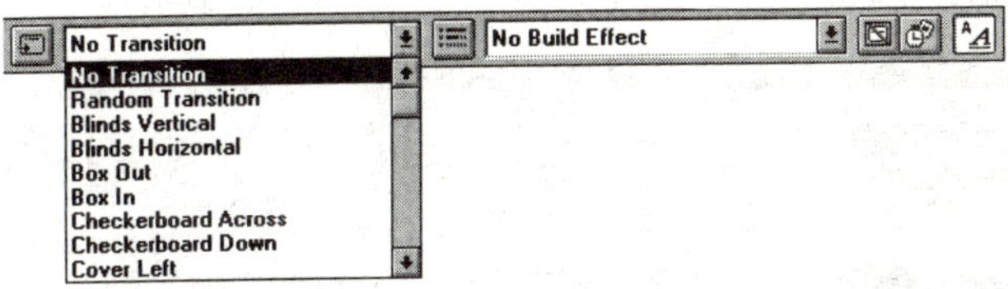

3 Select transition effects for the slides, varying them to get a reasonable idea of the possibilities.

Build

To select a Build effect for a slide, first select the required slide by clicking on it and then click on the *Build* button on the Slide Sorter toolbar. You can also open the *Tools* menu and select *Build*. The *Build* dialog window appears.

If a point is to change colour when the following point appears, click on the *Dim Previous Points* check box. You can then choose a colour from the subsequent drop-down list. If you want a point to appear with a special effect, click on the *Effect* check box and select the relevant effect from that drop-down list. If you only click on the first box, *Build Body Text*, the slide is built in a simple, straightforward way.
You can also open the same list of effects by clicking on the drop-down list next to the *Build* button on the Slide Sorter toolbar.

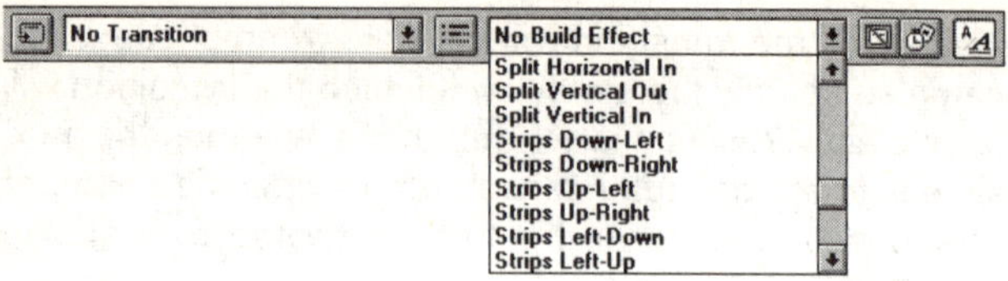

4 Apply various building techniques to all the slides.

When you have made all specifications, your screen, in the Slide Sorter View, will look something like this:

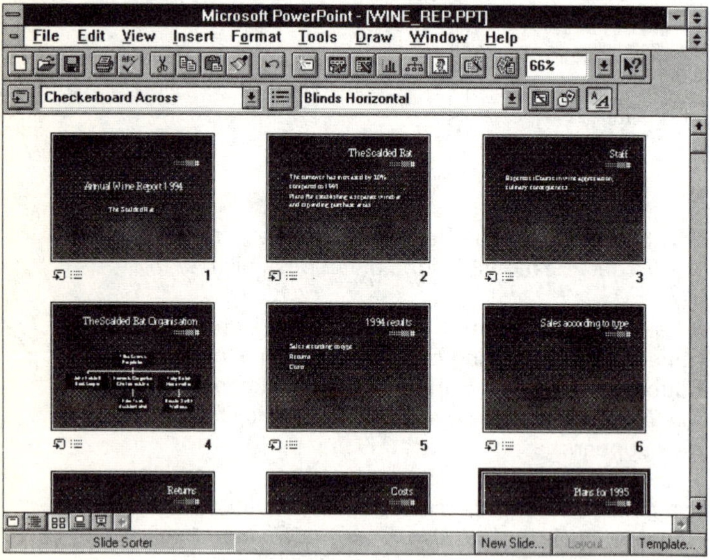

To start up the slide show, open the *View* menu and select *Slide Show*. The *Slide Show* dialog box appears in which you can specify which slides you wish to see and how the switch from one slide to the next is to be regulated.

You can also draw on a slide during the show if you want to add extra information or emphasise certain aspects. When the slide is displayed, move the mouse a little. The mouse pointer appears, along with a small box containing a pencil in the lower right-hand corner. Click on this box if you want to draw on the slide. The mouse pointer then assumes the shape of the pencil. Click on the box once more to switch back to the mouse pointer; you can then proceed to the next slide.

You can allow other people to view your presentation, even if PowerPoint is not installed on their own computers. The PowerPoint Viewer program, supplied along with the Microsoft Office package, makes this possible. You can (and may) copy this diskette and give it along with your presentation.

Exercise
Close the WINE_REP.PPT presentation and close PowerPoint.

Procedure:
1 Open the *File* menu and select *Save*.
2 Open the *File* menu and select *Exit*.

6 Working with Microsoft Access 2.0

This chapter deals with Microsoft Access 2.0 which is the Microsoft Office application for creating databases. As you read through this chapter, you will discover that Microsoft Access 2.0, with its ease of operation, is particularly user-oriented. The creation of tables, queries, forms, reports macros and modules is simple and straightforward, while the functions provided are more sophisticated and effective than those provided by other more extensive database programs.

If you wish to learn more about the integration of Microsoft Access databases with files created in other applications, consult the corresponding sections in chapters 10 to 13.

6.1 New in version 2.0

Version 2.0 provides enormous possibilities for creating complex and advanced databases. Even those who have no experience with databases can easily find their way in Access.

If you are already acquainted with Access, but not with the most recent version, the following list provides a concise overview of the new features available:

- Builder functions: The new Builder functions enable you to specify, for example, properties for expressions, queries and colours.
- Input Masks: By adding Input Masks to fields in which data have to be entered according to a fixed pattern, the input of data can take place more quickly and with increased reliability.

- Table Wizard: The Table Wizard provides an extensive number of example tables and fields from which you can compile new tables.
- Query Wizards: The new Query Wizards enable you to compile complex queries.
- Relationships Window: The Relationships Window displays the relationships between the tables and the database.
- AutoForm: The *AutoForm* function enables you to create a form quickly and easily.
- AutoReport: The *AutoReport* button enables you to create a report quickly and easily.

6.2 Working with databases

A database is a collection of data. This can consists of all sorts of data, such as the addresses of customers, turnover figures, a CD collection or information about the family.

In Access, the data is stored in tables. Access is referred to as a relational database, in other words, a database in which it is possible to (temporarily) link data from different data tables. A relational database makes it easy to search for, analyse, update and combine data.

A database can be made up of six types of components:

- tables: data about a certain topic are stored in rows (records) and columns (fields)
- queries: data based on certain selection criteria are gathered from one or more tables to form a query; you can use these data in a form or print them in a report
- forms: in forms, you can display, edit or enter data from individual records in tables or queries
- reports: you can gather data from the database in reports in order to print or analyse them

- macros: a macro can be constructed to execute certain tasks automatically
- modules: program code, written in Access Basic and used to adapt and automise working with the database, is stored in modules.

Data are stored in rows and columns within a table. The rows are the *records* and the columns are the *fields*. A record is, for example, a collection of data about one person or about an event. A field is a category of data, such as 'surname': in a database all surnames of customers, for example, will be listed in one column.

When tables in a database are linked to one another, there has to be at least one so-called 'primary key'. The primary key is a field or combination of fields that uniquely identifies each record in a table.
This will be dealt with in more detail in section 6.4.

6.3 Starting up Access

Microsoft Access

You can start up Access by clicking on the *Microsoft Access* icon in the Microsoft Office group under the Program Manager, or by clicking on the *Microsoft Access* button on the Microsoft Office toolbar.

Microsoft Access

Exercise
Start up Access (if it is not yet running) in one of the ways mentioned above.

Microsoft Access makes severe demands on your computer. If your system does not possess sufficient memory, Access may not work as it should. In that case, it is advisable to close any other opened applications.

When started up, the *Welcome to Microsoft Access* window appears. You can remove it from the screen by opening the Control menu (click on the small button in the upper left-hand corner) and select *Close*. If you do not want to be welcomed each time you start up this application, click on the *Don't display this startup card again* box in the lower right-hand part of the window.

The Cue Cards in Access provide a great deal of useful information about diverse tasks and components. They can also assist you in executing commands.

When Access has been started up and the welcome window has been closed, an empty window is shown on the screen. You can now create a new database or open an existing one.

We shall create a new database in this chapter.

6.4 Creating a new database

New Database

To create a new database, click on the *New Database* button on the Database toolbar, or open the *File* menu and select *New Database*. The *New Database* dialog window appears.

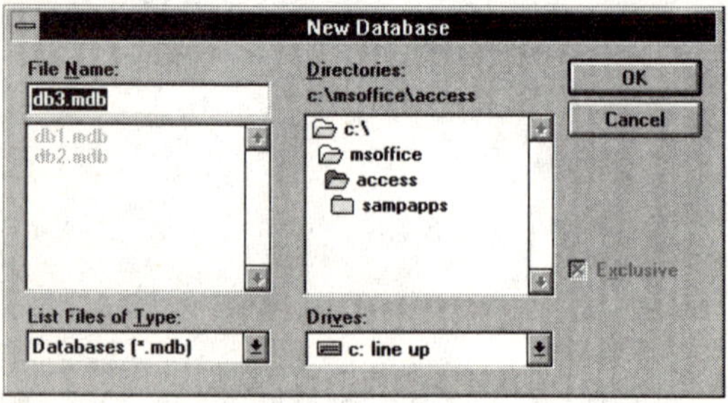

Specify the directory, along with the appropriate drive, in which you wish to save the new database. Type the name for the new database in the *File Name* text box.

Exercise
We shall now create a new database under the name RESTAUR.MDB.

Procedure:

1 Open the *New Database* dialog window.
2 Enter the name RESTAUR in the *File Name* box and specify a directory and drive of your choice. We have created (via the Windows File Manager) the directory *docs* as a subdirectory of *access* for our documents.
3 Click on *OK*.

The extension MDB is automatically added to the file name if you have specified (or accepted the default setting) *Databases (*.mdb)* in the *List Files of Type* box in the lower left-hand section of the dialog window.

The database window appears on the screen:

The database window displays six object buttons with the names *Table*, *Query*, *Form*, *Report*, *Macro* and *Module*. When the *Table* button is activated by clicking on it, the tables in the database are displayed at the right-hand side. The word *Tables* appears above the list. A similar registration takes place when the other buttons are activated. When the database window is opened, you can also select one of the top six options from the *View* menu to produce the same result.

6.4.1 Creating a new table

You can create a new table, import information from a file or include an existing table. In the following exercises, we shall create a new table.

If you know exactly which fields you wish to include in the new table, you can construct the table yourself right from the beginning. If you are not so sure, you can make use of the Table Wizard which will assist you in creating tables.

Exercise
We shall now create a new table containing data about the staff in the restaurant.

Procedure:

1. Click on the *Table* button in the database window and then click on the *New* button.
2. The *New Table* dialog window appears, in which you can choose whether to create a new table yourself or to activate the Table Wizards to help you.
3. Click on the *Table Wizards* button.

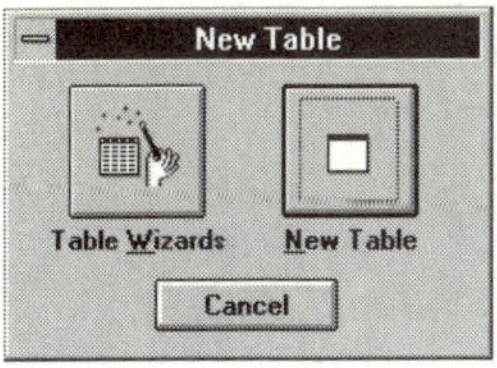

The first *Table Wizard* window appears.

4 Click on the *Employees* category from the *Sample Tables* list at the left-hand side of the window.

The fields in the *Sample Fields* list are automatically adjusted.

5 Select the following fields and move them to the *Fields in my new table* list by clicking on the name and then on the button with the arrow pointing to the right. Do this field by field. If you place a field in the right-hand list by accident, select that field and click on the button with the arrow pointing to the left. (The button with the double arrow places **all** the fields in the right-hand box in one go.) Make sure that the fields are entered in the following order of sequence:

- NationalEmplNumber
- FirstName
- LastName
- Address
- City
- PostalCode
- HomePhone
- Birthdate
- DateHired
- Salary

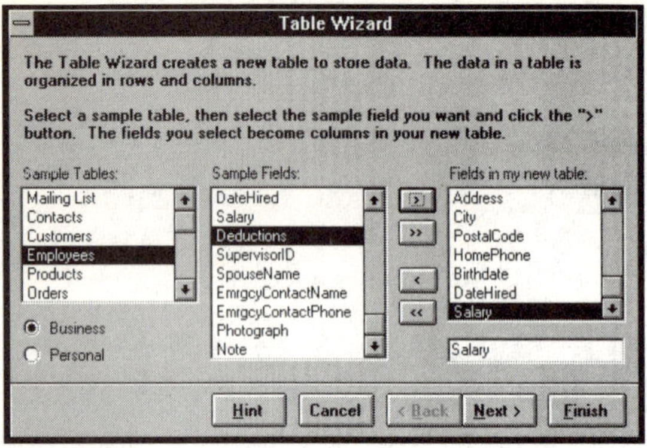

6 Click on the *Next* button.
7 Assign the name *Employees* to the table. Let Microsoft Access set a primary key and click on the *Next* button.
8 In the following window, select the option *Enter data directly into the table* and click on the *Finish* button.

You can always alter the table design later if required. The staff data should now be entered in the table.

The opened *Table: Employees* is now displayed on the screen. No data have been entered as yet. The table is shown in the Datasheet View as indicated on the status

---

Empl ID	NationalEmpl Number	First Name	Last Name	Address	
1	HH123456H	John	Falstaff	1597 Henry Estate	Shrewsbury
2	FR149723F	Francois	Gargantua	1534 Rabelais Road	Chinon
3	RH666666T	Friar	Tuck	3 Forest Groves	Nottingham
4	TN159888S	Toby	Belch	12 Illyria Gardens	Knightsbridge
5	MR222333L	Bessie	Smith	1 Empress Avenue	Bluesbury

bar. You cannot alter the table design in this mode; if you want to do so, you have to activate the Design View by pressing the *Design View* button at the extreme left of the toolbar.

The word 'Counter' is displayed in the ID field. A counter field is a field in which a new record is automatically allocated a number which consecutively follows the number of the previous record.

6.4.2 Entering data in a table

You enter data in a table by typing them. Press Tab to move on to the next field, or click on the next field to activate it. When you go to the next record, the data in the previous record are saved automatically. The pencil symbol in front of the record on which you are working indicates that the record is not yet saved. Pressing Enter or Tab at the end of one record will move you on to the next record.

Exercise
We shall now create a table by entering the following data:

Postal Code	Home Phone	Birthdate	Date Hired	Salary
SH6 4PH	0173-888-8181	01/05/61	11/11/91	1245.80
CH2 1PA	0153 212 2221	30/10/55	01/01/90	1950.65
NO6 2RH	0115-333-3131	03/03/67	06/07/92	1362.85
KN2 3OL	0171-555- 69999	18/12/54	01/01/90	1735.00
BL3 9MR	0193-223-3443	19/12/71	06/07/93	1010.45

Table: Employees

EmployeesID	NationalEmplNu	First Name	Last Name	Address	City
1	HH123456H	John	Falstaff	1597 Henry Estate	Shrewsbury
2	FR149723F	Francois	Gargantua	1534 Rabelais Rd.	Chinon
3	RH666666T	Friar	Tuck	3 Forest Groves	Nottingham
4	TN159888S	Toby	Belch	12 Illyria Gardens	Knightsbridge
5	MR222333L	Bessie	Smith	1 Empress Avenue	Bluesbury
(Counter)					

Record: 1 of 5

Table: Employees

City	Postal Code	Home Phone	Birthdate	Date Hired	Salary
Shrewsbury	SH6 4PH	(0173) 888 8181	01/05/61	11/11/91	£1,245.80
Chinon	CH2 1PA	(0153) 212 2221	30/10/55	01/01/90	£1,950.65
Nottingham	NO6 2RH	(0115) 333 3131	03/03/67	06/07/92	£1,362.85
Knightsbridge	KN2 0OL	(0171) 555 6999	18/12/54	01/01/90	£1,735.00
Bluesbury	BL3 9MR	(0193) 223 3443	19/12/71	06/07/93	£1,010.45

Record: 1 of 5

Note

When you come to enter the postal codes, you may run into difficulty (depending on the original settings for the program) with the field design. This is because the structure of this field is set to a fixed style of postal codes (to help avoid mistakes). To change it to suit your personal requirements, activate the Postal Code field and then click on the *Design View* button at the extreme left-hand side of the toolbar. The *Field Properties* window opens showing the current field properties for all the fields in the record. The Input Mask field has the structure *>LL00\0LL* (letter, letter, number, number, space, number, letter, letter), which means that it will not accept input with a different structure. Go to the Input Mask line by clicking on it and delete the code there. Then click on the *Datasheet View* button (2nd from the left on the toolbar) to return to the original Datasheet View. Proceed in the same way if you also have difficulties with the telephone numbers.
The dates also have a built-in structure. You only have to type the numbers.

In this Datasheet View, you can adjust the column widths by clicking on the column dividing lines (between the headings) and dragging them to the required positions.

Double click on the Control menu button in the datasheet window to close the table. This will return you to the database window in which the name of the new table is displayed.

Exercise

We shall now create a new table called Stock using the Table Wizard. It is to be based on the *Product* example table and will contain the following fields:

- ProductName
- UnitsInStock
- UnitsOnOrder
- UnitPrice

Procedure:

1 Open the *File* menu and select *New, Table*.

2 The database window appears. Click on *Table Wizards*.

3 Click on *Products* in the *Sample Tables*. The *Sample Fields* change automatically.

4 Select the required fields (named above) and move them one by one to the *Fields in my new table* box by clicking on the button with the arrow pointing to the right.

5 Click on *Next*.
6 Specify a name for the table, *stock*. Allow Access to set the primary key. Click on *Next*.
7 Activate the *Enter data directly into the table* option and click on *Finish*.

Enter the following data so that the table looks something like this:

Table: stock

stockID	Product Name	Units In Stock	Units On Order	Unit Price
1	South African	32	72	£3.15
2	Californian	18	144	£3.45
3	Bordeaux	38	36	£3.10
4	Chablis	14	36	£5.35
5	Riesling	19	36	£2.05
6	Algerian	9	36	£2.95
7	Rioja	17	18	£3.45
8	Bordeaux Red	21	144	£3.20
9	Cotes du Rhone	29	144	£3.15
10	Chianti	25	72	2.80
(Counter)				

Record: 10 of 10

6.4.3 Opening a table

Open

Open

The data in a table are automatically saved when you close it. If you wish to open a table after it has been closed, select its name in the table window and click on the *Open* button. You can also double click on the name to open it.
The same method is used to open queries, forms, reports, macros and modules.

6.4.4 Changing the table design

If you wish to alter the design of a table, you should open it in the Design View mode. This can be done in two ways:

- When the table is closed and the database window is visible, select the required table by clicking on it and then click on the *Design* button.

Design View

- When the table is opened in the Datasheet View, click on the *Design View* button on the toolbar or select *Table Design* from the *View* menu.

Exercise
We shall open the Employees table in the Design View.

Procedure:
1 Click on *Employees* in the *Tables* list.
2 Click on the *Design* button.

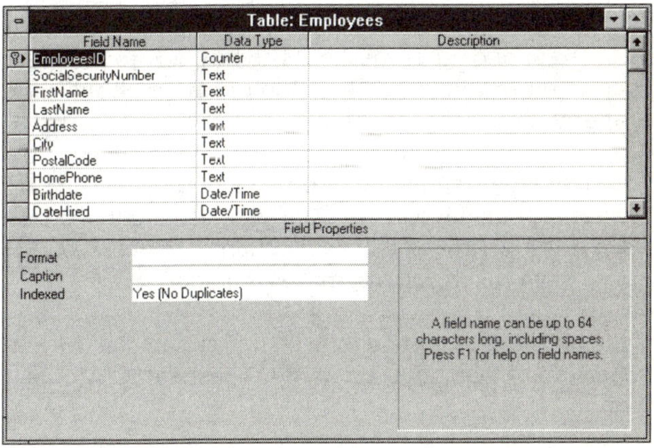

You can make the following modifications to a table design:

- add, move or remove a field
- change the data type of a field (text, date, counter etc.)
- specify the properties
- specify or remove a primary key
- create or remove an index

The FieldName list shows all the field names in this table. The Data Type list indicates which type of data the field contains. The key symbol indicates which field is used for the primary key.

When you click on a field, the lower *Field Properties* section is adjusted to the corresponding field. The *Caption* line in this section shows the name of the field in the table and in any form which may be used. If you do not specify any other name, the field name is used.

Click on several of the field names just to have a look at the corresponding properties. The box next to the Field Properties provides additional information about each property.

The data type of a field can be changed by clicking on the appropriate field in the Data Type list and then clicking on the arrow which subsequently appears. A list opens from which you can make a choice.

If you enter a description for a field, it appears at the left-hand side of the status bar in the Datasheet View or in a form.

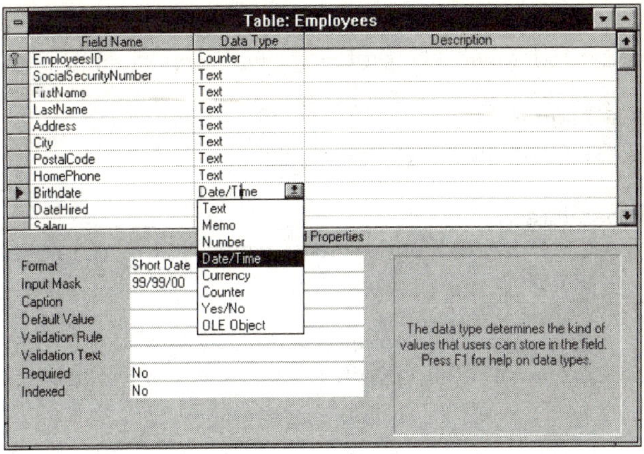

The *Input Mask* field property enables you to specify a pattern to which any input has to conform. For example, you could specify that a date should always conform to the pattern 99-99-00. If a value is entered which does not fulfil this condition, a message appears on the screen.

The easiest way of compiling an input mask is to use the *Input Mask Wizard*. Click on the relevant field name and then on the *Input Mask* line in the *Field Properties* section. A small button appears to the right of the text box. Clicking on it opens the *Input Mask Wizard*. Select the appropriate name from the *Input Mask Name* list and click on *Next*.

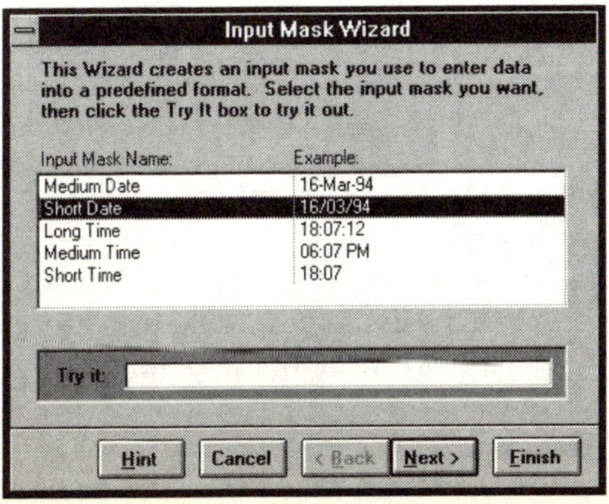

You can make further specifications in the subsequent Wizard windows. Click on *Finish* when you are satisfied.

Exercise
Close the table in the Design View.

Procedure:
1 Click on the Control menu symbol at the left of the title bar.
2 Select *Close*.
3 Click on *Yes* if you have made changes you wish to preserve, otherwise *No*. The database window appears once more.

Exercise
We shall now create a new table with the following data:

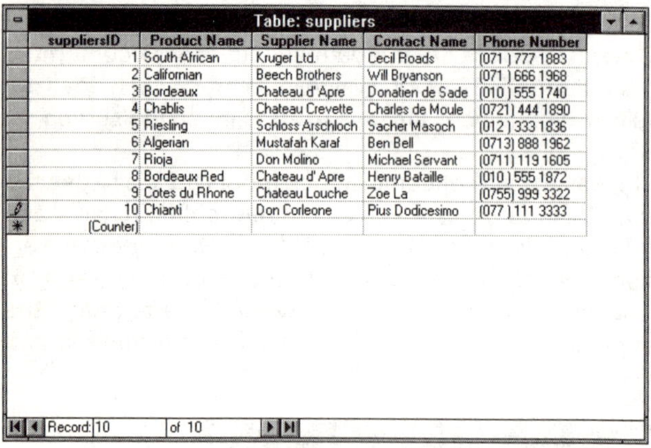

Table: suppliers

suppliersID	Product Name	Supplier Name	Contact Name	Phone Number
1	South African	Kruger Ltd.	Cecil Roads	(071) 777 1883
2	Californian	Beech Brothers	Will Bryanson	(071) 666 1968
3	Bordeaux	Chateau d' Apre	Donatien de Sade	(010) 555 1740
4	Chablis	Chateau Crevette	Charles de Moule	(0721) 444 1890
5	Riesling	Schloss Arschloch	Sacher Masoch	(012) 333 1836
6	Algerian	Mustafah Karaf	Ben Bell	(0713) 888 1962
7	Rioja	Don Molino	Michael Servant	(0711) 119 1605
8	Bordeaux Red	Chateau d' Apre	Henry Bataille	(010) 555 1872
9	Cotes du Rhone	Chateau Louche	Zoe La	(0755) 999 3322
10	Chianti	Don Corleone	Pius Dodicesimo	(077) 111 3333
(Counter)				

Record: 10 of 10

Procedure:
1 Click on the *New* button in the database window.
2 Click on *Table Wizards*.
3 Click on *Products* in the *Sample Tables* list.
4 Place the *ProductName* in the new table by clicking on the button with the arrow pointing to the right.

5 Click on *Suppliers* in the *Sample Tables* list.
6 Place *SupplierName* and *ContactName* and *Phone-Number* in the new table.
7 Click on *Next*.
8 Specify the name *suppliers* for the new table.
9 Click on *Finish*.
10 Enter the data as shown in the figure above.

6.5 Relationships between tables

You can define relationships between the various tables when working with databases. These relationships are used, for example, when creating queries.

In the following exercise, we shall define a relationship between the *stock* and *suppliers* tables.

Exercise
We shall define relationships between the tables in the RESTAUR database.

Database Window

Procedure:
1 Click on the *Database Window* button on the toolbar to display the database window if necessary.
2 Click on the *Relationships* button on the toolbar.

Relationships

Clicking on this button opens the *Add Table* dialog box if you have not defined any relationships as yet.

Add Table

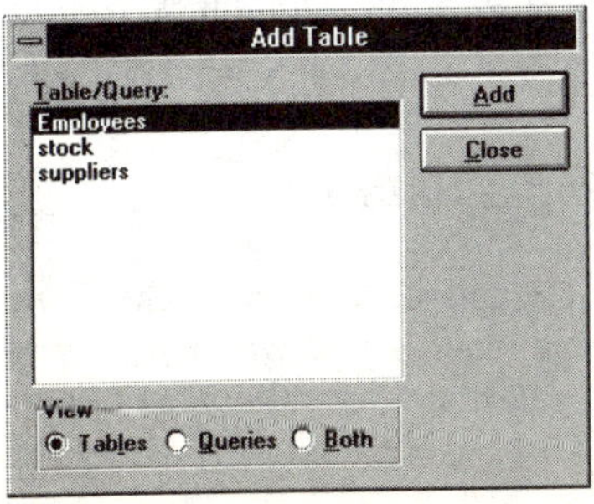

3 Click on the name *suppliers* in the list and then on the *Add* button.
4 Click on the name *stock* and then on the *Add* button.
5 Click on *Close*.

The *Relationships* window is opened.

6 Relationships can now be created by dragging the fields from one table to the fields which are to be related in the other table. When you release the mouse button, a new *Relationships* window appears with the headings *Table/Query* and *Related Table/Query*. The specified fields are shown in the list. Click on the *Create* button. This creates the required link:

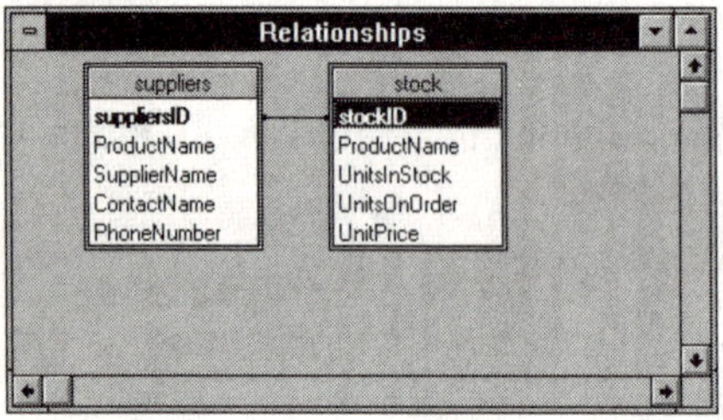

7 Close the *Relationships* window by double clicking on the Control menu button and choose *Yes* when you are asked if you wish to save the layout changes.

6.6 Closing and opening a database

If you enter data in the Datasheet View or in the Form View, the data are automatically saved when you move on to the next record. If you make alterations to the design of a database object (table, form, query etc.), you will be asked whether or not you want to save the changes when you leave the Design View.

Note
You can always close an opened database object, regardless of the view mode, by selecting *Close* from the *File* menu. Data are automatically saved but changes to the design are not. If you want to close a database object after changing the design, you will be asked if you want to save the alterations. If you have not saved the database object at all, you will be asked to specify a name for the object.
You can also close a database object by double clicking on the Control menu button.

6.6.1 Closing and opening a database

You can close an active database by opening the *File* menu and selecting the *Close Database* command. If you have made alterations to the design of components of the database and have not saved them as yet, you will be asked whether or not you wish to save these.

6.6.2 Opening a database

Open Database

You can open an existing database by clicking on the *Open Database* button on the Database toolbar or by opening the *File* menu and choosing the *Open Database* command.

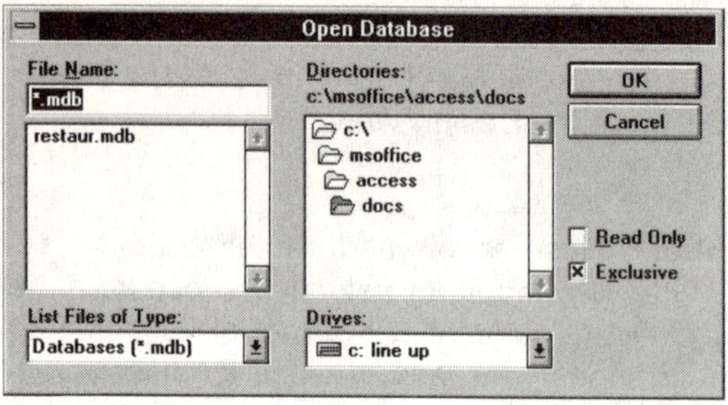

Select the required database from this window. The two check boxes enable you to determine whether a database is to be opened with the Read Only attribute, which means that the database can be examined but not altered, and the Exclusive option determines that the database can only be used by one user. These options are useful in a multi-user environment.

6.7 Working in the database window

In the database window, you can rename and copy database components and remove database objects.

6.7.1 Renaming database objects

To rename a database object such as a table or a form, proceed as follows:

- Select the object in the database window.
- Open the *File* menu and select *Rename*. The *Rename* dialog window appears.
- Type a new name in the text box and click on *OK*.

Note
If you change the name of a database object, you will also have to alter any references to that object. If you have

based a form on a table for instance, you will have to change the name of the table in the *RecordSource* property of the form. You cannot change the name of an open database object.

6.7.2 Copying database objects

You can save a database object in the database window under another name in the same database; you can also copy it to another database.

To copy a database object, proceed as follows:

Copy

Paste

- Select the object in the database window.
- Click on the *Copy* button on the toolbar or open the *Edit* menu and select *Copy*.
- If you wish to copy the object to another database, close the currently active database (Control menu button and then *Close*) and open the destination database by clicking on the *Open* button or by selecting *Open* from the *File* menu.
- When the destination database is opened, click on the *Paste* button on the toolbar or select *Paste* from the *Edit* menu.
- The *Paste* dialog window appears. Assign a name to the object being copied and click on *OK*.

6.7.3 Removing database objects

To remove an object from the database window, select the object and open the *Edit* window. Select *Delete* or press the Del key. A box appears asking if you really want to delete the object. If you are sure, click on *OK*.

6.8 Forms

A form displays a record from a database. One form shows one record. You can also add controls such as text boxes and check boxes, and also display data in an illustrative way.

6.8.1 Creating a new form using the AutoForm button

You can click on the *AutoForm* button to create a form based on the selected table quickly and easily.

Exercise
For practice, we shall create a new form based on the *stock* table.

Procedure:

Database Window

AutoForm

1 Activate the database window, if it is not yet active, by clicking on the *Database Window* button on the Table Datasheet or Table Design toolbar.
2 Select the *stock* table and click on the *AutoForm* button on the Database toolbar.

Access immediately creates a new form with the name *stock*.

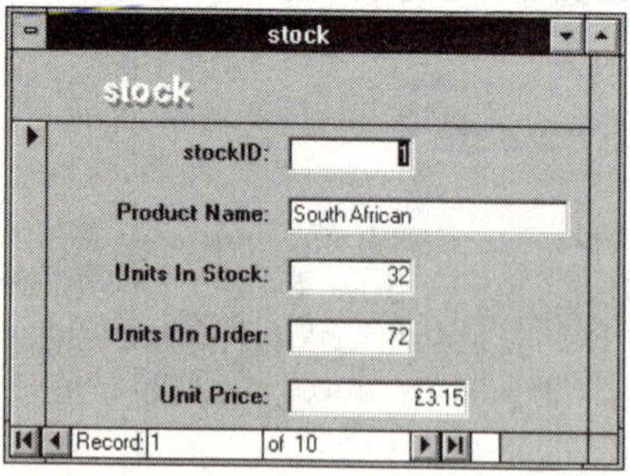

The status bar at the bottom of the form indicates which record (of how many) is currently being displayed. Clicking on the buttons on this bar will switch you to another record:

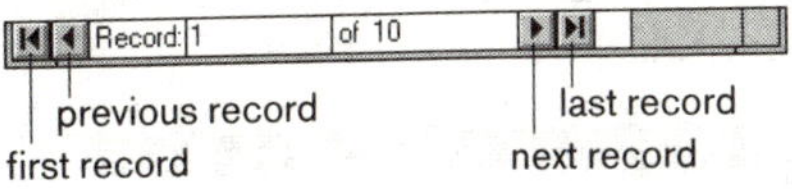

New

You can easily insert a new record by clicking on the *New* button on the Form View toolbar. You then switch to the next box to enter data by pressing Tab or Enter. You can also click on the relevant box using the mouse. When you move on to the next record or close the form, the data are saved automatically.

You can switch quickly and easily to a different view mode by clicking on the first three buttons on the toolbar:

button	**view**
	Design View
	Form View
	Datasheet View

6.8.2 Changing the form design

Design

If you wish to change the design of a form, click on the *Design View* button on the toolbar. If the form has been saved and closed, click on the *Form* button in the database window and select the appropriate form from the list. Then click on the *Design View* button.

Exercise
We shall examine our form in the Design View.

Clicking on the *Design View* button produces the following window (we have moved the Toolbox to the right-hand side of the screen).

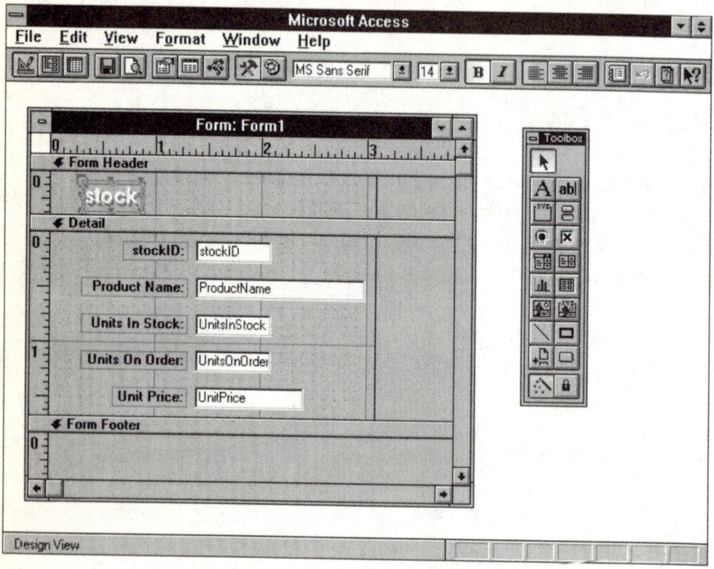

In this Design View, you can move the fields by dragging them to a different position. Click on the required field first to activate it. If you want to move the text box and corresponding text at the same time, click on these as well. When you drag these, the mouse pointer assumes the shape of a hand. When the mouse pointer assumes the shape of a hand with a pointing forefinger, you can move that component separately.

Properties

If you wish to change the properties of the form components (referred to as *controls*), double click on the component you wish to change. This opens a dialog window for that item. You can also select a component and then click on the *Properties* button on the Form Design toolbar, or open the *View* menu and select *Properties*. By changing the properties, you can determine how (the size for instance) and when (Visible Yes/No, Display When etc.) the components of the form are displayed.

The following figure shows the properties of the *ProductName* text box (the actual text box at the right not the label at the left). The source of this item (the *Control Source* property) is the ProductName field from the *stock* table which provides the data for this form. You can specify a source for this item by clicking on the *Control Source* property and then on an item in the list which shows the fields in the *stock* table.
If you click on the button behind the arrow, the *Expression Builder* window appears, which enables you to compile expressions. An expression is a collection of operators, constants, characters, functions, field names, controls and properties which combine like an equation to produce one result or value when applied.

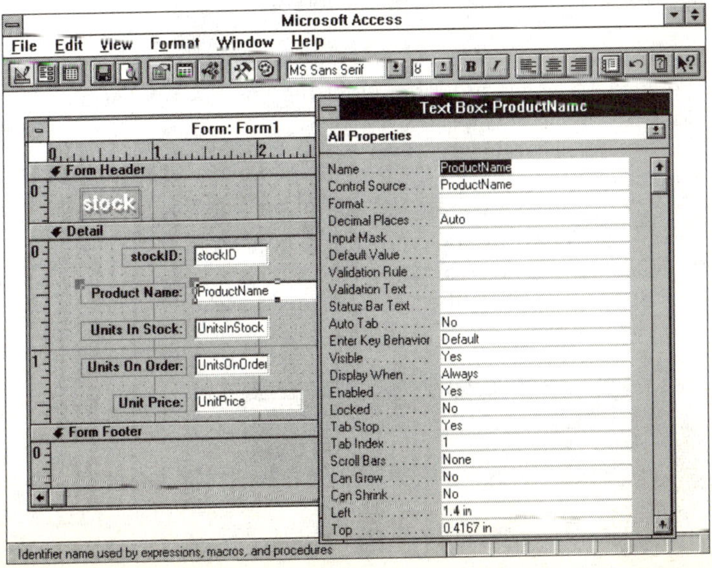

There is a toolbox available in the Form Design View which enables you to place controls in a form. This can be very convenient. These controls can be text boxes, check boxes, drop-down lists etc.

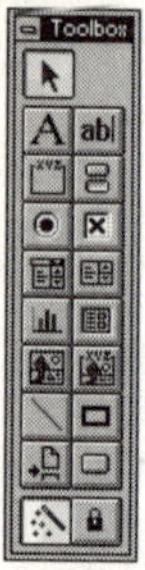

Save

When you close the form, by double clicking on the Control menu button for instance, a window automatically appears in which you are asked if you want to save the form. To save a form in between times, to be sure you will not lose it, you can also select *Save* from the *File* menu or click on the *Save* button on the toolbar.

Exercise
We shall now save the form under the name *stock* and close it.

Procedure:
1 Close the *Properties* window (if still open) by double clicking on the Control menu button.
2 Click on the *Save* button on the toolbar.
3 Specify *stock* in the *Save As* dialog window and click on *OK*.

4 Click on the *Database Window* button on the toolbar to show the RESTAUR database window. If you click on the *Forms* button in this window, you will see that *stock* has been created.

6.8.3 Creating a new form using the Form Wizards

Exercise
We shall make use of the form Wizards to create a new form.

Procedure:

1 Open the database window and click on the *Form* button.

2 Click on the *New* button. The *New Form* window appears. Click on the arrow pointing downwards at the right of the *Select A Table/Query* text box.
3 Select *Employees* from the subsequent list.
4 Click on the *Form Wizards* button.

5 The *Form Wizards* window appears. Select *Single-Column* from the list and click on *OK*.
6 The *Single-Column Form Wizard* window appears. Select all the fields shown in the *Available Fields* list by clicking on the button with the two arrows. Click on the *Next* button.

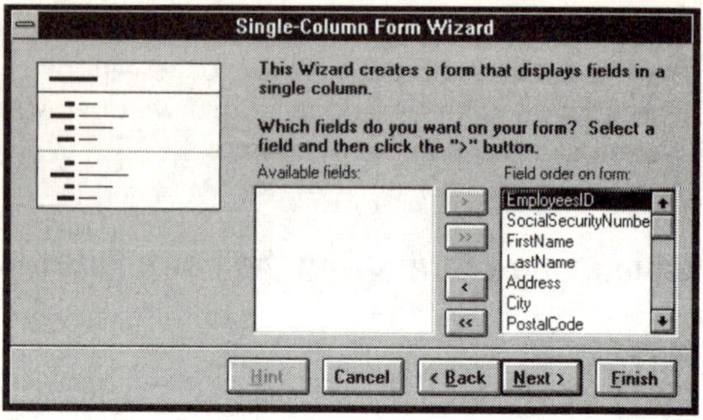

7 Select the *Embossed* option from the next dialog window and click on *Next*.
8 The title of your form, *Employees*, is already entered in the next dialog window. Accept this and activate the *Open the form with data in it* option if necessary. Click on *Finish*.

The form is now created and subsequently displayed on the screen.

9 Examine the form and then close it by double clicking on the Control menu button of the form.
10 A message box appears, asking if you want to save the changes. Click on *Yes*.
11 The *Save As* dialog window appears. Type the name **Employees** and click on *OK*.

The database window appears, showing the newly-created Employees form.

6.9 Working with data

You can easily search for and replace data in databases. You can also filter or sort data according to specified criteria so that you can obtain a selection of records you wish to examine, while all the others are excluded.

6.9.1 Searching for data

Find

If you want to look through one field, click on the field selector and then on the *Find* button on the toolbar.

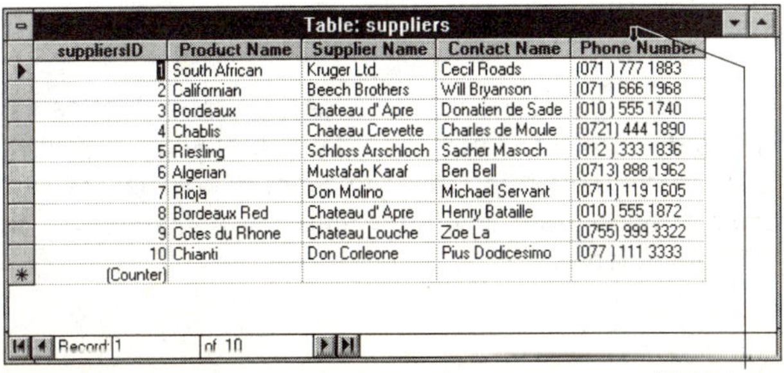

Table: suppliers

suppliersID	Product Name	Supplier Name	Contact Name	Phone Number
1	South African	Kruger Ltd.	Cecil Roads	(071) 777 1883
2	Californian	Beech Brothers	Will Bryanson	(071) 666 1968
3	Bordeaux	Chateau d' Apre	Donatien de Sade	(010) 555 1740
4	Chablis	Chateau Crevette	Charles de Moule	(0721) 444 1890
5	Riesling	Schloss Arschloch	Sacher Masoch	(012) 333 1836
6	Algerian	Mustafah Karaf	Ben Bell	(0713) 888 1962
7	Rioja	Don Molino	Michael Servant	(0711) 119 1605
8	Bordeaux Red	Chateau d' Apre	Henry Bataille	(010) 555 1872
9	Cotes du Rhone	Chateau Louche	Zoe La	(0755) 999 3322
10	Chianti	Don Corleone	Pius Dodicesimo	(077) 111 3333
(Counter)				

Record: 1 of 10

field selector

The *Find in field* dialog window then appears. Specify what you are looking for in the *Find What* box. You can also specify other search options such as Where you want to search, in which Direction, whether or not the Whole Field should be matched or only a Part of it (drop-down list) etc.

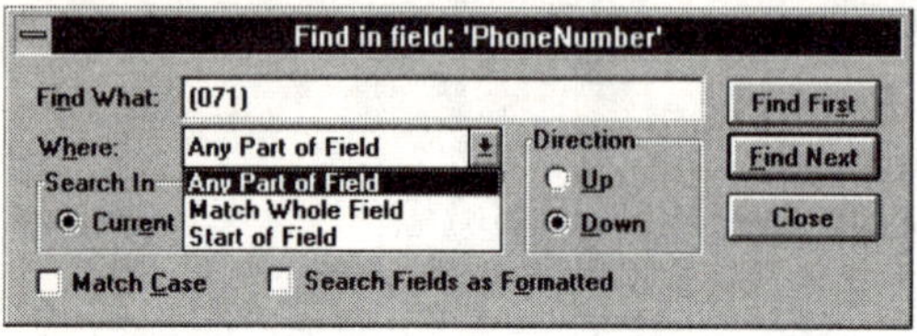

Our figure shows a search for all inner London telephone numbers among the suppliers.

6.9.2 Replacing data

If you want to replace the data in one field, click on the field selector for that field. Then select the *Replace* option from the *Edit* menu.

The *Replace* dialog window is opened. In principle, this works in just the same way as the *Find* dialog window. Specify, in the *Replace With* box, the text or value which is to replace the sought text or value.

6.9.3 Sorting records

If you wish to sort records in a table or form, first select the field you want to sort. In a datasheet you can simply click on the field selector. If you want to sort several columns at once, hold down the Shift key while clicking on the field selectors.

Then click on the sort buttons on the toolbar:

Sort Ascending

Sort Descending

You can also open the *Records* menu and select *Quick Sort* followed by *Ascending* or *Descending* in the subsequent submenu.

6.9.4 Filtering records

You can apply a filter to display and sort only those records you require. Filters are temporary. When you deactivate a filter, it disappears, but you can save a filter as a query which enables you to use it again in the future.

Edit Filter/ Sort

To create a filter, click on the *Edit Filter/Sort* button on the toolbar. A window is opened showing the active table, query or form.

Exercise
For practice, we shall create a filter for the Employees table.

Procedure:

1 Open the Employees table.
2 Click on the *Edit Filter/Sort* button on the toolbar.

Edit Filter/ Sort

The *Filter* window appears on the screen.

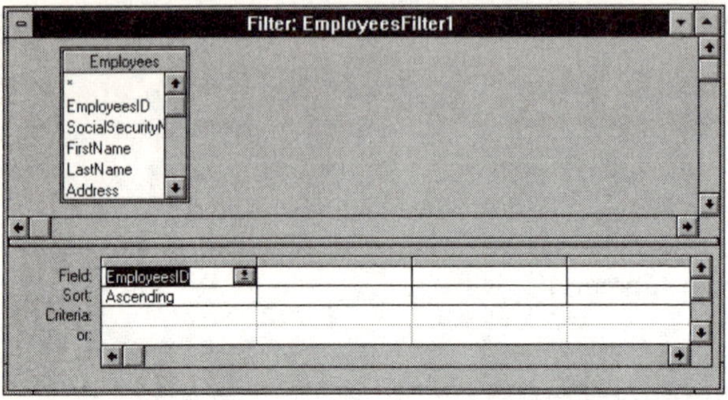

3 Double click on the FirstName, LastName, DatedHired and Salary fields.

4 Click on the *Sort* line in the newly-created LastName column and place *Ascending* in the box by clicking on the arrow and selecting this option from the drop-down list.

5 In the DateHired field, on the *Criteria* line, enter **>=1-1-92** so that all records which satisfy the condition of coming after the 1st of January 1992 will be displayed.

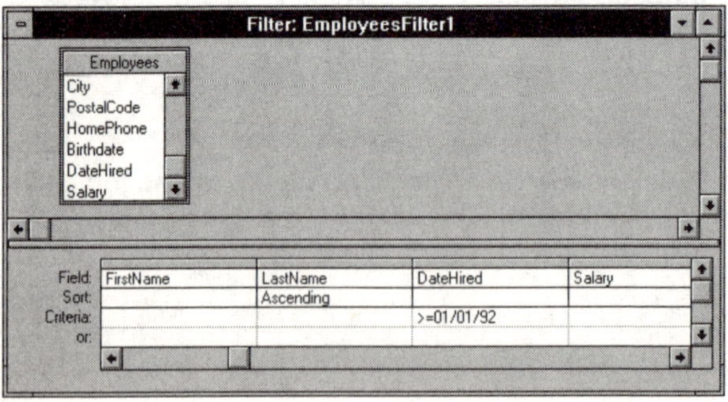

Apply Filter/ Sort

6 Click on the *Apply Filter/Sort* button to implement the filter you have just specified.

The table window appears displaying only the records of the employees who have been engaged since the first of January 1992. The records have been sorted according to surname as specified.

Show All Records

7 Click on the *Show All Records* button on the toolbar to show all records in the table once more.

Save

If you wish to save a filter as a query, open the *File* menu while the *Filter* window is displayed on the screen and select the *Save As Query* option. You can also click on the *Save* button while the *Filter* window is open.

To close the *Filter* window, double click on the Control menu button of the window.

6.10 Creating a query

A query is actually also a kind of filter. The main differences with a 'normal' filter are:

- a query can be saved
- data from **different** tables can be included in a query
- the criteria in a query are often more complex than in a 'normal' filter.

A query can provide answers to questions such as: 'Which wines have been ordered in crates of twelve dozen and who is the contact person?'. As mentioned, a query enables you to examine and edit data from different tables. In addition, it can also serve as the basis for a form, a report or a chart. The result of a query is referred to as a dynaset, into which fields from various tables can be adopted.

Exercise

Create a new query for the RESTAUR database which will show which wines are on order, the name of the supplier and the contact person.

Procedure:

1 Open the database window.

2 Click on the *Query* button.

3 Click on the *New* button.

The *New Query* window appears.

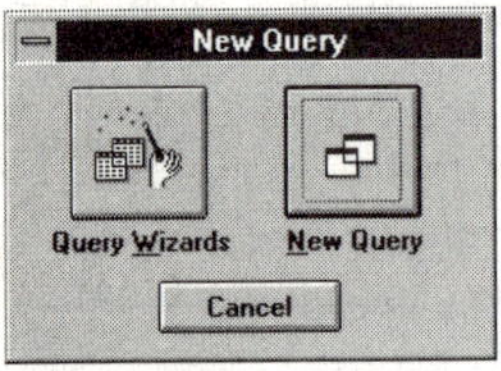

4 Click on the *New Query* button.

5 Click on the name *suppliers* in the subsequent list and then on the *Add* button.

6 Click on *stock* and then on the *Add* button.

7 Click on the *Close* button.

The relationship between the two tables is shown in the *Select Query* window which then appears. In the lower part of this window, you can add fields to be used for sorting and which you want to display in the dynaset. To add a field here, double click on its name in the upper part of the window.

8 Complete the query as follows by selecting three fields from the *suppliers* table and the UnitsOnOrder field from the *stock* table. Activate the *Sort* line under *ProductName* and select *Ascending* from the drop-down list. Place the condition **>0** on the *Criteria* line so that only current orders will be displayed.

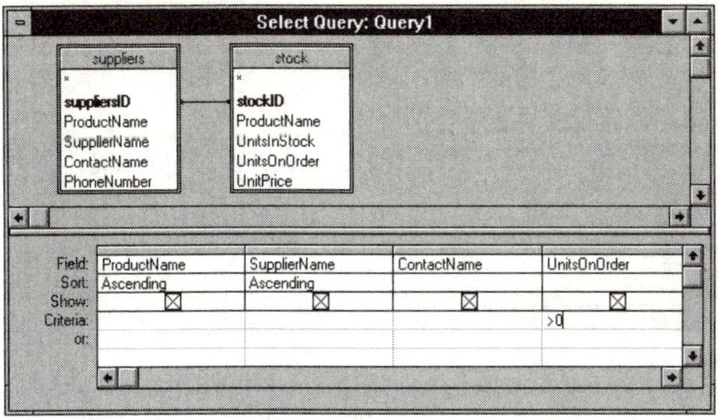

Run

9 When you have completed the query window, click on the *Run* button on the toolbar to actually start the query. The result is then displayed in a separate window.

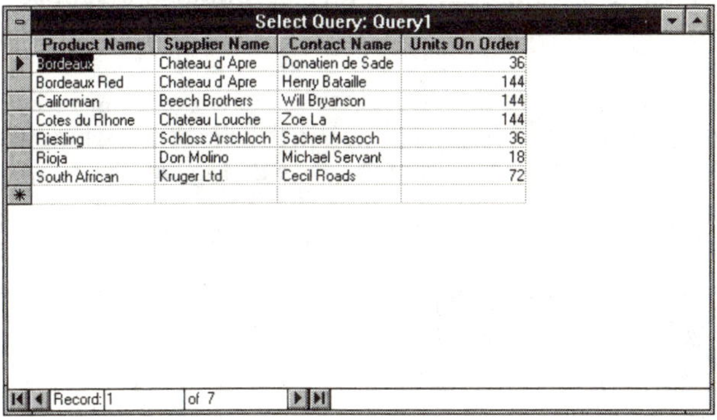
Select Query: Query1

Product Name	Supplier Name	Contact Name	Units On Order
Bordeaux	Chateau d' Apre	Donatien de Sade	36
Bordeaux Red	Chateau d' Apre	Henry Bataille	144
Californian	Beech Brothers	Will Bryanson	144
Cotes du Rhone	Chateau Louche	Zoe La	144
Riesling	Schloss Arschloch	Sacher Masoch	36
Rioja	Don Molino	Michael Servant	18
South African	Kruger Ltd.	Cecil Roads	72

Record: 1 of 7

10 When you have examined the query and are satisfied, click on the Control menu button of the query window to close the query.

A dialog window then appears asking if you wish to save the query.

11 Answer *Yes.*
12 The *Save As* window appears. Enter the name **orders** and click on *OK*.

The *Orders* query is then shown in the database window.

6.11 Creating reports

In a report, you can examine and print data from a database. You can show only specific chosen data or certain specified groups of records. You can also format the data to your own requirements.

Exercise
We shall create a report in which the total orders are shown, along with data about the product, the supplier and the contact person.

Procedure:

1 Click on the *Report* button in the database window.
2 Click on the *New* button in the dialog window.

The *New Report* window appears.

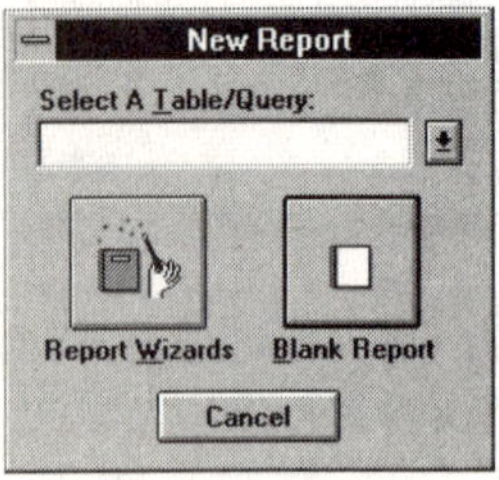

3 Click on the arrow pointing downwards and select the *orders* query. Click on the *Report Wizards* button.

4 In the subsequent window, click on the *Groups/Totals* option from the list. Click on *OK*.
5 In the *Groups/Totals Report Wizard* window, select all the available fields for the report by clicking on the button with the double arrow. Then click on the *Next* button.
6 In the subsequent window, in which you are asked how you want to group the records, simply click on *Next*. Accordingly, no fields are selected.
7 In the next window, in which you are asked how you wish to sort the data, select *UnitsOnOrder*. Click on the name and then on the button with one arrow pointing right. Click on *Next*.
8 In the next window, you can choose which style you wish to apply to the report. Select *Executive* and, in the *Orientation* section, select *Landscape*. The *Line Spacing* should be 1/12 in. Click on the *Next* button.
9 Enter the name **orders** for the report and remove any crosses in the check boxes. The last window will look like this:

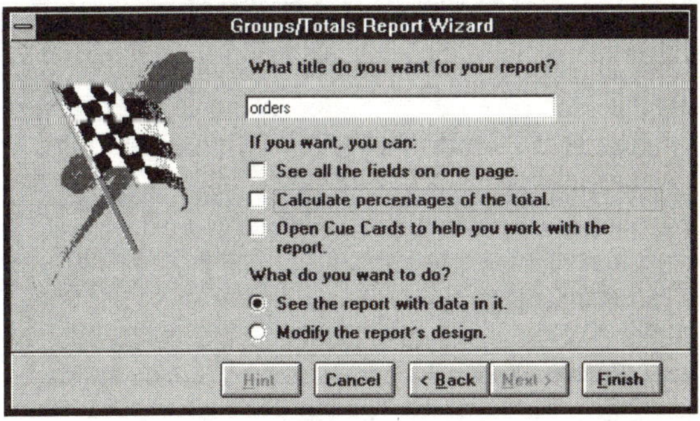

10 Click on the *Finish* button.

The report is created automatically. The total number of units on order is calculated and shown in the report (we have narrowed the fields a little to display all data on the screen at once).

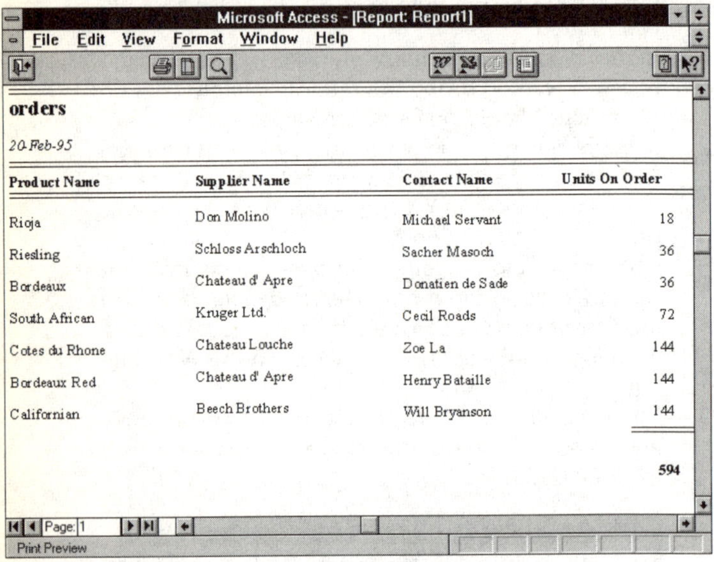

orders

20-Feb-95

Product Name	Supplier Name	Contact Name	Units On Order
Rioja	Don Molino	Michael Servant	18
Riesling	Schloss Arschloch	Sacher Masoch	36
Bordeaux	Chateau d' Apre	Donatien de Sade	36
South African	Kruger Ltd.	Cecil Roads	72
Cotes du Rhone	Chateau Louche	Zoe La	144
Bordeaux Red	Chateau d' Apre	Henry Bataille	144
Californian	Beech Brothers	Will Bryanson	144
			594

11 Close the window by clicking on the Control menu button.

A window appears in which you are asked if you want to save the changes.

12 Click on *Yes*.
13 Enter the name **orders** in the name box in the *Save As* window. Click on *OK*.

The *orders* report is shown under the Reports category in the database window.

6.12 Printing database objects

Print

By selecting the *Print* command from the *File* menu, or the *Print* button from the toolbar, you can print the currently active datasheet, form, query, report or module. This also applies to the object selected in the database window. The *Print* dialog window is opened, in which you can make further specifications referring to the print job. If you select *Print Setup* from the *File* menu, you can make further specifications about the printer and printer port.

If you wish to print only a selection of the records, you should select them first in the datasheet. If you wish to print the entire datasheet, you do not need to make a prior selection.

Print Preview

If you select the *Print Preview* option from the *File* menu, or click on the *Print Preview* button on the toolbar, an example of how the document will look when it comes out of the printer is displayed on the screen.

Exercise

We shall now close the RESTAUR database and also close down Access.

Procedure:

1 Click on the Control menu button in the database window.
2 Click on *Close*. The database window is closed.
3 Open the Microsoft Access *File* menu and select *Exit*. Access is closed down.

7 Working with Microsoft Mail

A component of Microsoft Mail is supplied along with the Microsoft Office package, which enables you to link to a Microsoft Mail system.

Microsoft Mail is a program which allows you to send messages to other users in a network. If you are connected to a network and Microsoft Mail is installed on your computer, the *File* menu in all applications will contain the *Send* command, and the applications Word, Excel, and PowerPoint will also contain the *Add Routing Slip* command. These commands enable you to send a message along with an attached document and to send a document to a number of other people for examination.

Microsoft Mail

If the Microsoft Office Manager is activated on your computer, you can start up Mail by clicking on the appropriate button on the Microsoft Office Manager toolbar. You can also double click on the Microsoft Mail icon under the Program Manager. The exact location of the Mail program group will depend on the configuration of your computer. It may be located in Main or the Network group.

Microsoft Mail

7.1 Enclosing a document in a Mail message

You can attach a document to a message which you wish to send via Mail.

Exercise
We shall send a copy of the RESTAUR.DOC document to another user in our network.

Procedure:

1 Start up Mail and log in, giving the password if necessary.

Compose

2 Click on the *Compose* button on the toolbar, open the *Mail* menu and select *Compose Note.*

The *Send Note* window appears.

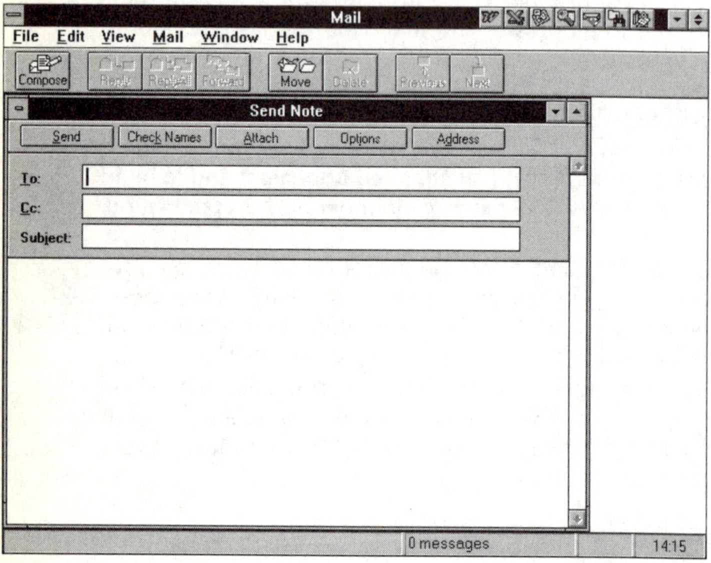

3 Type the user name of the person who is to receive the note, or click on the *Address* button to open the *Address* window from which you can select a name.

4 Type **Test** in the *Subject* box, and in the message section, **This is a test. If you click on the following icon, the REST.DOC file will be opened in Microsoft Word.**

5 Click on the *Attach* button.

The *Attach* window appears.

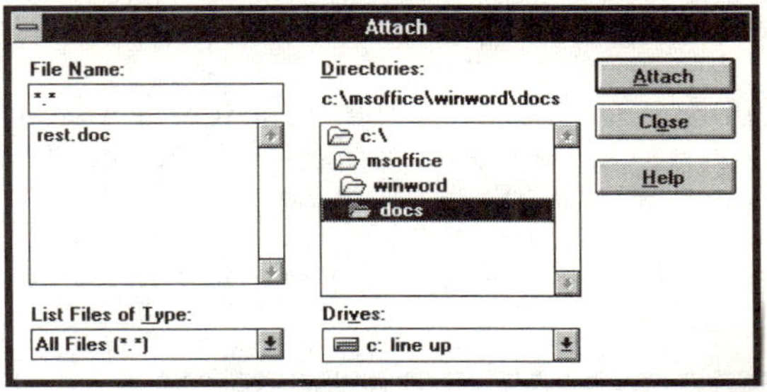

6 Select the REST.DOC file from the directory where you stored it.
7 Click on the *Attach* button.
8 Click on *Close*.

The *Attach* window is closed and the message window appears again. A Word icon has been adopted into the message window, with the appropriate file name displayed underneath.

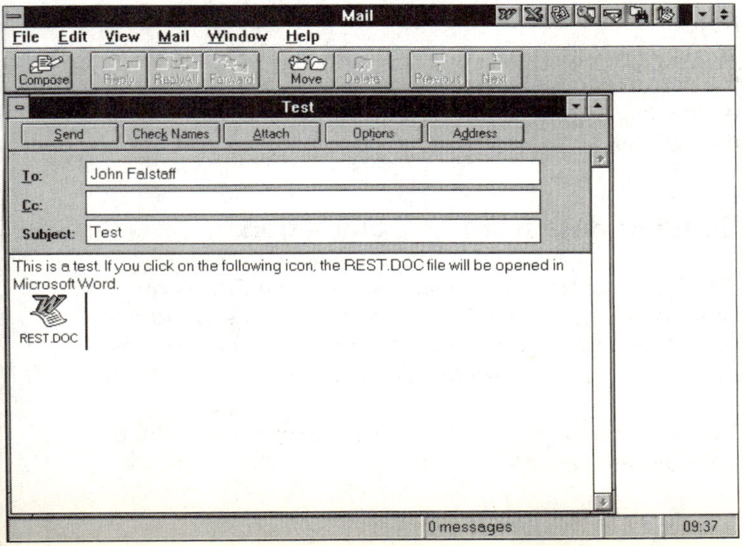

If Word is installed on the receiving computer, the user will be able to read the message by double clicking on the icon. Word is started up and the file is opened.

If the receiver wishes to read the message at a later date, he/she can store the attachment by opening the *File* menu and selecting *Save Attachment*.

In that case, the *Save Attachment* dialog window is opened.

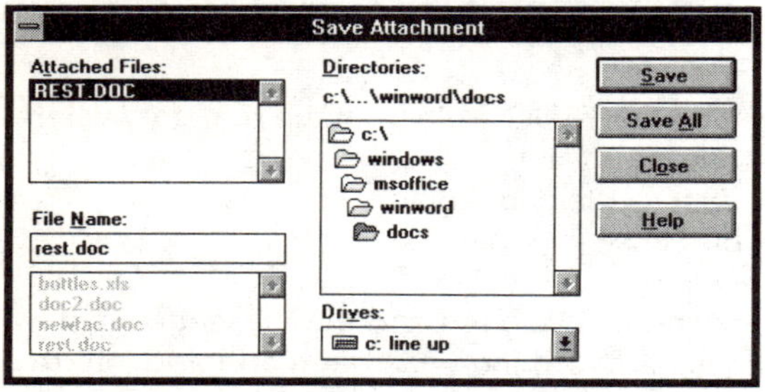

Note
You can also send so-called *courtesy copies* to others in the network so that they can take note of any correspondence. In that case, enter the name(s) of the recipient(s), divided by a semi-colon if necessary, in the *Cc* text box.

7.2 Sending data from an application

If Mail is installed on your workstation, the *File* menu of all the Microsoft applications will contain the *Send* option. Word, Excel and PowerPoint will also provide the *Add Routing Slip* or *Routing Slip* options.

The *Send* option enables you to send an opened document or database object to another user in the network.

Exercise
For practice, we shall send the Word document called REST.DOC to another user in your network.

Procedure:
1 Start up Word and open the REST.DOC.
2 Select *Send* from the *File* menu.

This will start up Mail if it has not already been activated.

3 Sign in to Mail.

The *Send Note* dialog window appears.

4 Specify the name of the recipient, type a few words about the subject matter and enter the required text in the message section.

The icon of the Word document has been placed in the message box automatically. If the recipient of the message double clicks on the icon, the file is automatically opened in Word (if this program has been installed on the receiving computer).

7.3 Circulating documents

You can send messages to others in the network from Word, Excel and PowerPoint. To do so, open the *File* menu and select *Add Routing Slip* or *Routing Slip*. The recipients can then add remarks to the document and send it on to other users, or return it to you.

Exercise
We shall send the REST.DOC to various users in the network.

Procedure:

1 Start up Word and open the REST.DOC if that has not already occurred.
2 Open the *File* menu and select *Add Routing Slip*.

The *Routing Slip* dialog window appears.

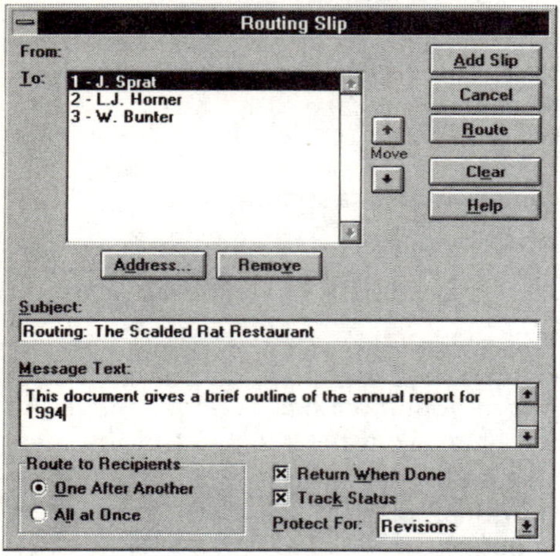

3 Enter the names of users who are connected to your network in the *To* box. If you click on the *Address* button, the *Address* window will appear from which you can choose the desired names.

The *Move* buttons enable you to change the order of sequence of the names in the *To* list. This order determines the message route.

In the lower section of the window, the *One After Another* option specifies that the document is sent to the recipients one by one. When a user has read the document, he/she can add remarks and send it on to the next person in the list by opening the *File* menu and choosing

Send. The message is then automatically passed on. The *All at Once* option from this section will send the message to all recipients at once.

If the *Return When Done* check box has been activated, the document is automatically returned to the sender when everyone has had a look at it. If *Track Status* is activated, the sender can keep track of who has received the document at any given time. When the message is passed on, the sender is informed of this.

4 Click on the *Route* button to send the message.

8 Microsoft Office Manager

Microsoft Office

The Microsoft Office Manager is a toolbar by means of which you can quickly start up Microsoft Office applications, or switch from one opened application to another. The Microsoft Office Manager is activated by clicking on the Microsoft Office icon in the Microsoft Office group under the Program Manager.

If you regularly work with Microsoft Office, it is advisable to include the Microsoft Office icon in the StartUp group window under the Program Manager. Then the Microsoft Office Manager will be automatically activated when you start up Windows.

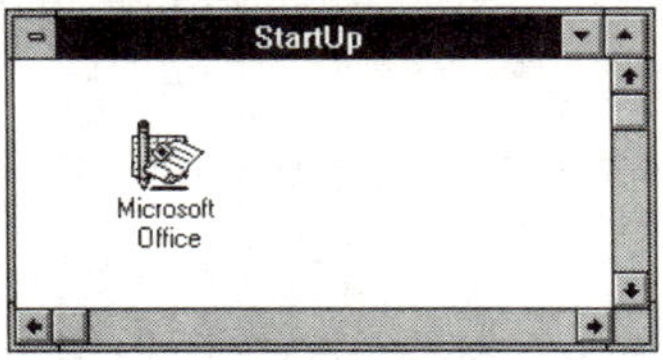

To close the Microsoft Office Manager click on the Microsoft Office icon at the extreme right of the Microsoft Office Manager toolbar and select *Exit* from the menu which appears.

8.1 Starting up applications by means of the Microsoft Office Manager

The Microsoft Office Manager toolbar, once it has been activated, is shown in all applications. You can adjust the toolbar to your own requirements by adding or removing buttons. If you have a network card, your toolbar will initially look like this:

The buttons on the toolbar have the following functions:

button	**function**
	starts up or activates Word
	starts up or activates Excel
	starts up or activates PowerPoint
	starts up or activates Access
	starts up or activates Mail
	opens the *Find File* window which enables you to search for files conforming to certain criteria.
	opens the Microsoft Office menu

To start up an application, simply click once on the corresponding button on the toolbar. To switch between opened applications, click on the required application button.

If you want to start up a second version of an application, hold down Ctrl while clicking on the application button on the Microsoft Office Manager toolbar.

8.2 Arranging the application windows on the desktop

You can easily (re)arrange the application windows on the desktop. Accordingly, you can arrange the display so that you can view several windows at once, which is very convenient if you wish to transfer or copy data from one application to another.

To arrange two application windows on the desktop, activate the first window, press and hold down Shift and click on the icon of the second application on the Office Manager toolbar. Both applications are then displayed on the screen one above the other.

The following figure shows the Word and Excel application windows on the desktop:

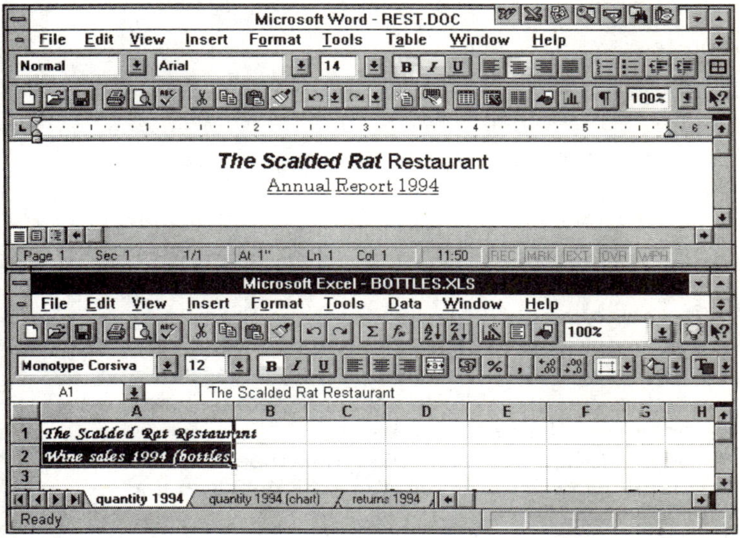

8.3 Closing down applications by means of the Microsoft Office Manager

You can close down an application by selecting *Exit* from the *File* menu. You can also use the Microsoft Office Manager to close down applications. This is done by pressing and holding down the Alt key while clicking on the application button on the Microsoft Office Manager toolbar.

8.4 The Microsoft Office menu

Microsoft Office

The Microsoft Office menu is opened by clicking on the Microsoft Office button on the Microsoft Office toolbar.

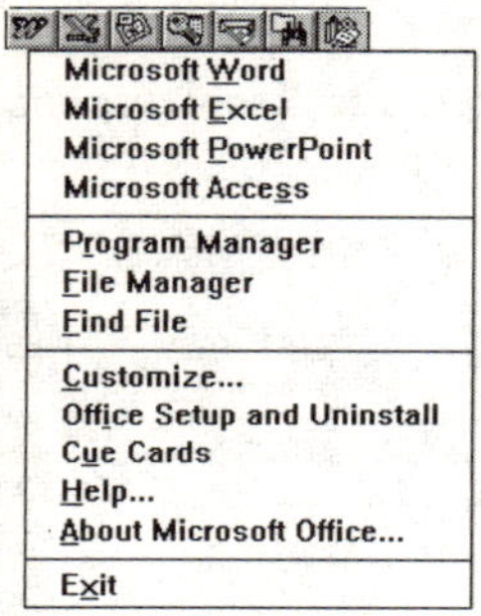

- The first four options, as you see, activate the applications of the same name.
- The next two options switch you to the Program Manager and the File Manager.
- Selecting *Find File* activates the file finding function which is convenient if you cannot remember where a certain file is located.
- The *Customize* option enables you to specify settings for your work environment. We shall deal with this in more detail in the following section.
- The *Office Setup and Uninstall* option enables you to start up Office or remove it from your computer. We dealt with this in chapter 1.
- The *Cue Cards* option activates information sheets which help you in the tasks that you are implementing at any given moment. They remain on the screen while you are working so that you have easy reference.
- The *Help* option opens the list of contents in the Microsoft Office Help function. This not only provides help about working with Office, it also gives access to the Help functions in Word, Excel, PowerPoint and Access.

- The *About Microsoft Office* option provides a quick summary of the Microsoft Office version and your computer system.
- The *Exit* option will close down the Microsoft Office Manager.

8.5 Customizing the Microsoft Office Manager

When you select the *Customize* option from the *Microsoft Office* menu, the *Customize* dialog window is opened in which you can modify the Microsoft Office toolbar, the menu and the way Microsoft Office is displayed on the screen.

8.5.1 Customizing the Microsoft Office Manager toolbar

If you wish to alter the settings applying to the toolbar, click on the *Toolbar* tabsheet in the *Customize* dialog window.

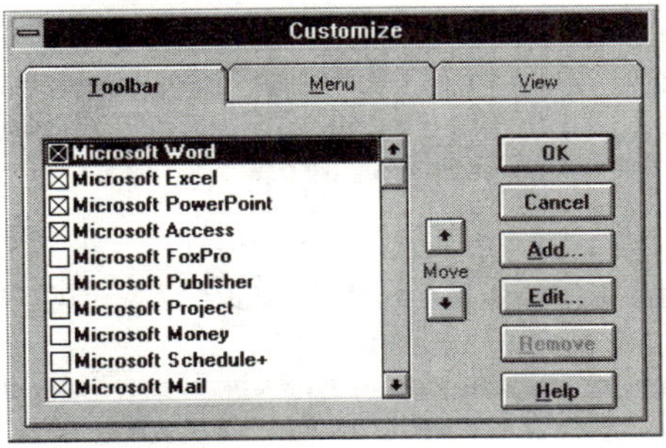

If you want to move a button to a different place on the toolbar, select the name of the button from the tabsheet, and click on one of the *Move* buttons to move the application button to the required position.

If you wish to add a button, click on the check box in front of the application name shown in the list. If you want to add a button for an application that is not shown in the list, select the name from the list at which point the new application is to be inserted (the new application is placed after the selected name). Then click on the *Add* button. The *Add Program to Toolbar* dialog window is opened. Enter the command which activates the program in the *Command Line* box and the directory where the program is to create its documents in the *Working Directory* box. You can select these from existing file and directory lists by clicking on the *Browse* button. Click on *OK* to confirm the specifications.

If you wish to modify the program item settings, select the corresponding name from the list and click on the *Edit* button. The *Edit Program Item* appears in which you can specify the required settings. You can make changes to the description, command line or working directory. You can also activate the program in a particular way by specifying additional parameters, such as opening an application along with a document or with a special style etc.

To remove a button from the toolbar, remove the cross from the check box next to the list of names. To remove an added program from the list altogether, select the program and click on the *Remove* button.

8.5.2 Customizing the Office menu

If you wish to make modifications to the *Microsoft Office* menu, activate the *Menu* tabsheet in the *Customize* dialog window.

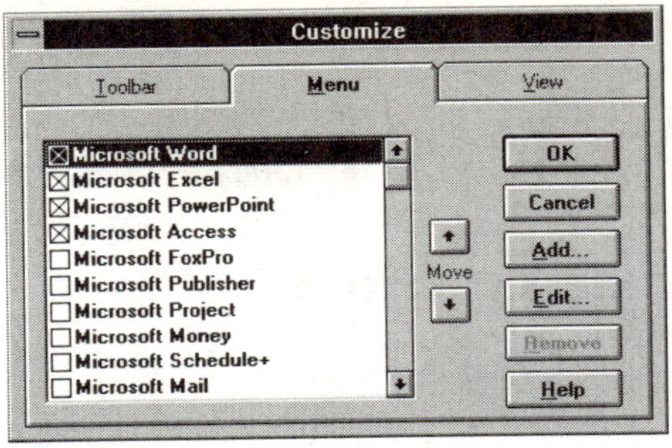

If you wish to move a menu option to another position in the menu, select the option from the list and click on one of the *Move* arrows.

To add an option to the menu, click on the check box adjacent to the required program item. If you want to add a program that is not shown in the list, select the program item under which you want to insert the new item. Then click on the *Add* button. The *Add Program to Menu* dialog window appears. Specify the program to be added to the list or click on the *Browse* button and select the required program from the directory and file lists displayed. Click on *OK* to confirm the specifications and close the dialog window.If you want to change the settings of a program listed in the menu, select the program from the list and click on the *Edit* button. The *Edit Program Item* dialog window is again opened. You can specify settings for the way in which the program is to be started up or run. Click on *OK* to confirm the specifications and close the dialog window.

To remove a menu option from the Microsoft Office menu, remove the cross in the check box next to the option, by clicking on it. If you have added an option and want to remove it again, select it from the list and click on the *Remove* button.

8.5.3 Customizing the toolbar display

Altering the settings on the *View* tabsheet in the *Customize* dialog window enables you to modify the way the Microsoft Office toolbar is shown on the screen.

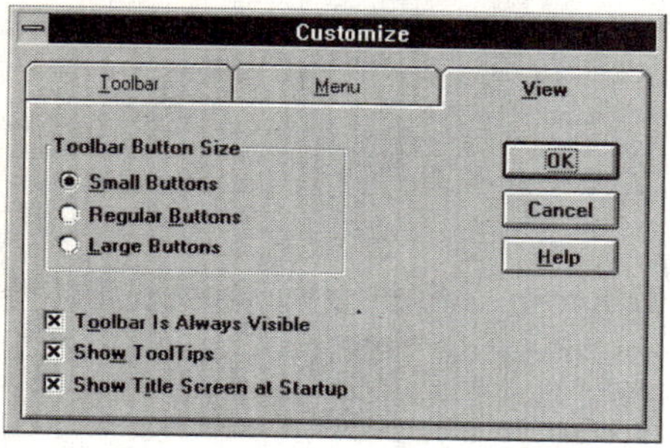

- The *Toolbar Button Size* section provides options for the size of the buttons shown.
- The *Toolbar Always Visible* option ensures that the toolbar is shown in all Microsoft Office applications.
- If the *Show Tool Tips* option is active, information will be given when the mouse pointer rests on any of the toolbar buttons.
- If the *Show Title Screen at Startup* option is active, the opening screen is always shown when Microsoft Office is started up.

9 Making optimal use of Microsoft Office

The great virtue of Microsoft Office lies in the fact that, in addition to each individual application supplying an enormous amount of practical features, the applications work in a harmonious and coordinated way, as if they form one single program. All applications can be active simultaneously so that it is easy and straightforward to move or copy data from one application to the other. Moreover, you can also link, embed, import and export data. Microsoft Office also provides diverse Help programs which can, in principle, be opened from all applications.

9.1 Moving and copying data

There are various ways to move and copy data. You can move and copy data not only within documents but also within and between applications.

9.1.1 Drag-and-drop

Prior to being able to make use of the drag-and-drop function in Word and Excel, you may have to make adjustments to the settings. This is done by opening the *Tools* menu and selecting *Options*. Activate the *Edit* tabsheet and ensure that the *Drag-and-Drop* check box is activated. You do not need to activate an option in PowerPoint and Access prior to using the drag-and-drop feature, but in Access you can only drag and drop in the Design View mode.

To move selected data, simply drag them to the new position. To copy selected data, hold down the Ctrl key while dragging. This method applies to moving and copying data within an application, either within a document or from one document to another. You can also use it to move or copy data from certain applications to others.

You can use this drag-and-drop method to move or copy data from Word to Excel, PowerPoint and Access. From Excel you can drag and drop data to Word, PowerPoint and Access. You can move or copy data from the Slide Sorter View in PowerPoint to Word, Excel and Access. It is not possible to drag data from Access to a different application.

Exercise
We shall copy data from an Excel worksheet to a Word document.

Procedure:

1 Start up Word by clicking on the *Word* button on the Microsoft Office Manager toolbar. Open the REST.DOC document and place the insertion point at the first blank line under the heading 'Wine Sales - Turnover 1994'.
2 Press and hold down the Shift key and click on the *Excel* button on the Microsoft Office Manager toolbar. The windows from both applications are now shown on the screen, one under the other.
3 Open the BOTTLES.XLS document in Excel.
4 In the BOTTLES.XLS document, activate the *quantity 1994* tabsheet.
5 Select the range A4:G19.
6 Press and hold down the Ctrl key and drag the selected data to the insertion point in the Word document. You can drag the selected data when the mouse pointer has assumed the shape of an arrow pointing diagonally leftwards (this occurs when the mouse pointer is on the frame of the selected data). A copy of the selected data is added to the Word document.

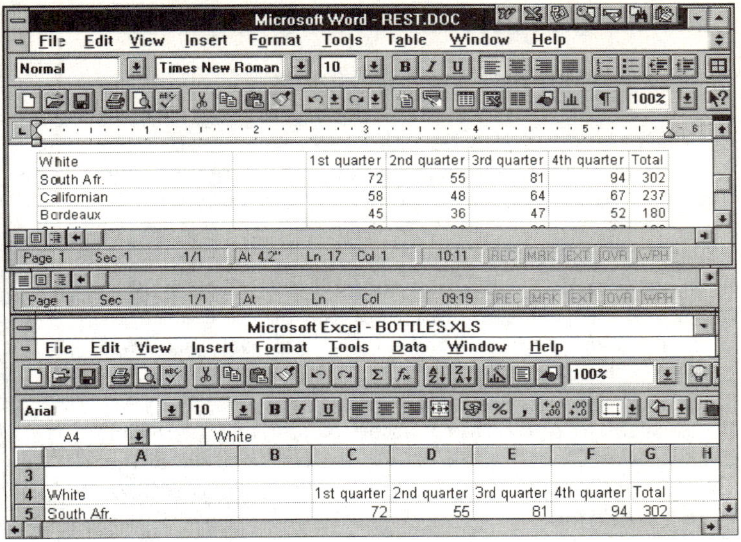

Click on the *Maximize* button at the right of the title bar to gain a good overview of the data in the REST.DOC document.

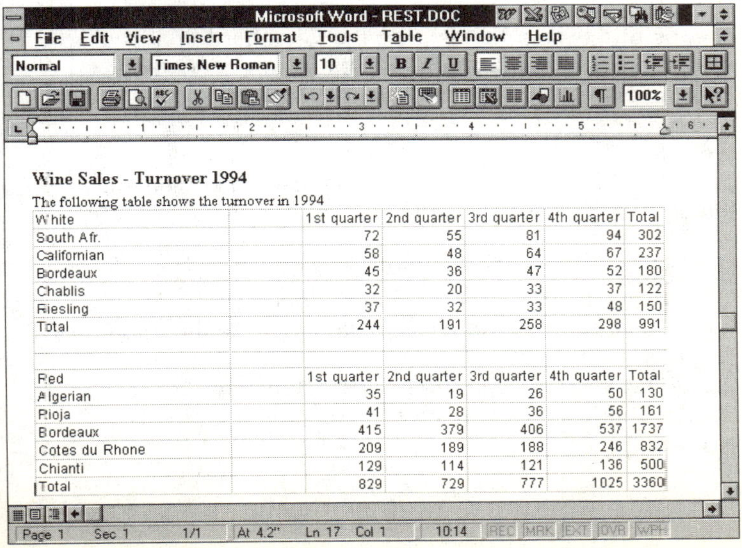

Wine Sales - Turnover 1994

The following table shows the turnover in 1994

White	1st quarter	2nd quarter	3rd quarter	4th quarter	Total
South Afr.	72	55	81	94	302
Californian	58	48	64	67	237
Bordeaux	45	36	47	52	180
Chablis	32	20	33	37	122
Riesling	37	32	33	48	150
Total	244	191	258	298	991
Red	1st quarter	2nd quarter	3rd quarter	4th quarter	Total
Algerian	35	19	26	50	130
Rioja	41	28	36	56	161
Bordeaux	415	379	406	537	1737
Cotes du Rhone	209	189	188	246	832
Chianti	129	114	121	136	500
Total	829	729	777	1025	3360

9.1.2 Cut, Copy and Paste

In addition to the drag-and-drop method, you can make use of the *Cut, Copy* and *Paste* buttons to copy or move data. This method can be used to move or copy data within a document, from one document to another within the same application and from one application to another.

Cut

If you wish to move data, first select the data you want to move and then click on the *Cut* button on the toolbar, or open the *Edit* menu and select *Cut*. The data are then copied to the Clipboard.

Copy

If you want to copy data instead of just moving them, click on the *Copy* button on the toolbar instead of the *Cut* button or open the *Edit* menu and choose *Copy* from the *Edit* menu.

Paste

Then place the insertion point at the position where the data are to be inserted and click on the *Paste* button on the toolbar, or open the *Edit* menu and select *Paste*.

A copy of the data remains on the Clipboard until you place new data there or until you close down Windows. You can copy or move them to various locations.

Exercise
We shall copy the chart we made in Excel to supplement the data we have just copied to Word.

Procedure:
1 Switch to the BOTTLES.XLS document in Excel and click on the *Maximize* button to make the document screen-filling.
2 Activate the *quantity 1994 (chart)* tabsheet.
3 Double click in the chart to select it. It acquires a wider frame.

4 Click on the *Copy* button on the toolbar. The data are copied to the Clipboard.
5 Switch to the Word document, REST.DOC, and place the insertion point under the data we inserted in the previous exercise (press Enter if necessary).
6 Click on the *Paste* button. The chart is inserted as the following figure illustrates (zoomed out to 50% to show data and chart).

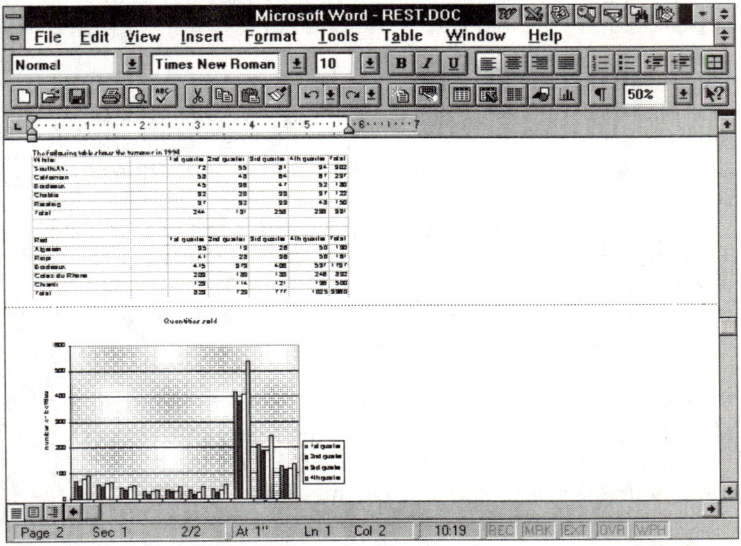

9.2 Linking and embedding data

Data which have been inserted into another application and saved there are regarded as being an object. In this way, an object can be a table, a chart etc.

Objects can be copied to other documents in three ways: they can be copied, linked or embedded.

When an object is **copied**, the data contained are simply copied to the new document. They can only be edited by means of the functions available in the new document.

When an object is **linked**, the data are displayed in the destination document but they are *stored* in the source document. Any alterations to these data in the source document are automatically transferred to the destination document. Therefore, if you want to alter the data, you should do that in the source document.

When you **embed** an object, the data are stored in the document to which they have been copied. However, a link is created to the application in which the data were created. If you want to alter the data in the embedded object, you do that in the destination document, in other words, in the document to which they have been copied. To do this, however, you need to activate the application which you used to create the object initially. This is done by double clicking on the embedded object. Then you can make the required modifications.

When data are linked to a file, the size of the destination file scarcely increases. This is because only the *structure* of the data is stored in the destination file; the actual data themselves are not stored in the destination file.

Linked data can only be examined if the source file is available. If this file cannot be found, the user cannot gain access to the linked data.

When data are embedded, the file containing the data does increase considerably in size. This is because the embedded data are stored in the destination file. As mentioned, if the user wishes to modify the data, the application in which the data were initially created must be available.

9.2.1 Linking data

In the following exercise, we shall link data from an Excel file to a Word file.

Exercise

We shall link data from the BOTTLES.XLS file to the REST.DOC document in Word.

Procedure:

1 Ensure that Word and Excel have both been started up and open the REST.DOC and BOTTLES.XLS documents.

2 Activate the *returns 1994* tab sheet in Excel.

3 Select the range A4:G19.

Copy

4 Copy the selected data by clicking on the *Copy* button on the Standard toolbar or by opening the *Edit* menu and selecting *Copy*.

Microsoft Word

5 Click on the *Microsoft Word* button on the Office Manager toolbar to activate Word.

6 Move the insertion point to the first blank line under the heading 'Wine Sales - Returns 1994'.

7 Open the *Edit* menu and select *Paste Special*.

The *Paste Special* window appears.

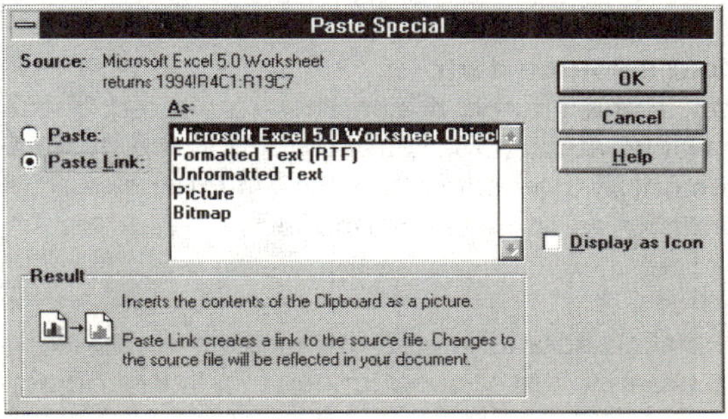

8 Activate the *Paste Link* option button and select *Microsoft Excel 5.0 Worksheet Object* from the list. Click on *OK*.

The selected data from the worksheet are linked to the Word document and a copy is shown at the specified position in the text.

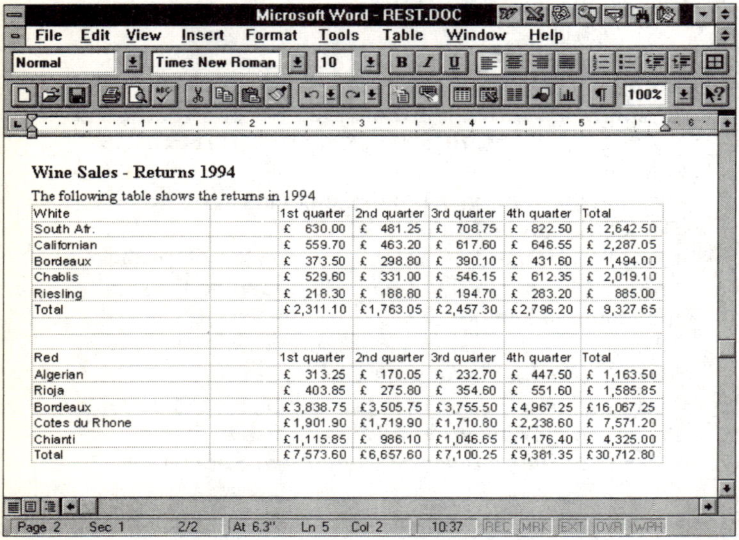

Wine Sales - Returns 1994

The following table shows the returns in 1994

White		1st quarter	2nd quarter	3rd quarter	4th quarter	Total
South Afr.		£ 630.00	£ 481.25	£ 708.75	£ 822.50	£ 2,642.50
Californian		£ 559.70	£ 463.20	£ 617.60	£ 646.55	£ 2,287.05
Bordeaux		£ 373.50	£ 298.80	£ 390.10	£ 431.60	£ 1,494.00
Chablis		£ 529.60	£ 331.00	£ 546.15	£ 612.35	£ 2,019.10
Riesling		£ 218.30	£ 188.80	£ 194.70	£ 283.20	£ 885.00
Total		£2,311.10	£1,763.05	£2,457.30	£2,796.20	£ 9,327.65
Red		1st quarter	2nd quarter	3rd quarter	4th quarter	Total
Algerian		£ 313.25	£ 170.05	£ 232.70	£ 447.50	£ 1,163.50
Rioja		£ 403.85	£ 275.80	£ 354.60	£ 551.60	£ 1,585.85
Bordeaux		£3,838.75	£3,505.75	£3,755.50	£4,967.25	£16,067.25
Cotes du Rhone		£1,901.90	£1,719.90	£1,710.80	£2,238.60	£ 7,571.20
Chianti		£1,115.85	£ 986.10	£1,046.65	£1,176.40	£ 4,325.00
Total		£7,573.60	£6,657.60	£7,100.25	£9,381.35	£30,712.80

Changing the source data

If the data in the source document are altered, these changes will be automatically transferred to the destination document. If the destination document is closed, it will be modified as soon as it is opened.

Exercise

We shall make alterations to the Microsoft Excel worksheet and examine the consequences to a linked object.

Procedure:

1 Activate the *returns 1994* worksheet in the BOTTLES.XLS document in Excel.
2 Change the formula in cells C5 to F5 so that the selling price of the exquisite South African wine is raised from £8.75 to £9.00. This is done by activating the first cell (C5) and pressing F2 to edit the formula. Press Enter to confirm the changes. Alter each cell in turn so that the final values become £648, £495, £729 and £846. The Total will change automatically.
3 Activate the Word document. You will see that the proper values have been transferred to the table in REST.DOC.

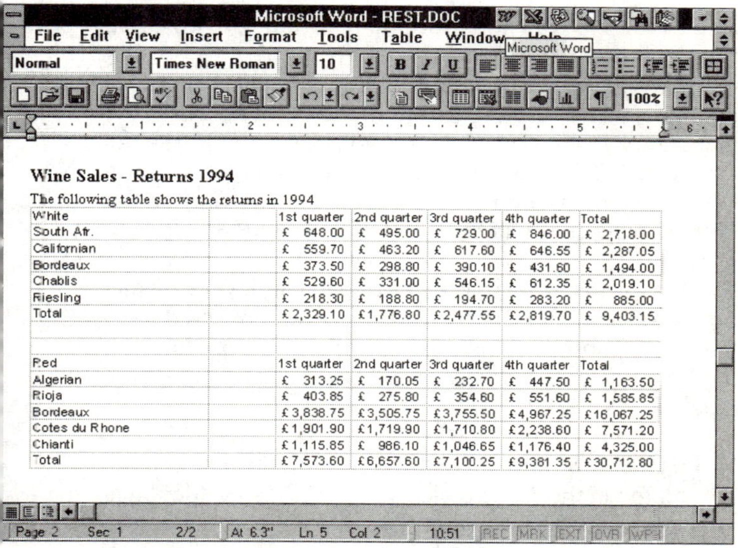

Wine Sales - Returns 1994

The following table shows the returns in 1994

White		1st quarter	2nd quarter	3rd quarter	4th quarter	Total
South Afr.		£ 648.00	£ 495.00	£ 729.00	£ 846.00	£ 2,718.00
Californian		£ 559.70	£ 463.20	£ 617.60	£ 646.55	£ 2,287.05
Bordeaux		£ 373.50	£ 298.80	£ 390.10	£ 431.60	£ 1,494.00
Chablis		£ 529.60	£ 331.00	£ 546.15	£ 612.35	£ 2,019.10
Riesling		£ 218.30	£ 188.80	£ 194.70	£ 283.20	£ 885.00
Total		£2,329.10	£1,776.80	£2,477.55	£2,819.70	£ 9,403.15
Red		1st quarter	2nd quarter	3rd quarter	4th quarter	Total
Algerian		£ 313.25	£ 170.05	£ 232.70	£ 447.50	£ 1,163.50
Rioja		£ 403.85	£ 275.80	£ 354.60	£ 551.60	£ 1,585.85
Bordeaux		£3,838.75	£3,505.75	£3,755.50	£4,967.25	£16,067.25
Cotes du Rhone		£1,901.90	£1,719.90	£1,710.80	£2,238.60	£ 7,571.20
Chianti		£1,115.85	£ 986.10	£1,046.65	£1,176.40	£ 4,325.00
Total		£7,573.60	£6,657.60	£7,100.25	£9,381.35	£30,712.80

Modifying a link

You can alter a link you have made. This is done by selecting the linked data in the destination file and then choosing *Links* from the *Edit* menu. The *Links* dialog window appears.

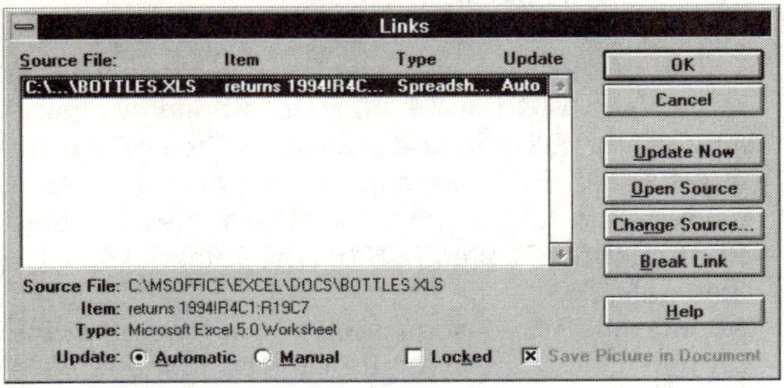

Select the link you wish to modify (in our example, we have only created one link up to now).
You can, for instance, change an automatic link into a manual link by clicking on the *Manual* option button. A manual link is a link which is only updated when you select the *Update Link* option from the shortcut menu (when the linked data have been selected) or when you click on the *Update Now* button in the *Links* dialog window.

To break a link, open the *Links* dialog window, (*Edit* menu, *Links*) and click on the *Break Link* button. The data in the destination document remain there as a picture but they cannot be modified or linked to the source data again.

You can also protect a link by activating the *Locked* option button in the *Links* dialog window. This protection is temporary and ensures that the link cannot be changed during this time. To lock a link in Excel, activate the *Manual* option button.

9.2.2 Embedding objects

If you insert Excel data in Word by means of the *Cut* or *Copy* and *Paste* commands, they are inserted as a Word table and can only be editing by means of the Word functions. Therefore, if you wish to make use of the functions in the application in which the data were created, select the *Paste Special* option instead of *Paste* from the *Edit* menu, or use the drag-and-drop method.
If you drag Excel data to a Word document, for example, the data are embedded. You can edit them using Excel functions by double clicking on the object in Word. (Section 9.1.1 discusses drag-and-drop in detail.)

To embed an object which contains no data as yet, select the *Object* command from the *Insert* menu.

Embedding objects using Paste Special
To embed objects, select the data in the source file and then click on the *Copy* button or select *Copy* from the *Edit* menu. Then activate the destination file, place the insertion point at the position where the data are to be inserted and select *Paste Special* from the *Edit* menu. Activate the *Paste* option button in the dialog window and select the object that you want to embed from the list. Click on *OK*.

When you want to edit an embedded object, double click on the object. The functions of the original application used to create the object are activated so that you can make modifications.

Embedding new objects
To embed a new object, place the insertion point at the position where the object is to be situated and select *Object* from the *Insert* menu. The *Object* dialog window appears.

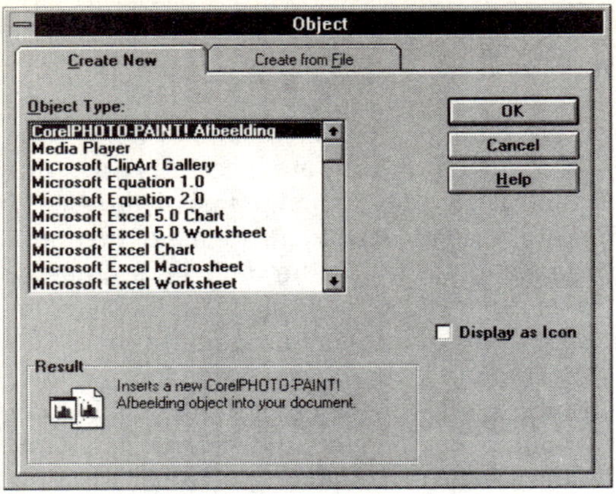

Activate the *Create New* tabsheet if you wish to insert a new object. Select the required Object Type from the list.

If you want to insert an existing file, activate the *Create from File* tabsheet. You can then select the required file.

Note
The can use the *Picture* option from the *Insert* menu if you want to insert a figure which has been created in a different application. The figure can also be linked using that command.

Editing an embedded object
If you double click on an embedded object - depending on the situation - either the original application will be opened in its own window or the menus and toolbars in the destination document will be replaced by those in the original application. You can then use these menus and toolbars to edit the embedded object.

If the object is opened in a separate application window, you must choose the *Exit* command from the *File* menu to return to the destination document. If only the menus and toolbars have been replaced, click on the area outside the object to return to the destination document.

It may occur that you are not able to edit an object by double clicking on it. In that case, select the object and open the *Edit* menu. The name of the object (type) should be shown there. Select this option and click on *Edit* from the subsequent submenu if you want to edit the object within the document.

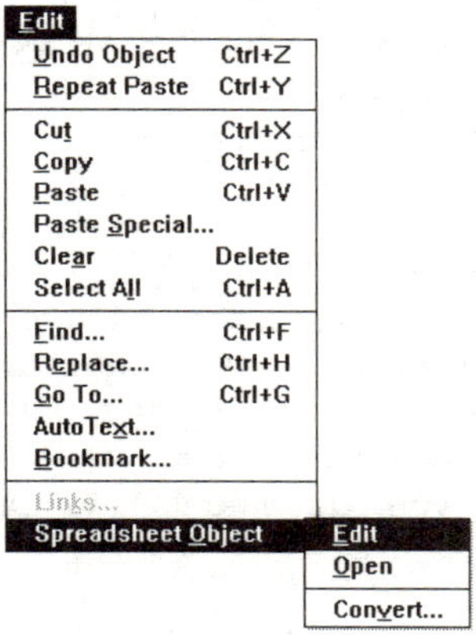

9.3 Importing and exporting documents

In Microsoft Office, you can convert the file layout of one application to a layout which can be read by another application. Accordingly, they gain a layout which can be directly edited in the new application, or which can be examined by other computer users who may not possess the original application.

To convert a document to another file layout, open the document in the application in which it was created and then open the *File* menu. Select *Save As* and specify the required type in the *Save File as Type* section at the bottom of the dialog window. We refer to this as 'exporting'.

If you wish to convert a file which has been saved in a different application, open the *File* menu in the application in which you are working and select *Open*. Select the type of file you want to open from the *List Files of Type* section. We refer to this as 'importing'.

We shall deal with importing and exporting in practical examples in chapters 10 to 13 where documents will be read into, and used in, other applications.

9.4 Shared Help programs

There are a number of utility programs available in Microsoft Office which can be used in various applications. These programs, such as the Microsoft Organization Chart, with which you became acquainted in section 5.7.2, enable you to improve your documents and to make them more attractive.

The following utility programs are available in Microsoft Office:

ClipArt Gallery	This is a program which will insert illustrations into documents. More than 1000 illustrations are supplied.
Organization Chart	This is a function which inserts organization structure charts into a document.
Equation	This program enables you to insert mathematical comparisons into a document quickly and easily.
WordArt	You can create special effects with text in Word.

Graph	Using Graph, you can create charts and insert them into a document.

In the following exercises, the ClipArt Gallery and Word-Art will be applied to make files more attractive.

9.4.1 Inserting illustrations

Exercise
We shall add a picture to the REST.DOC file to make it more attractive.

Procedure:
1 Ensure that Word and the REST.DOC document are opened.
2 Open the *Insert* menu and select *Frame*.

In order to be able to move a picture quickly and easily, it is convenient to have it in a frame, although this is not strictly necessary. Having it in a frame also enables you to place text around the illustration.

A window appears in which you are asked whether you wish to activate the Page Layout View.

3 Click on *Yes*. The mouse pointer acquires the shape of a plus sign (if not, open the *Insert* menu again and select *Frame* once more).
4 Drag the mouse from the margin at the left-hand side of the title towards the centre to create a frame as shown in the figure overleaf:

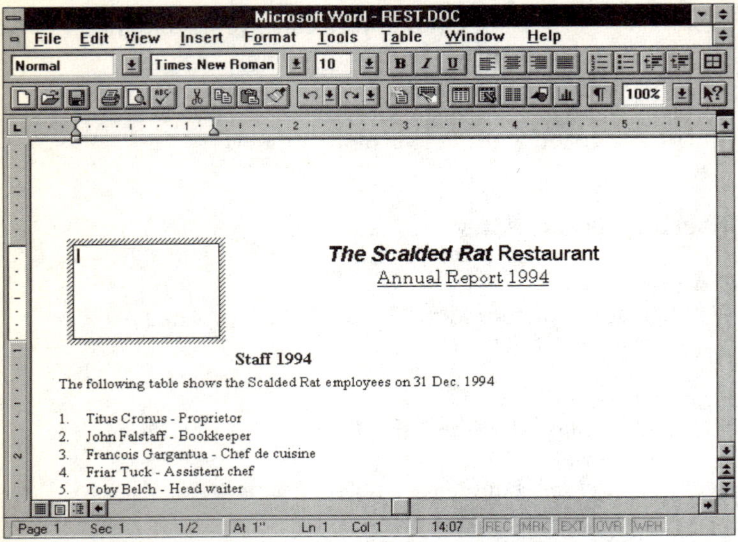

5 The insertion point should be flashing in the frame (if not, click in the frame). Open the *Insert* menu and select *Object*.

6 Activate the *Create New* tabsheet and select *Microsoft ClipArt Gallery* from the *Object Type* list.

7 Click on *OK*.

The *Microsoft ClipArt Gallery* dialog window is opened. If you have not already worked with the ClipArt Gallery, the illustrations will have to be read in. This may take a few minutes. Click on *OK* if asked.

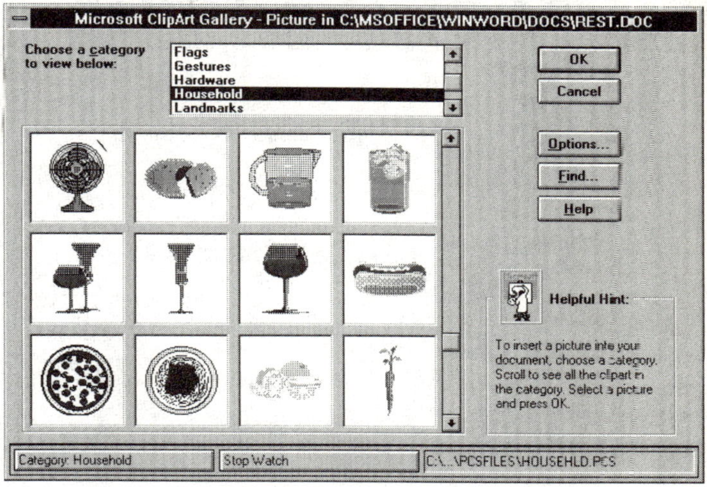

7 Activate the *Household* category in the upper part of the window and select the picture of the wine glasses by clicking in it.
8 Click on *OK*.

A (large) copy of the wine glasses picture is inserted into the document.

9 Select the object by clicking on it.
10 Drag the sizing handle in the lower right-hand corner upwards to the left to make the illustration smaller. Drag it until it attains a reasonable size.
11 Click anywhere outside the picture.

12 Your document will then look something like this:

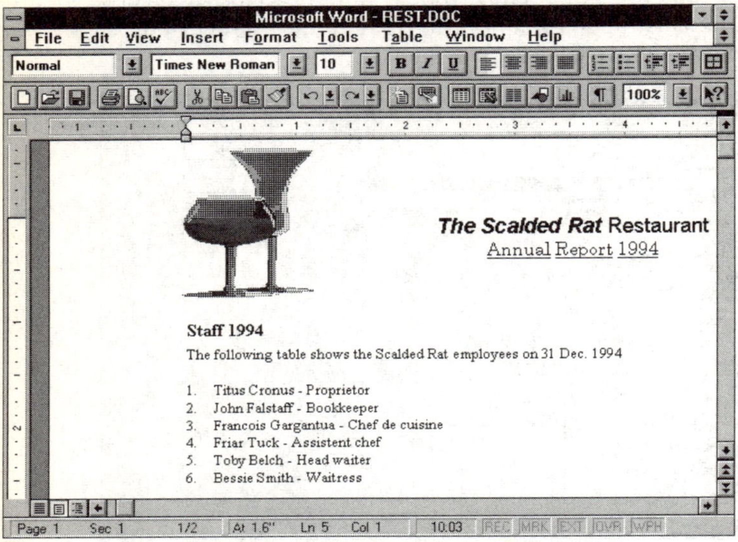

Exercise

We shall now insert a picture from the ClipArt Gallery into a PowerPoint slide.

Procedure:

1 Start up PowerPoint and open the WINE_REP.PPT file.

2 Activate the first slide in the slide display.

New Slide

3 Click on the *New Slide* button at the bottom of the window.

4 Move to the last slide in the *AutoLayout* section by clicking on the scroll arrow. Select the last slide, the blank slide and click on *OK*.

This will insert a blank slide after slide number 1.

5 When the new slide 2 is shown on the screen, open the *Insert* menu and select *Clip Art* from the *Insert* menu.

The *ClipArt Gallery* dialog window is opened once more.

6 Select the wine glass picture from the *Household* category again and click on *OK*.

The picture is added to the slide. You can move the picture to another position by dragging it, or you can alter its size by clicking on and dragging the sizing handles.

Exercise
We shall add illustrations to a table and to forms.

Procedure:

1 Start up Microsoft Access and open the RESTAUR.MDB database.

2 Click on the *Table* button if necessary.

3 Select the *stock* table and click on the *Design* button.

4 Add a new field called *Illustration* to the FieldName list by typing its name in the first empty box. Enter *OLE Object* in the Data Type list.

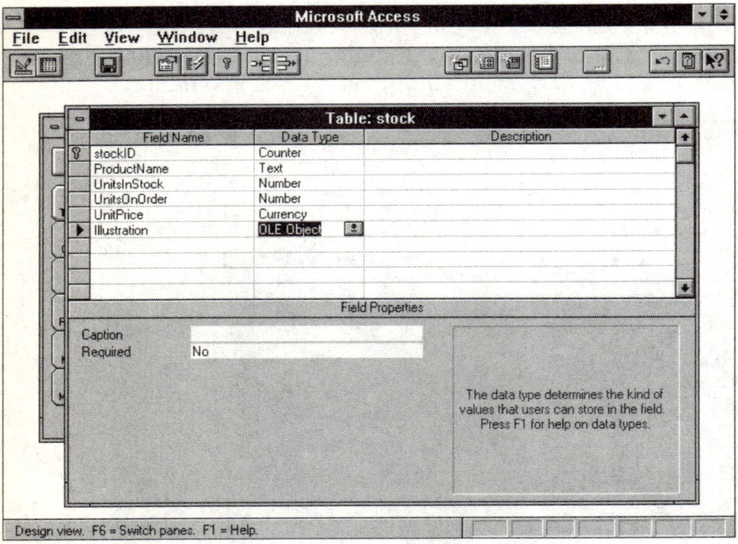

Datasheet View

5 Click on the *Datasheet View* button on the toolbar.

6 If you are asked if you wish to save the changes to the design, answer *OK*.

7 At the extreme right-hand side of the table a new field has been added, Illustration. You can widen it if you want by dragging the right-hand edge. Activate this field for the first record and open the *Edit* menu. Select *Insert Object*. A dialog window appears.

8 Activate the *Create New* option button if necessary and select *ClipArt Gallery* from the list of *Object Types*.
9 Click on *OK*.
10 Select the map of the African Continent from the *Maps - International* category and click on *OK*.

The text 'Microsoft ClipArt Gallery' is inserted in the *Illustration* field of the first record.

11 Repeat this process for the other records, choosing an appropriate map or picture to suit each one.

Tip
You can also copy the contents of the *Illustration* field to all the other records. You can then alter the contents of each field by double clicking on it. This directly opens the *ClipArt Gallery* in which the previously selected category is still active. This makes it easier and quicker to select a suitable picture.

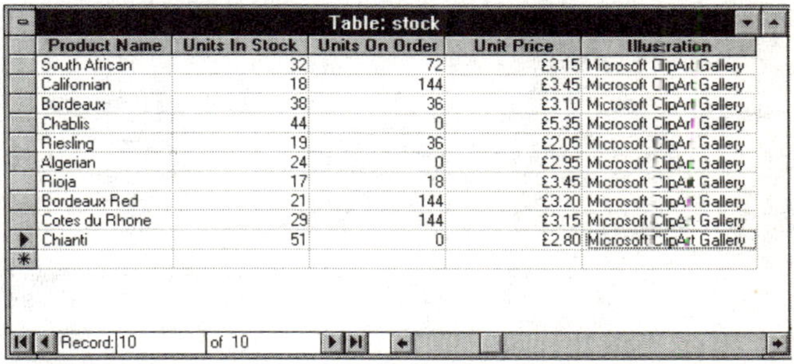
Table: stock

Product Name	Units In Stock	Units On Order	Unit Price	Illustration
South African	32	72	£3.15	Microsoft ClipArt Gallery
Californian	18	144	£3.45	Microsoft ClipArt Gallery
Bordeaux	38	36	£3.10	Microsoft ClipArt Gallery
Chablis	44	0	£5.35	Microsoft ClipArt Gallery
Riesling	19	36	£2.05	Microsoft ClipArt Gallery
Algerian	24	0	£2.95	Microsoft ClipArt Gallery
Rioja	17	18	£3.45	Microsoft ClipArt Gallery
Bordeaux Red	21	144	£3.20	Microsoft ClipArt Gallery
Cotes du Rhone	29	144	£3.15	Microsoft ClipArt Gallery
Chianti	51	0	£2.80	Microsoft ClipArt Gallery

Record: 10 of 10

12 Close the table by clicking on the *Database Window* button on the toolbar.

13 Click on the *Form* button in the database window.

14 Select the *stock* form and click on the *Design* button. The design window appears along with the Toolbox.

15 Activate the Toolbox.

Bound Object Frame

16 Click on the *Bound Object Frame* button in the Toolbox.

When you move the mouse pointer, you see that it has assumed the shape of a plus sign along with a copy of the *Bound Object Frame* button.

17 Drag the mouse to create a box as shown in the figure below:

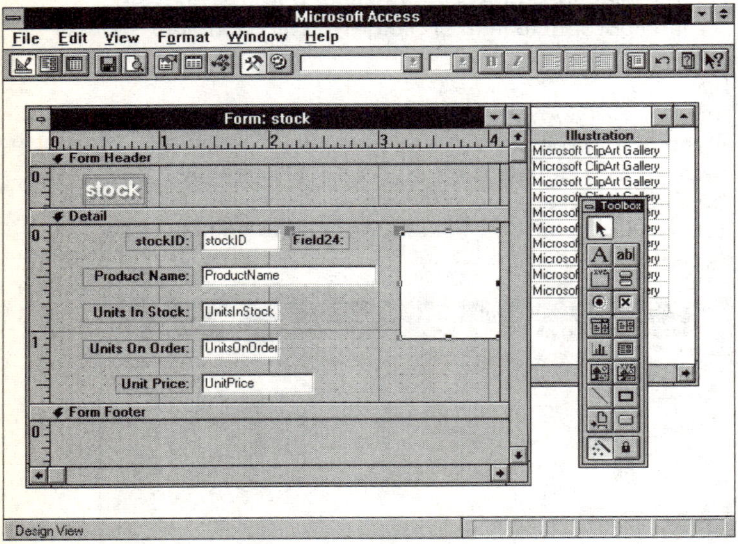

Properties

18 You will see that a label box showing 'Field' along with a number has appeared on the form. Activate this by clicking on it and select the *Properties* button from the toolbar.

19 Activate the *Caption* line and type **Illustration**. Enter **No** in the *Visible* line underneath and enter **0.75 in.** in the *Width* line. Close the *Properties* window via the Control menu button.

20 Select the new frame and click on the *Properties* button on the toolbar again.

21 Activate the *Control Source* line and select the *Illustration* field name from the list. Activate the *Size Mode* line and select *Stretch* from the drop-down list. Close the *Properties* window via the Control menu.

Form View

22 Click on the *Form View* button on the Standard toolbar.

23 If you are asked if you wish to save the changes made, reply *Yes*.

In the Form View, the chosen illustration will be shown on each form. If you wish to insert a picture in a new record later, select the frame in which the picture is to be placed and open the *Edit* menu. Select *Insert Object* and then activate *Microsoft ClipArt Gallery* to open the gallery.

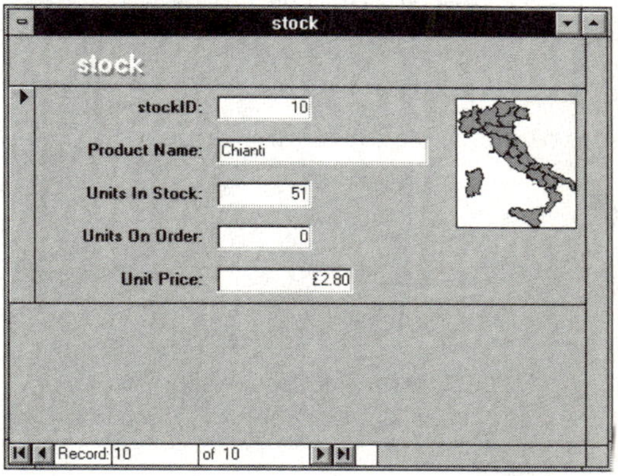

9.4.2 Using WordArt to create text effects

You can use WordArt to create attractive effects with your texts. We shall use the following exercise to create a WordArt object in Word.

Exercise
We shall create a WordArt object in REST.DOC Word document.

Procedure:
1 Activate Word and the REST.DOC document in the Normal View.
2 Place the insertion point just above the 'Staff 1994' heading and press Ctrl+Enter to force a page break.
3 Place the insertion point at the end of the first page.
4 Open the *Insert* menu and select *Object*.
5 Activate the *Create New* tabsheet if necessary and select *Microsoft WordArt* from the list.
6 Click on *OK*.

The *Enter your text here* dialog window appears.

7 Type the text **Ratify the Rumour** to replace the original text (Your Text Here) in the box.
8 Close the *Enter Your Text Here* dialog box using the Control menu button.
9 Select the object by clicking in the selection area in the left margin and open the *Edit* menu. Select *WordArt Object*.
10 Select *Open* from the submenu.
11 Open the *Choose a Shape* drop-down list by clicking on the arrow. A dialog window appears. Select *Wave 2* from the list by clicking on it.

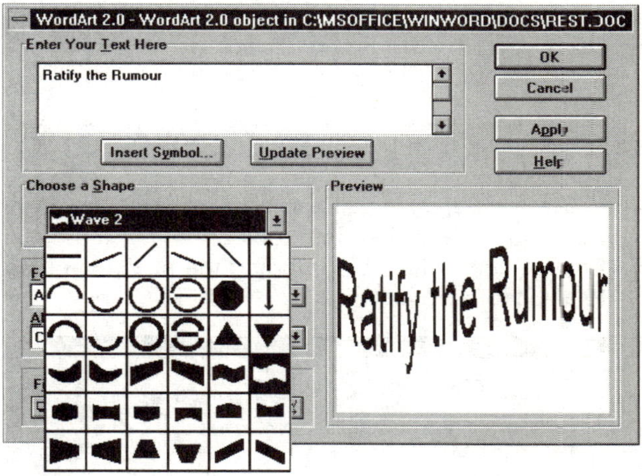

12 In the *Fill* section at the bottom of the window, click on the first button to give the text a shadow. The *Shadow* dialog window appears. Select the last shadow in the row and then click on *OK*.
13 Click on *OK* once again to actually enter the specifications in the Word document.

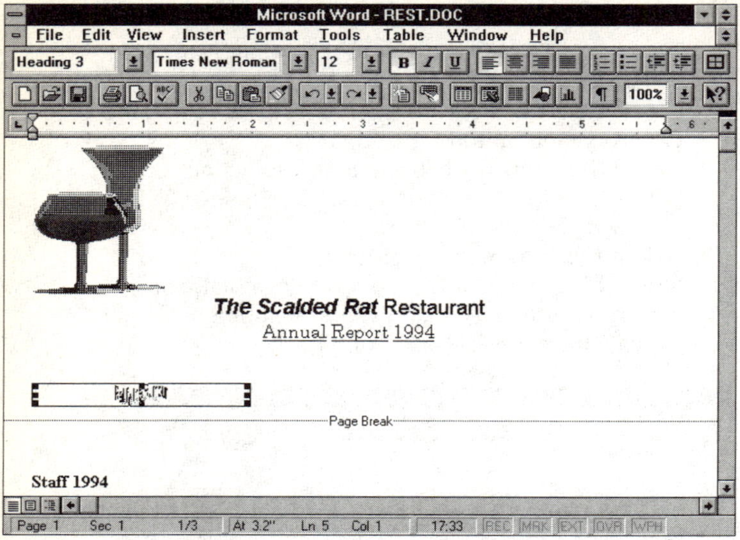

14 While the object is still activated, click on the *Center* button on the Standard toolbar.

15 Enlarge the textbox by dragging the sizing handles to a suitable position.

10 Integration: adopting data into Word documents

The next four chapters discuss the possibilities of creating documents compiled from various applications. In this chapter, we shall deal with adopting data into Word.

10.1 Adopting Excel data into a Word document

It is quite easy to insert, embed or link data from Excel in(to) Word in order to clarify data or passages of text. Excel charts can also be used to present data more clearly.

10.1.1 Inserting Excel data as a Word table

If you move or copy data from Excel to Word by means of the *Cut* or *Copy* and *Paste* commands, the data are inserted in Word as a table. You cannot modify them using the Excel editing functions; you can only use the Word functions.

Exercise
We shall insert data from an Excel worksheet into a Word document where they will be regarded as a table.

Procedure:
1 Start up Word and open the REST.DOC file.
2 Place the insertion point in the empty line above the heading 'Stock on 31 Dec. 1994'.
3 Press Enter twice to insert two blank lines.
4 Type the text **Purchase prices per sort 1994**, press Enter and type on the following line the text

The following table gives a summary of the purchase prices according to sort:

5 Format the text 'Purchase prices per sort 1994' in the Heading 3 style.

6 Place the insertion point in the empty line under 'The following table...'

7 Start up Excel, open the BOTTLES.XLS document and activate the *purchase 1994* worksheet.

Copy

8 Select the range A4:G19 and click on the *Copy* button on the Standard toolbar, or select *Copy* from the *Edit* menu.

Paste

9 Switch over to Word by clicking on the *Word* button on the Office toolbar, and click on the *Paste* button or select *Paste* from the *Edit* menu.

The Excel cells are inserted as a Word table in the REST.DOC document.

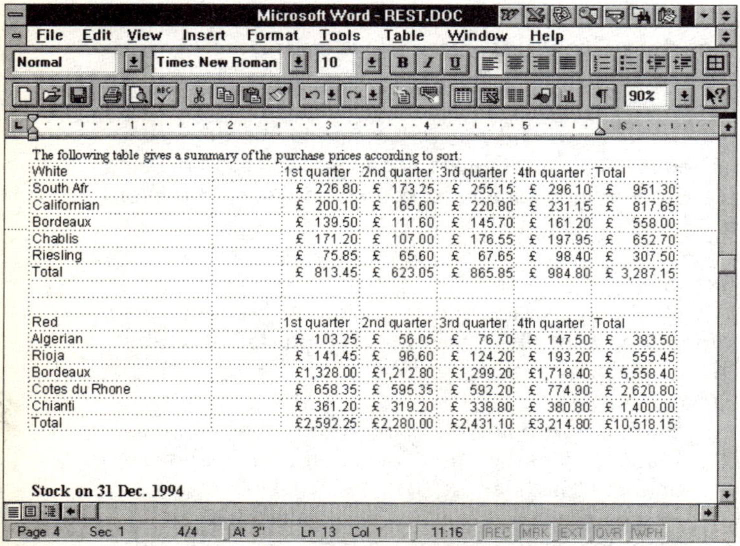

The following table gives a summary of the purchase prices according to sort:

White		1st quarter	2nd quarter	3rd quarter	4th quarter	Total
South Afr.		£ 226.80	£ 173.25	£ 255.15	£ 296.10	£ 951.30
Californian		£ 200.10	£ 165.60	£ 220.80	£ 231.15	£ 817.65
Bordeaux		£ 139.50	£ 111.60	£ 145.70	£ 161.20	£ 558.00
Chablis		£ 171.20	£ 107.00	£ 176.55	£ 197.95	£ 652.70
Riesling		£ 75.85	£ 65.60	£ 67.65	£ 98.40	£ 307.50
Total		£ 813.45	£ 623.05	£ 865.85	£ 984.80	£ 3,287.15
Red		1st quarter	2nd quarter	3rd quarter	4th quarter	Total
Algerian		£ 103.25	£ 56.05	£ 76.70	£ 147.50	£ 383.50
Rioja		£ 141.45	£ 96.60	£ 124.20	£ 193.20	£ 555.45
Bordeaux		£1,328.00	£1,212.80	£1,299.20	£1,718.40	£ 5,558.40
Cotes du Rhone		£ 658.35	£ 595.35	£ 592.20	£ 774.90	£ 2,620.80
Chianti		£ 361.20	£ 319.20	£ 338.80	£ 380.80	£ 1,400.00
Total		£2,592.25	£2,280.00	£2,431.10	£3,214.80	£10,518.15

Stock on 31 Dec. 1994

10.1.2 Embedding a new Microsoft Excel worksheet in Word

In the previous exercise, you inserted Excel data into Word but you did not embed them. Imagine that you prefer to embed the data instead of merely inserting them.

Exercise
We shall now undo the previous exercise. Subsequently, we shall embed the Excel data in the Word document.

Procedure:

Undo

1 Click on the *Undo* button on the Standard toolbar. The table will then immediately disappear from the Word document (if you have not implemented any other actions since the *Paste* command). You could also open the Undo list by clicking on the arrow next to the *Undo* button; then you can choose the *Paste* command.

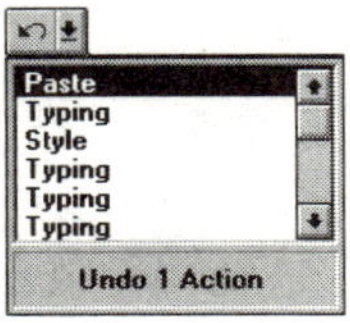

2 Activate Excel, the BOTTLES.XLS document and the *purchase 1994* worksheet.
3 Select the range A4:G19 if necessary.

Copy

4 Click on the *Copy* button or select *Copy* from the *Edit* menu.
5 Switch to Word, ensure that the insertion point is at the required position and select *Paste Special* from the *Edit* menu.
6 Activate the *Paste* option button in the subsequent *Paste Special* dialog window and select *Microsoft Excel 5.0 Worksheet Object* from the list. Click on *OK*.

The table is then embedded as an Excel table. You can modify it by means of the Excel editing functions by double clicking on it.

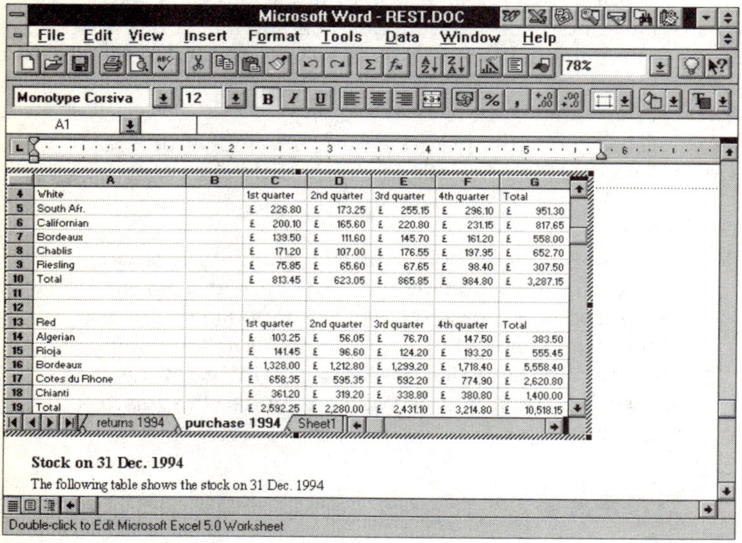

Note

If you had selected the *Paste Link* option button instead of *Paste* in the *Paste Special* dialog box, the selected range would not be embedded in the Word document; it would have been *linked* instead. This means that if the data are altered in the original document in Excel, the alterations would be passed on to the table in Word. Section 9.2.1 also deals with this topic in detail.

10.1.3 Linking a chart in Excel to a Word document

In the following exercise, we shall create a link between a chart in an Excel worksheet and a Word document. If the chart in the original worksheet is modified, the changes are automatically passed on to the version in Word. Accordingly, the data are always up to date.

Exercise

In section 9.1.2, we *copied* the chart in BOTTLES.XLS to the REST.DOC Word document. We shall now remove it from the Word document (if you do still have it), and then we shall *link* the chart instead so that any changes to the original will also be transferred to the chart in Word.

Procedure:

1 First activate Word and the REST.DOC.

2 Move to the chart and select it by clicking on the selection area in the left margin. The entire chart is selected. Press Del to remove it from the Word document. Now we can begin to insert a linked chart.

3 Place the insertion point under the table which shows the turnover in 1994 (inserted in section 9.1.1). Press Enter twice to insert two blank lines.

4 Type the text **Turnover Chart - 1994**, press Enter and type the text **The following chart shows the turnover per sort in 1994:**. Press Enter again.

5 Apply the Heading 3 style to the text 'Turnover Chart - 1994'.

6 Place the insertion point under the text 'The following chart...'.

7 Switch to Excel and activate the *quantity 1994 (chart)* worksheet.

8 Click on the chart to activate it.

Copy

9 Click on the *Copy* button on the Standard toolbar, or select *Copy* from the *Edit* menu.

10 Switch to Word and select *Paste Special* from the *Edit* menu.

11 Activate the *Paste Link* option button in the *Paste Special* dialog window. Select *Microsoft Excel 5.0 Chart Object* from the list and click on *OK*.

The chart is inserted into the Word document as a linked object.

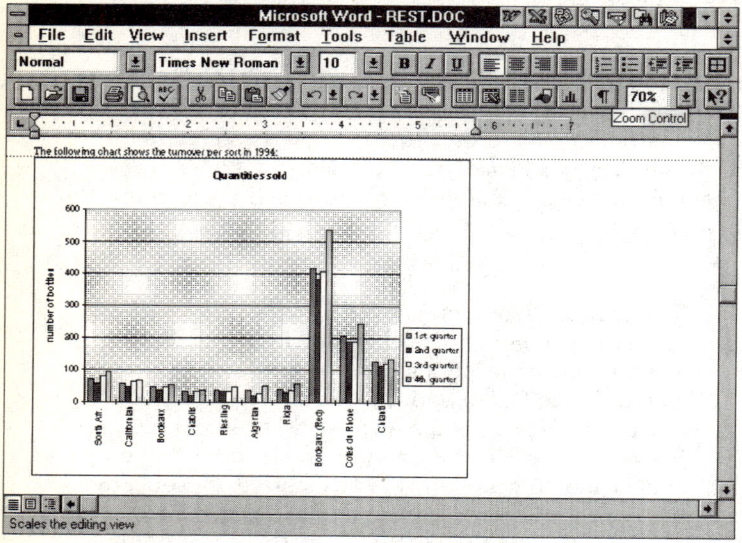

Note

Linked data are actually stored in Word as fields. A field is visible either as code or as result. You can determine whether you see the code or the result by opening the *Tools* menu and selecting *Options*. The figures in this book show the results, but you can select *Field Codes* from the *View* tabsheet if you prefer to see the codes instead:

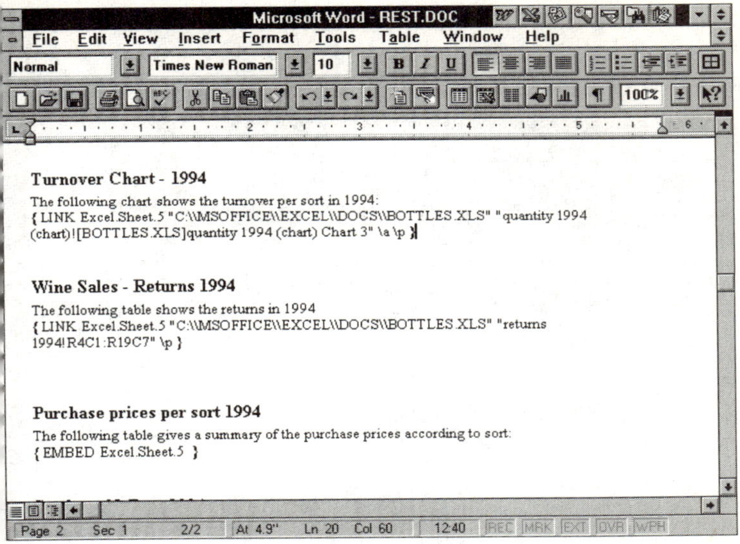

10.1.4 Inserting a new Microsoft Excel worksheet

Insert Microsoft Excel Work-sheet

The *Insert Microsoft Excel Worksheet* button is situated on the Standard toolbar. You can use this to embed a new Excel worksheet in a document.

When you click on this button, a small window containing a grid is opened. You can drag the mouse pointer across this grid to determine how many rows and columns the new worksheet is to consist of. You can always alter this later if necessary. Since the new worksheet will form an embedded object, you will be able to edit it using the Excel functions.

If you double click on the object which has been imported from Excel, the Excel toolbars, menus and commands become available (see also section 9.2.1).

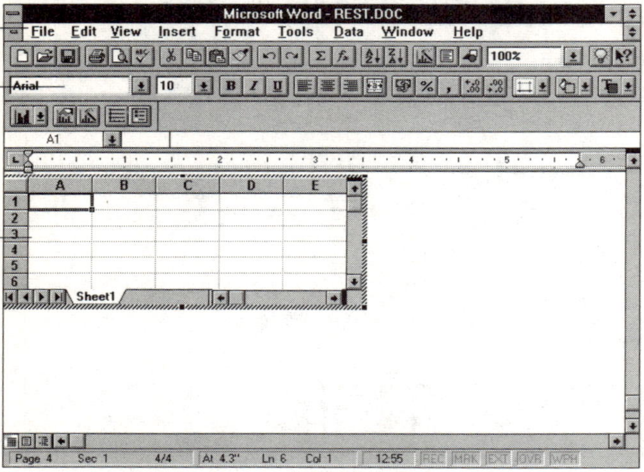

10.2 Adopting PowerPoint data into a Word document

It is possible to adopt slides from PowerPoint into a Word document. You can then examine the slides in Word by means of the PowerPoint Viewer utility program which is supplied along with Microsoft Office. We presume that you have installed the PowerPoint Viewer program. This program also enables users, who do not possess the PowerPoint program themselves, to examine PowerPoint slides.

10.2.1 Embedding PowerPoint slides in a Word document

If you wish to select certain slides in order to insert them into a Word document, you should activate the Slide Sorter View in PowerPoint to obtain a good overview.

Exercise
We shall now insert selected PowerPoint slides into a Word document.

Procedure:
1. Activate Word and the REST.DOC document. Press Ctrl+End to move the insertion point to the end of the document.
2. Press Enter twice to insert two blank lines.
3. Type the text **Presentation 1994**, press Enter and type **Double click on the next slide to activate the 1994 presentation** on the next line. Press Enter twice.
4. Apply the Heading 3 style to the 'Presentation 1994' text, and press Ctrl+End to move to the end of the document.
5. Activate PowerPoint, the WINE_REP.PPT document and switch to the Slide Sorter View.
6. Select slides number 1, 2, 3, 5 and 10 by clicking on them while holding down the Shift key.

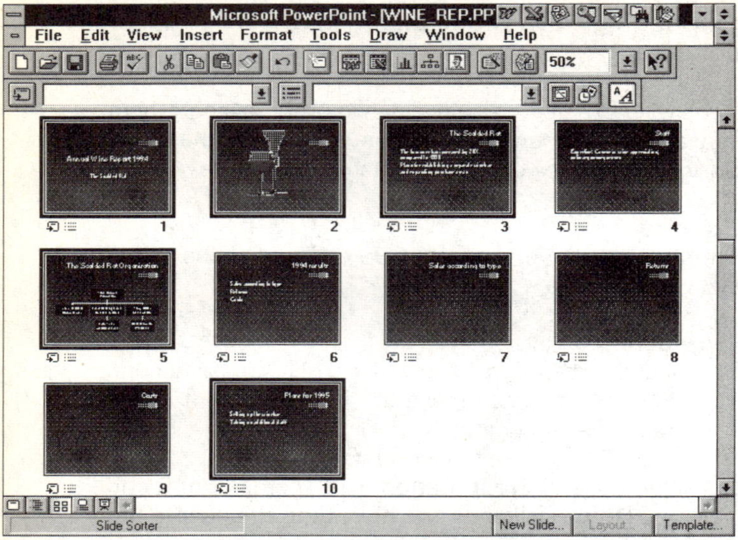

Copy

7 Click on the *Copy* button on the Standard toolbar or select *Copy* from the *Edit* menu.

8 Activate Word and select *Paste Special* from the *Edit* menu.

9 Activate the *Paste* option button in the subsequent dialog window and select *Microsoft PowerPoint 4.0 Presentation Object* from the list.

10 Click on *OK*.

Note

If you wish to make a link between the PowerPoint slides and the Word document, activate the *Paste Link* option button in the *Paste Special* dialog window. If, in a Word document, you wish to show an icon representing a PowerPoint presentation instead of a slide, activate the *Display as Icon* check box.

The first slide of the presentation is displayed in the Word document. Because the slide is rather large, it is advisable to shrink it a little by clicking on it and dragging it to a suitable size using the sizing handles.

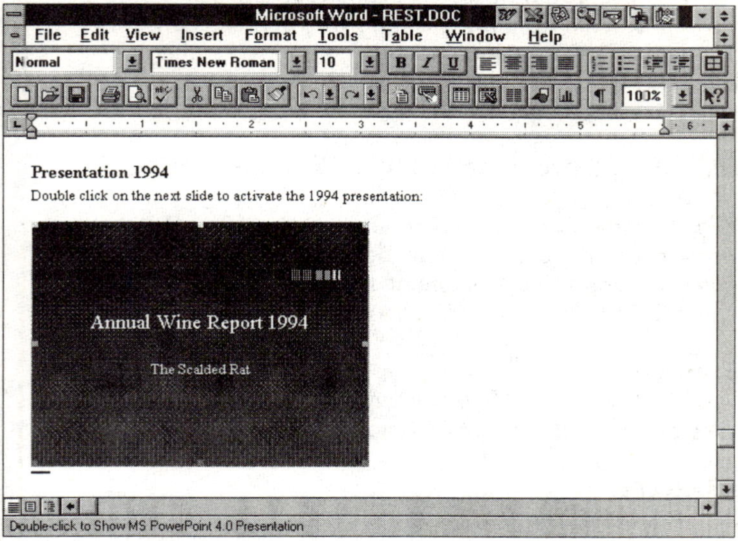

11 Double click on the slide to start the presentation.

The presentation fills the screen. When one slice has been sufficiently shown, press the mouse button to move on to the next. When you have reached the last slide, the Word document is returned to the screen. If you want to draw on the slide during the presentation, click on the pencil which appears in the lower right-hand corner when you move the mouse pointer and then draw by dragging the mouse pointer. Click on the small box again to restore the mouse pointer to the screen.

Note
You can also embed a complete slide shown in a Word document by placing the insertion point at the required

position in Word and selecting the *Object* option from the *Insert* menu. The *Object* dialog window appears. Activate the *Create from File* tabsheet and select the PowerPoint file from the files shown. Then click on *OK*. The entire PowerPoint file is then embedded in the document.

10.2.2 Exporting a presentation to a Word document

You can create a new Word document based on a PowerPoint presentation. This can be useful if you want to make a supporting document for a presentation. You can edit and format the data in Word.

Exercise
We shall create a Word document to provide an overview of a PowerPoint presentation.

Procedure:

1 Activate PowerPoint and the WINE_REP.PPT document.

Report It

2 Click on the *Report It* button.

3 If the *Convert File* appears, ensure that *Rich Text Format (RTF)* is selected and then click on *OK*.

The PowerPoint presentation appears on the screen as a Word text. You can now edit the text and save it as a Word document.

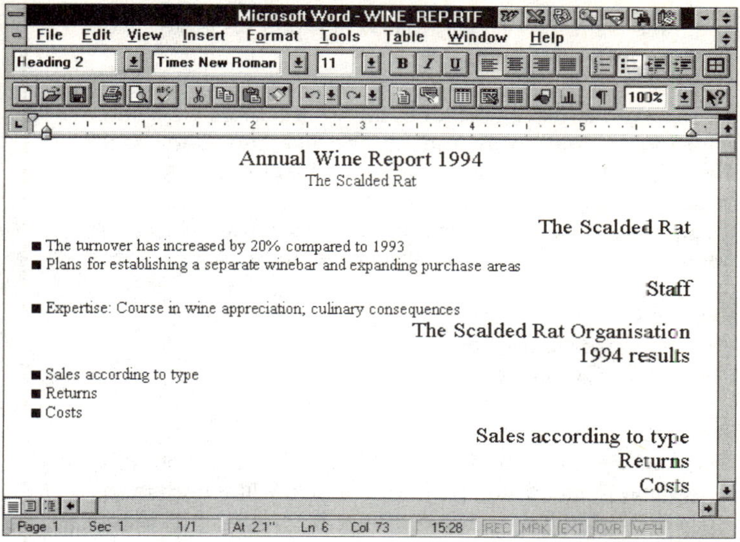

4 Edit the document as required. (As you see, the headings in our document are right-aligned which is not very convenient for a Word document.) Save the document as PRESVIEW.DOC.

10.3 Adopting Access data into a Word document

It is possible to insert data from an Access database into a Word document. If you insert an Access table into a Word document, you can edit it further as a Word table. In addition, you can convert data from objects created in Access to a layout which Word can interpret.

10.3.1 Inserting an Access table into a Word document

There are two ways in which you can insert an Access database table into a Word document. This table then becomes a normal Word table which can be edited using the Word functions.

If you only wish to insert a section of a table, select the appropriate section in Access and use the *Copy* and *Paste* commands to insert the data into Word.

If you wish to insert a complete table, use the *Database* command in Word to adopt the entire table.

Exercise
We shall insert a section of the *stock* Access table into the REST.DOC Word document.

Procedure:
1 Activate Word and the REST.DOC document, and place the insertion point on the blank line under the text 'The following table shows the stock on 31 Dec. 1994'.
2 Start up Microsoft Access, open the RESTAUR.MDB file and open the *stock* table.
3 Select the 'Product Name' and 'Units In Stock' columns by clicking on the 'Product Name' column heading, pressing and holding down the Shift key and clicking on the 'Units In Stock' column heading.

Copy

Paste

4 Click on the *Copy* button on the toolbar or select *Copy* from the *Edit* menu.
5 Activate Word and click on the *Paste* button on the Standard toolbar, or select *Paste* from the *Edit* menu.

The table is then inserted into the Word document as a Word table.

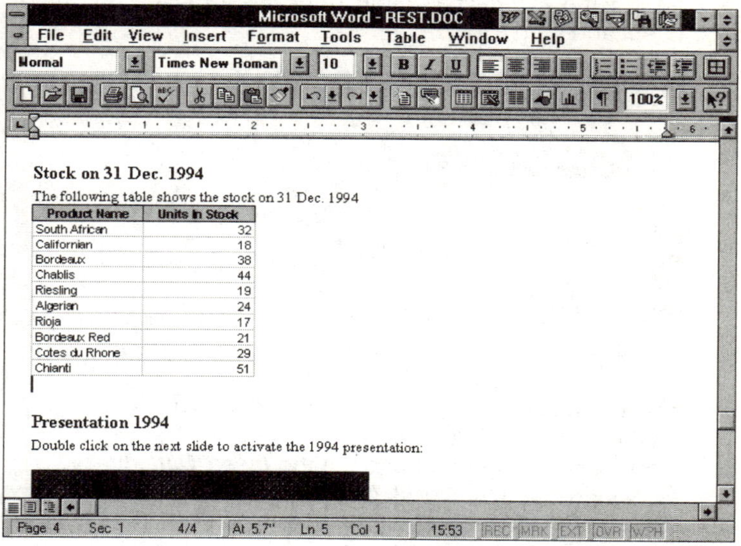

Exercise

We shall insert the complete *Employees* Access table into the REST.DOC Word document.

Procedure:

1 Activate Word and the REST.DOC document.
2 Place the insertion point in the empty line under the last name in list of staff under the first heading.
3 Open the *Insert* menu and select *Database*. The *Database* dialog window appears.
4 Click on the *Get Data* button. The *Open Data Source* dialog window appears.
5 Activate *MS Access Databases (*.mdb)* in the *List Files of Type* section and select the RESTAUR. MDB file (in our case, *c:\msoffice\access\docs*

restaur.mdb) and click on *OK*. The *Microsoft Access* dialog window appears.

6 Select the *Employees* table from the *Tables* tabsheet and then click on *OK*.

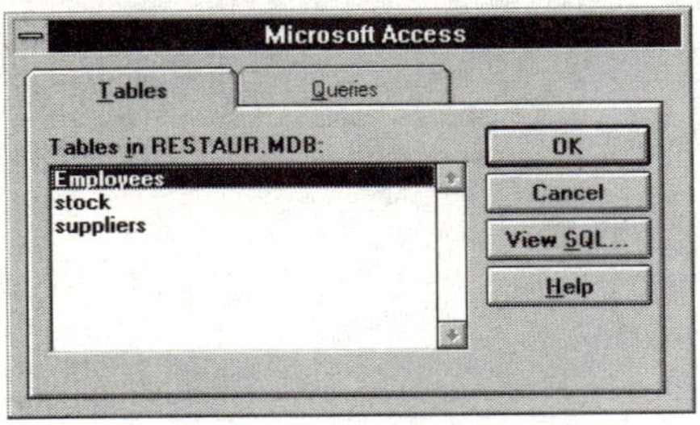

7 The *Database* dialog window appears again. Click on the *Insert Data* button.

8 Activate the *All* option button in the *Insert Data* dialog window and then click on *OK*.

Microsoft Word

10 Click on the *Microsoft Word* button on the Office Manager toolbar to switch to Word.

The table has been inserted as a Word table. You will probably have to make some formatting changes to display the table clearly. When you have done so, it will look something like this (we have reduced the font size in the table to show more information simultaneously):

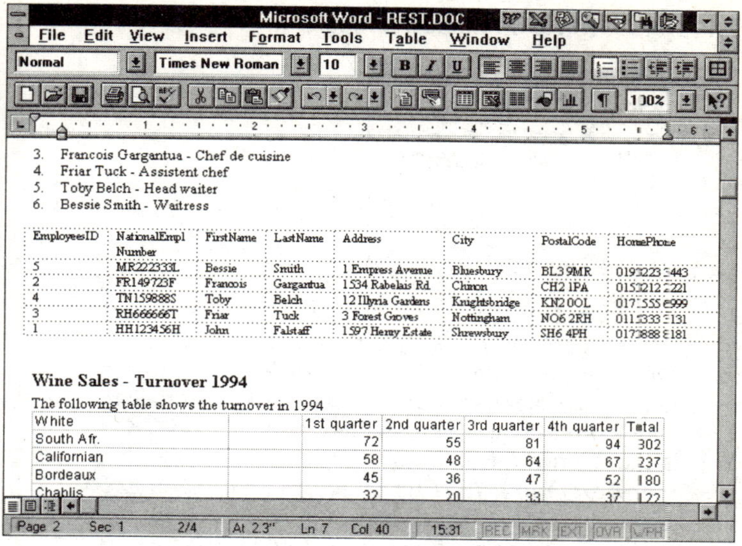

10.3.2 Converting Access data to Word format

It is possible to convert data from an Access object such as a form, report, table or query into a Word file.

Exercise

We shall convert the *orders* Access report into a Word document.

Procedure:

1 Activate Microsoft Access and the RESTAUR database and click on the *Report* button.

2 Select the *orders* report and click on the *Preview* button.

3 Open the *File* menu and select *Output To*.

The *Output To* dialog window appears.

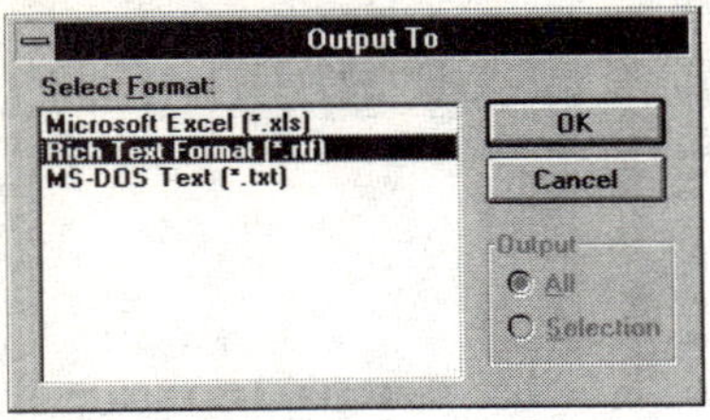

4 Select *Rich Text Format (*.rtf)* and click on *OK*.
5 Type the new name of the file, **orders.doc**, in the *Output To* dialog window. Click on the *AutoStart* check box to place a cross there and click on *OK*.
6 If the *Convert File* window appears, ensure that *Rich Text Format (RTF)* is selected and click on *OK*.

The report is then opened in Word. You can also insert the data into another document by copying them and pasting them in the other document.

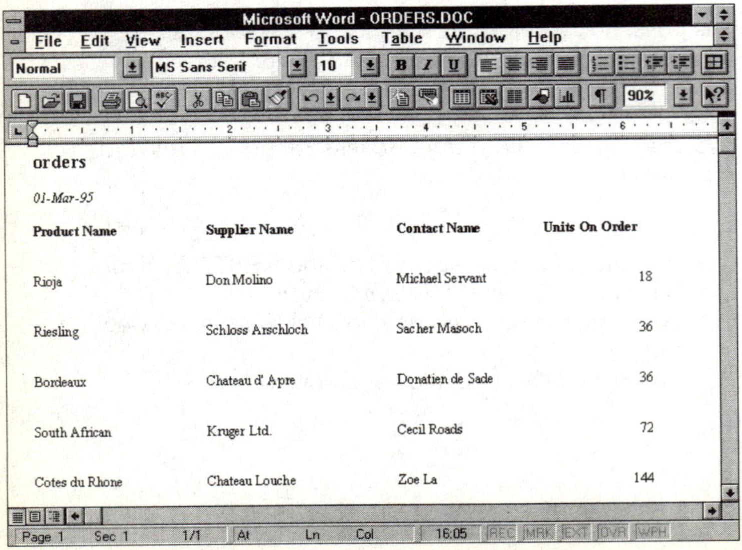

10.3.3 Creating form letters using Word and Access

Form letters are easily created in Microsoft Office by merging data from an Access file with a Word letter.

In the main document, the Word letter, you place the merge fields in which the specific personal data are to be inserted. Form letters can be created in both Word and Access. When working in Access, you can make use of the Mail Merge Wizard. In the following exercise, we shall create form letters in Word.

Exercise
We shall create a form letter to send to the employees of the Scalded Rat Restaurant.

Procedure:

New

1. Activate Word and click on the *New* button on the Standard toolbar to create a new file.
2. Open the *Tools* menu and select *Mail Merge*.

The *Mail Merge* dialog window appears:

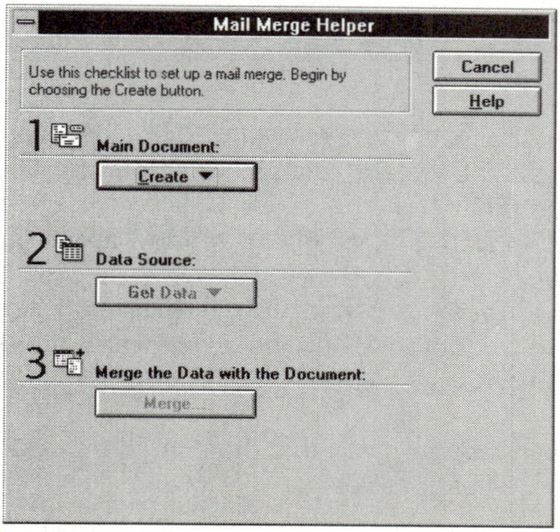

3 Click on the *Create* button under the *Main Document* heading.
4 Select *From Letters* from the submenu.
5 Select *Active Window* in the subsequent dialog box.

The *Mail Merge Helper* window appears again.

6 Click on *Get Data* in the *Data Source* section.
7 Select *Open Data Source* from the subsequent submenu.

The *Open Data Source* dialog window appears.

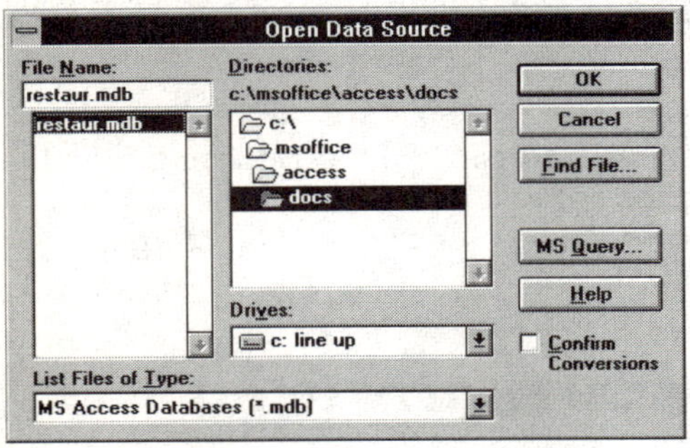

8 Select *MS Access Databases (*.mdb)* from the *List Files of Type* list. Select *restaur.mdb* from the list and click on *OK*.
9 If the *Confirm Data Source* dialog window appears, click on *OK*.
10 Activate the *Tables* tabsheet in the *Microsoft Access* dialog window, select the *Employees* table and click on *OK*.

A window appears advising you that the main document contains no merge fields as yet.

11 Select *Edit Main Document.*

The Word window appears along with the empty main document.

Type the following text in the Word window and format it as shown or according to your own wishes.
At various points in the letter, merge fields will be inserted, or merge fields will replace the initial text. This will be done in the steps to come.
When the actual merge takes place, the merge fields will be filled with specific personal data applying only to the recipient of the letter.

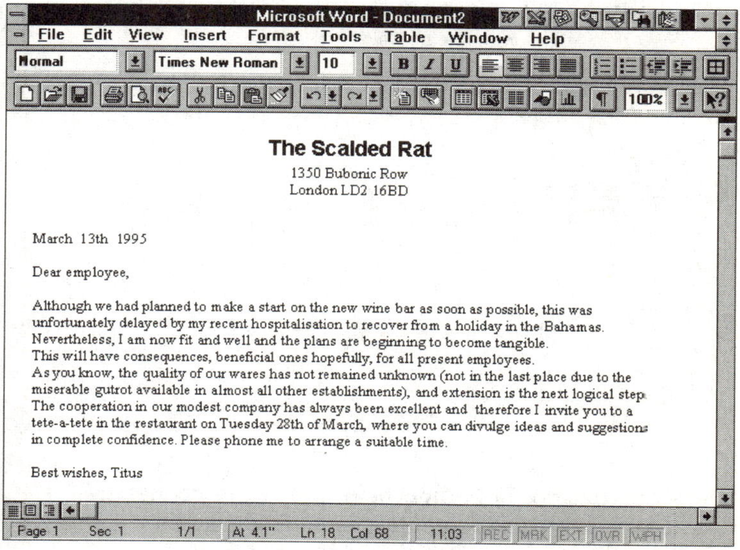

Note
Instead of typing the date at the top of your letter, you can place the date as a *field* in the letter. Then it will always give the current date according to the computer

when the letter is opened or printed again in the future. Placing a date field takes place as follows:

a) Place the insertion point at the required position.
b) Open the *Insert* menu and select *Date and Time*.
c) Select the desired format in the *Date and Time* dialog window.
d) Click on the *Insert as Field* check box.
e) Click on *OK*.

12 Create five empty lines above the date by pressing Enter and place the insertion point on the third of these.
13 Click on the *Insert Merge Field* button on the Mail Merge toolbar.

Insert Merge Field

A list is opened of all the fields available in the *Employees* database table.

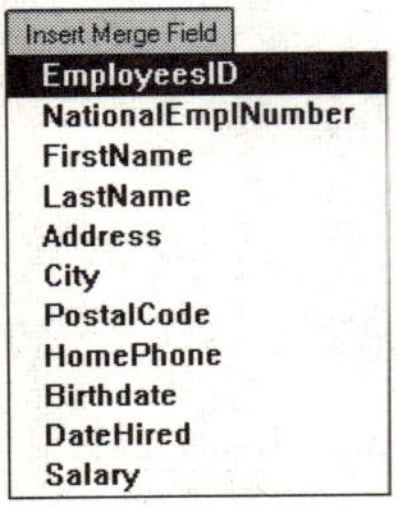

14 Click on the FirstName field, press the spacebar and click on the *Insert Merge Field* once again.
15 Click on the LastName field and press Enter.
16 Insert the Address field on the next line in the same way and press Enter again.
17 Insert the City and PostalCode on the next line, leaving a space between them.
18 Delete the word 'employee' behind 'Dear' and replace it with the FirstName field.

The document now looks like this:

«FirstName» «LastName»
«Address»
«City» «PostalCode»

March 13th 1995

Dear «FirstName»,

Although we had planned to make a start on the new wine bar as soon as possible, this was unfortunately delayed by my recent hospitalisation to recover from a holiday in the Bahamas. Nevertheless, I am now fit and well and the plans are beginning to become tangible.
This will have consequences, beneficial ones hopefully, for all present employees.
As you know, the quality of our wares has not remained unknown (not in the last place due to the miserable gutrot available in almost all other establishments), and extension is the next logical step. The cooperation in our modest company has always been excellent and therefore I invite you to a tete-a-tete in the restaurant on Tuesday 28th of March, where you can divulge ideas and suggestions in complete confidence. Please phone me to arrange a suitable time.

Best wishes, Titus

Exercise
We shall now merge the letter with the personal data in the database table.

Procedure:

1. Open the *Tools* menu and select *Mail Merge*. The *Mail Merge Helper* window appears.
2. Click on the *Merge* button in section 3 of the window.

The *Merge* dialog window appears.

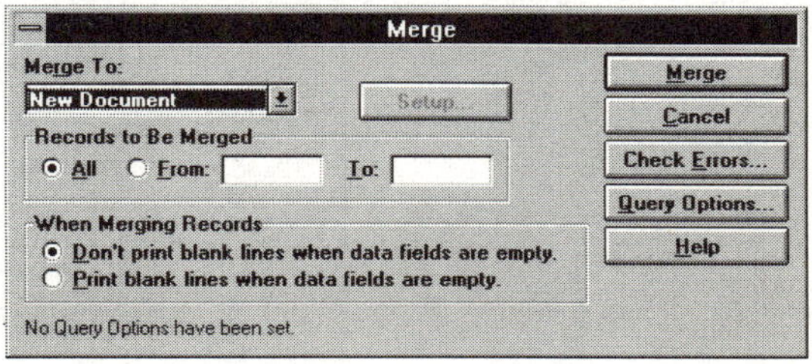

3 Ensure that the window is filled in as shown in the figure (all records to be merged to a new document). Then click on *Merge*.

The data are inserted into the merge fields. The form letters are displayed in a new Word document window. Each letter is displayed in a separate section. The figure below shows the dividing line between the first and the second letter. (The window is shown at a zoom percentage of 80%.)

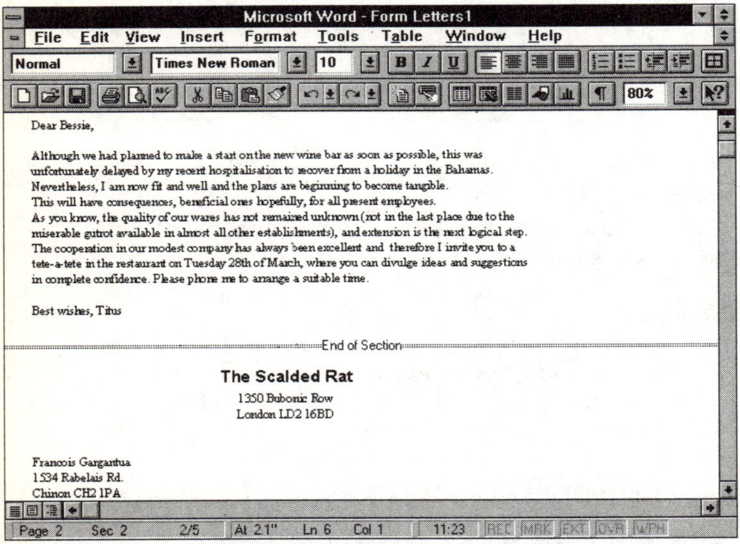

4 Save the merge document as LETTERS.DOC.

11 Integration: adopting data into Excel workbooks

In this chapter, we shall present a number of examples in which data created in other Microsoft Office applications are inserted into Excel workbooks.

11.1 Adopting Word data into an Excel workbook

Data from Word documents can be inserted into Excel worksheets in all kinds of ways. You can copy Word tables to worksheets, link tables and embed new Word text in a worksheet so that you can edit it later using the Word text formatting functions.

11.1.1 Copying a Word table to a worksheet

Imagine you have a table in Word which you want to use in Excel. You do not need the Word functions for table formatting in the Excel worksheet, so you do not need to embed the table as an object.

Exercise
We shall copy the Word table containing the employees' data to a new worksheet in the BOTTLES.XLS workbook in Excel.

Procedure:

1. Start up Word and open the REST.DOC document.
2. Place the insertion point in the table showing the employees in 1994.
3. Open the *Table* menu and select the *Select Table* option.

Copy

4 Click on the *Copy* button on the Standard toolbar or select *Copy* from the *Edit* menu.

5 Start up Microsoft Excel and open the BOTTLES.XLS workbook.

6 Activate Sheet 1 (or the next empty sheet in your workbook) and go the cell A1.

Paste

7 Click on the *Paste* button on the Standard toolbar or open the *Edit* menu and select *Paste*.

The table is inserted in the worksheet and has the features of a normal Excel range of cells. You can widen the columns to accommodate all the data.

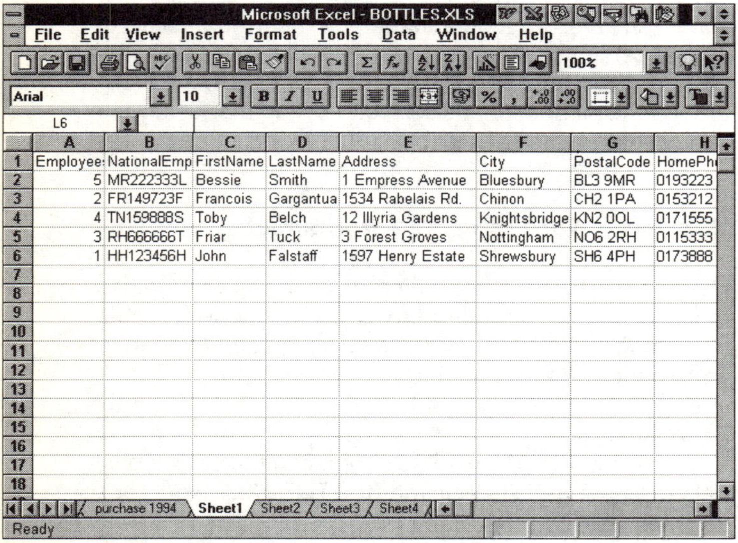

8 Change the name of the worksheet to Employees by double clicking on the Sheet1 tab at the bottom of the screen and then entering the name in the text box.

11.1.2 Linking Word data to a worksheet

If you wish to insert a Word table into an Excel workbook in such a way that the data will automatically be adjusted in Excel when the table is altered in Word, you should *link* the table to the Excel workbook.

To link a Word table to an Excel worksheet, proceed as follows:

Copy

- Select the table in the Word document.
- Click on the *Copy* button on the Standard toolbar or open the *Edit* menu and select *Copy*.
- Activate the required workbook in Excel and activate the cell where the upper left-hand corner of the table is to be placed.
- Open the *Edit* menu and select *Paste Special*.

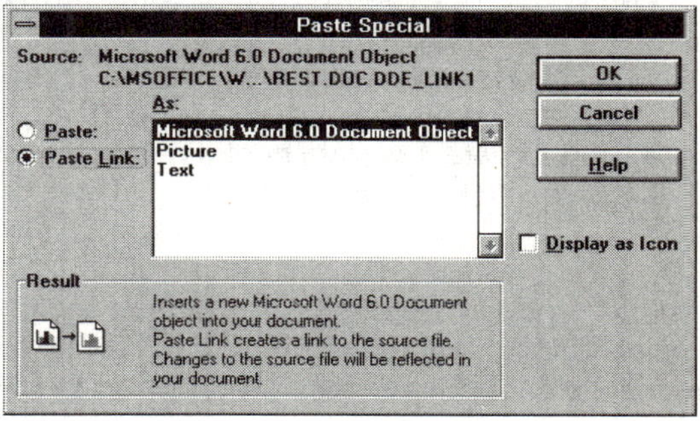

- The *Paste Special* dialog window appears. Activate the *Paste Link* option button, select *Microsoft Word 6.0 Document Object* and click on *OK*.

The table is inserted as a linked object into the Excel workbook. If you make any alterations to the table in Word, these will be automatically transferred to the cells in Excel.

11.1.3 Embedding Word text in a workbook

If you wish to insert text into a workbook and you also wish to make use of the formatting features provided by Word, you can embed the text as a Word object. Double clicking on it will activate the Word formatting features. You can use the *Copy* and *Paste Special* commands from the *Edit* menu to copy existing data from Word to an Excel workbook. In the following exercise, we shall create a new Word object in an Excel workbook.

Exercise

We shall embed a new Word object in the BOTTLES.XLS Excel workbook.

Procedure:

1 Activate Excel and the BOTTLES.XLS workbook.
2 Activate the *quantity 1994* worksheet and move the insertion point to cell J4.
3 Open the *Insert* menu and select *Object*. The *Object* dialog window appears.
4 Activate the *Create New* tabsheet if necessary and select *Microsoft Word 6.0 Document*. Then click on *OK*.

A small Word window appears on the screen at the insertion point. You can enter and edit text here. The toolbars and menus acquire the Word layout when this window is active.

5 Drag the window open in a downwards direction to make room for the text shown in the figure:

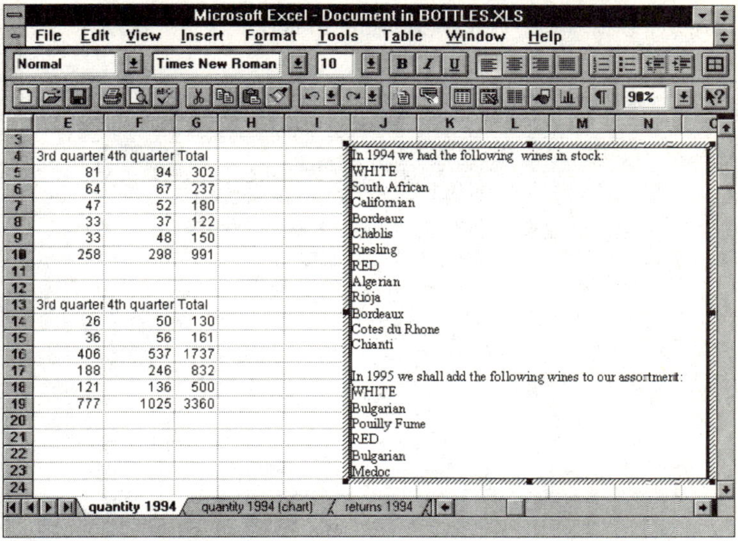

Bullets

Increase Indent

6 Select the items in the list of newly-created text and click on the *Bullets* button on the Formatting toolbar and on the *Increase Indent* button.

7 Click anywhere outside the Word window.

The window now looks something like this (at 85% zoom):

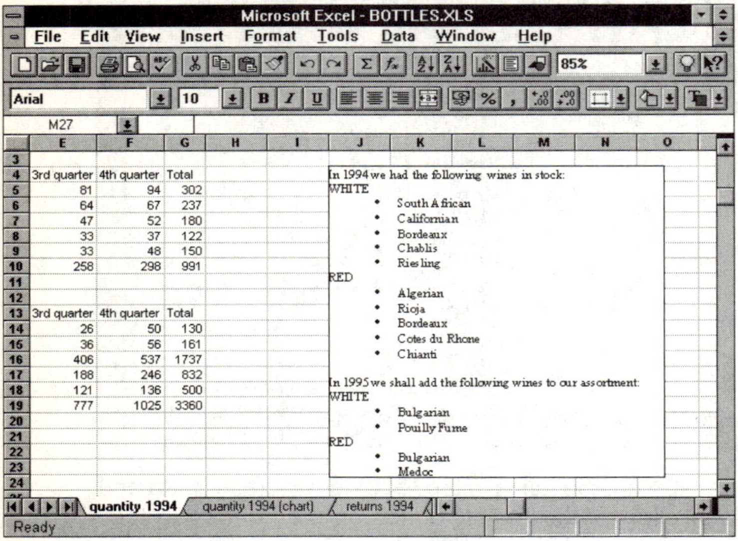

11.2 Adopting PowerPoint data into an Excel workbook

Just as with a Word document, you can also insert a whole or a part of a PowerPoint presentation into an Excel workbook. The PowerPoint Viewer enables you to examine the slides in the workbook. If you send the workbook to another user in your network, by means of Mail for example, that user will be able to view the presentation without actually having access to PowerPoint (as long as PowerPoint Viewer is available).

11.2.1 Embedding a complete PowerPoint presentation in a workbook

In the following exercise, we shall embed a complete presentation in a workbook. We shall then examine it.

Exercise

We shall embed the WINE_REP.PPT presentation in a new worksheet in the BOTTLES.XLS workbook.

Procedure:

1 Activate Excel, the BOTTLES.XLS workbook and the next new empty worksheet.
2 Double click on the worksheet tab and assign it the name **presentation 1994**.
3 Type **Presentation 1994** in cell A1.
4 Press F2, select the text and make it bold by clicking on the *Bold* button.
5 While the text is still selected, open the *Font Size* drop-down list on the Formatting toolbar and click on size 16.
6 Activate cell B3 and open the *Insert* menu. Select *Object*.
7 Activate the *Create from File* tabsheet and select WINE_REP.PPT from the list. (We stored it in the *docs* directory, a subdirectory of *powerpnt*.) Click on *OK*.

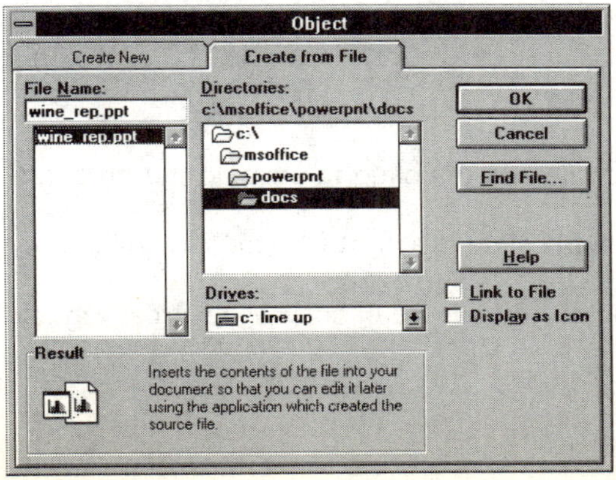

Notes
If you wish to link the presentation to the workbook, activate the *Link to File* check box in the *Object* dialog window. If you make changes to the presentation, they will be passed on automatically to the workbook.

The first presentation slide is displayed on the worksheet.

8 Drag the sizing handles until the slide fills the cells B3:E12.

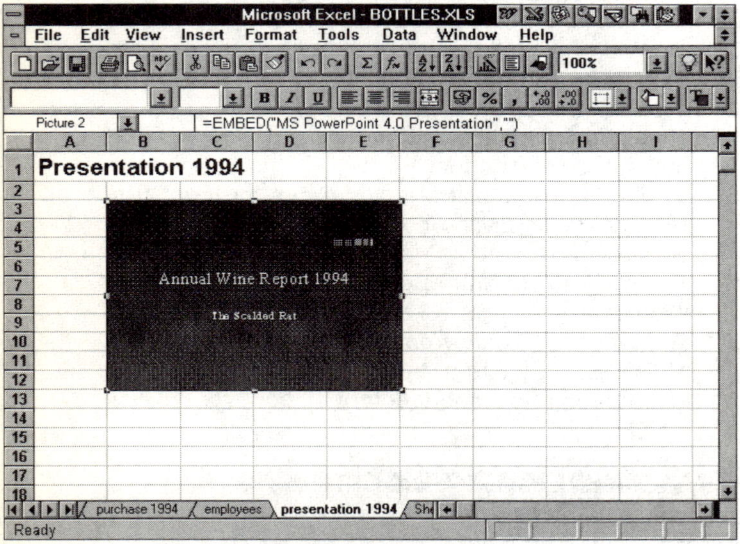

9 Double click on the slide to start up the presentation.
10 Click on the slide to activate the following slide.

When the last slide has been shown the Excel window reappears.

11.2.2 Embedding selected slides in a workbook

If you prefer, you can embed only a part of a presentation instead of the entire presentation.

Exercise
We decide not to display all the slides. Therefore, we shall embed only a few of them in the workbook.

Procedure:

1 Remove the presentation we have just adopted into the *presentation 1994* worksheet by activating it (click on it once) and then pressing the Del key.
2 Place the insertion point at the required position on the worksheet (B3 in our case).
3 Start up PowerPoint and open the WINE_REP.PPT presentation.
4 Activate the Slide Sorter View and select slides 1, 2, 3 5 and 10 by holding down the Shift key while clicking on the slides.

Copy

5 Click on the *Copy* button on the Standard toolbar or select *Copy* from the *Edit* menu.

Paste

6 Activate Excel and click on the *Paste* button or select *Paste* from the *Edit* menu.

The selected slides are inserted into the Excel worksheet. The first slide is displayed.

7 Adjust the size of the inserted slides to suit your requirements.

You can start up the presentation by double clicking on the embedded object.

11.3 Adopting Access data into an Excel workbook

It is possible to insert data from an Access database into a workbook so that you can edit and analyse them further in Excel.

11.3.1 Inserting data from Access into a worksheet

Imagine you wish to insert data from Access into an Excel worksheet. Often you will only need a part of the Access object. It is quite easy to copy the required data to Excel.

Exercise
We shall copy data from the *stock* database table to the BOTTLES.XLS worksheet.

Procedure:
1 Activate Excel, the BOTTLES.XLS workbook and go to the next empty worksheet.
2 Change the name of the worksheet by double clicking on the worksheet tab and entering the new name, **stock**.
3 Type **Stock on 31 Dec 1994** in cell A1.
4 Select the cell and place the text in boldface by clicking on the *Bold* button on the Formatting toolbar.
5 While the text is still selected, open the *Font Size* drop-down list and select size 12.
6 Go to cell A3.
7 Start up Microsoft Access and open the RESTAUR.MDB database.
8 Open the *stock* table and select the Product Name, Units In Stock and Units On Order columns by dragging the mouse pointer (arrow pointing downwards) across the column headings.

Copy

Paste

9 Click on the *Copy* button on the toolbar or select *Copy* from the *Edit* menu.

10 Activate Excel and ensure that cell A3 is still selected.

11 Click on the *Paste* button on the Standard toolbar in Excel, or select *Paste* from the *Edit* menu.

The records copied in Access have now been inserted into the worksheet. They have the normal Excel format and can be edited further by means of the Excel functions.

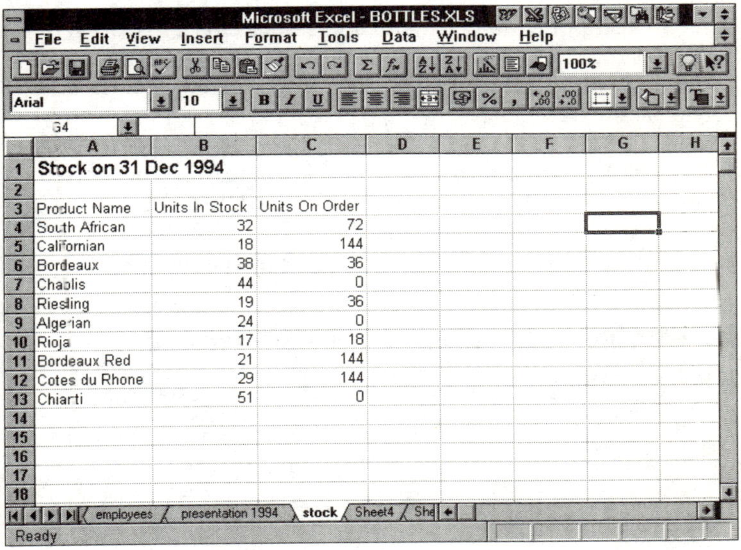

11.3.2 Exporting a database table to a new workbook

You can also create a completely new Excel workbook based on data exported from Access. In this process, the data are converted to a file layout which can be read by Excel.

Exercise

We shall export a query from the RESTAUR.MDB Microsoft Access database to a new Excel workbook.

Procedure:

1 Activate Access and the RESTAUR.MDB database.

2 Activate the database window and click on the *Query* button.

3 Select the *orders* query if necessary.

Analyze It with MS Excel

4 Click on the *Analyze It with MS Excel* button.

Note

You can also open the *File* menu and select *Output To* in order to export a database. The *Analyze It with MS Excel* command implements the *Output To* command and opens a new file in Excel.

The query is opened as a new workbook in Excel. A new name has been assigned automatically: ORDERS.XLS.

5 Save the workbook under the same name, ORDERS.XLS.

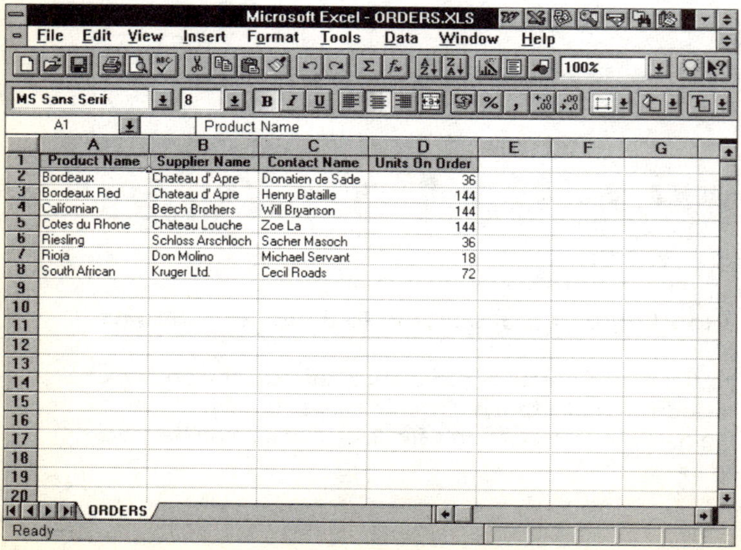

Note

You can easily create a PivotTable in Excel, based on an imported Access table. This is done by activating a cell in the Excel table, opening the *Data* menu and selecting *PivotTable*. The *PivotTable Wizard* dialog window is opened enabling you to create a pivot table.

Although a detailed description of the workings of pivot tables is beyond the scope of this book, this function does provide a quick and convenient method to compare and analyse data. You can obtain an excellent description of how this works along with a clear demonstration by opening the *Help* menu in Excel and selecting *Search for Help on*. Type *pivot tables, explained*, click on the *Show Topics* button and then on the *Go To* button.

12 Integration: adopting data into PowerPoint presentations

You can insert data from other Microsoft Office applications into PowerPoint presentations in order to supplement the information shown on the slides or simply to make the slides more attractive. In this chapter, we shall deal with how to integrate data from Word, Excel and Access into PowerPoint.

12.1 Adopting Word data into a PowerPoint presentation

You can create a new PowerPoint presentation based on a Word document. You can also insert passages of text or other elements from Word into a presentation.

12.1.1 Creating slides based on a Word outline

If you have applied a certain layout to a Word document in the Outline View, you can use this to create slides in PowerPoint. Each paragraph which has a Heading 1 layout style is accredited its own slide. Paragraphs with a lower heading level (down to Heading 5) become text on the slide, being indented according to level. If there is text which has no heading level in the Word document, it will not be imported into the slide. We shall illustrate this using a new Word outline.

Exercise
We shall create a slide show based on a Word outline.

Procedure:

1 Start up Word and open a new empty document.
2 Open the *View* menu and select *Outline* to activate the Outline View.

The Outline toolbar is shown across the top of the work area.

3 Use the Outline toolbar to apply various levels to the text in the document by clicking on the corresponding Heading level from the drop-down style list, click on the *Show Formatting* button (second from the right on the Outline toolbar) and type the following text:

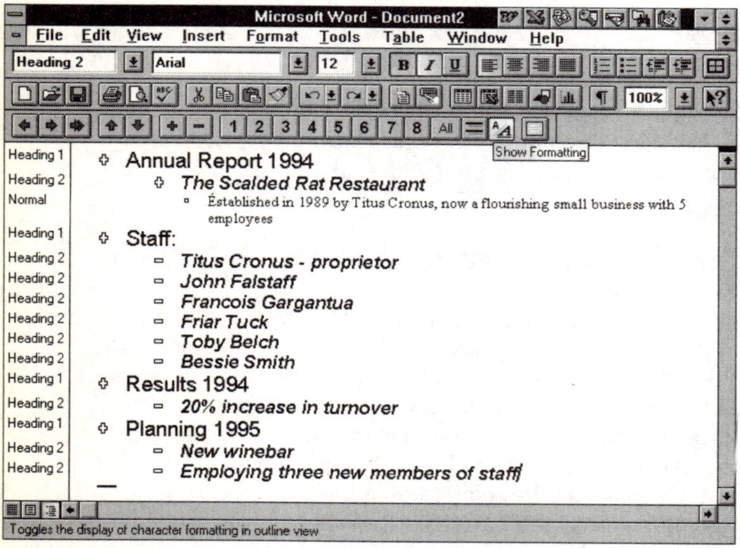

Note

We have displayed the style area in the left margin to help clarify the text layout. You can make this area visible by opening the *Tools* menu, selecting *Options* and activating the *View* tabsheet if necessary. Specify the required area width in the *Style Area Width* section. We specified 0.6".

4 Save the document as REST2.DOC and close it.

Open

5 Activate PowerPoint and click on the *Open* button on the Standard toolbar or open the *File* menu and select *Open*. If the *PowerPoint* dialog window appears, ensure that the *Open an Existing Presentation* option button is activated.

6 The *Open* dialog window appears. Select *Outlines* from the *List Files of Type* drop-down list. Open the appropriate directory and select the file REST2.DOC you have just created in Word. Click on *OK*.

The document is opened in PowerPoint in the Outline View.

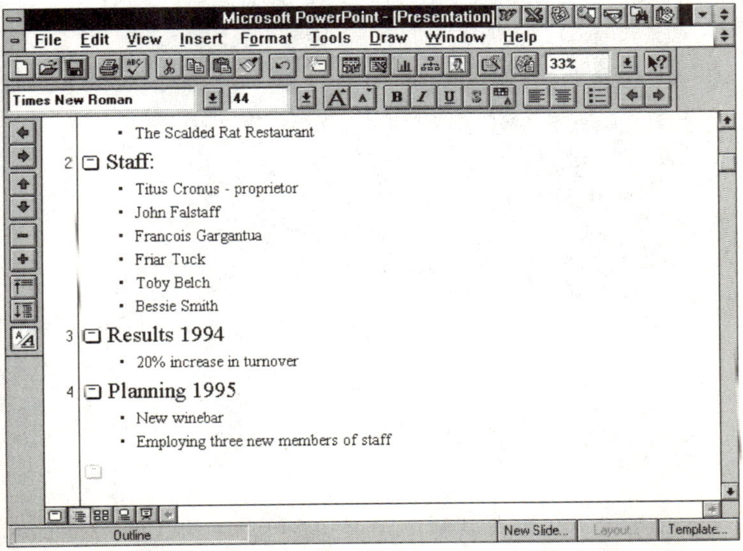

8 Activate the Slide View or Slide Sorter View to examine the slides.
9 Open the *Format* menu and select *Presentation Template*.
10 Activate the *sldshow* directory (subdirectory of *template*) and select the *tropics.ppt* file from the list. Click on the *Apply* button.

The new presentation is designed in accordance with the selected template.

11 Save the file as REST2.PPT

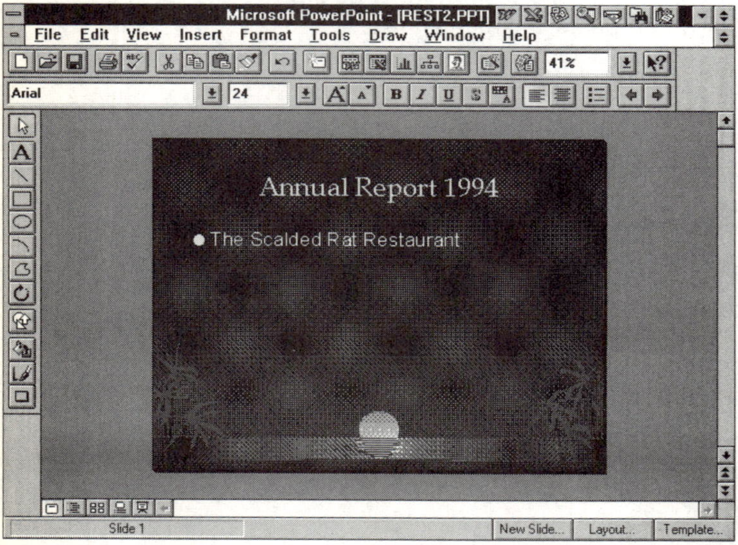

12.1.2 Adding data from a Word document to a presentation

Imagine that you have data in a Word outline and you wish to insert these as slides into an existing PowerPoint presentation. This is done by converting these data to the PowerPoint format. In that case, each paragraph with a Heading 1 style will become a new slide. Paragraphs with a lower heading level (down to Heading 5) are adopted as subordinate text into the slide.

Thus, to adopt text from a Word outline into an existing PowerPoint presentation, proceed as follows:

- Select, in PowerPoint, the slide which is to come after the newly-inserted slides.
- Open the *Insert* menu and select *Slides from Outline*.

The *Insert Outline* dialog window appears.

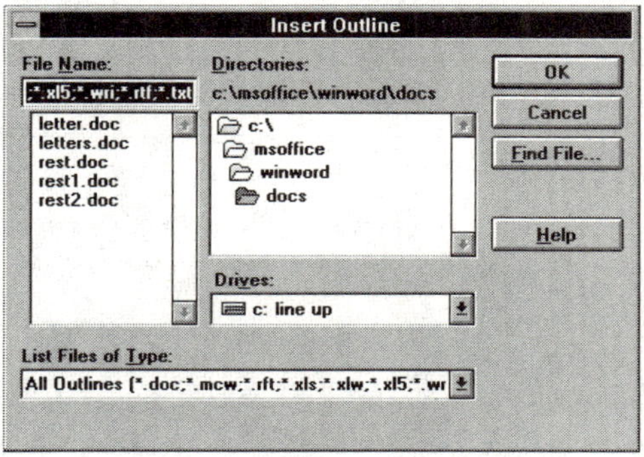

- Select the Word document you wish to use and click on *OK*.

12.1.3 Copying Word data to a slide

It is also possible to copy text or pictures from Word to a slide in PowerPoint.

Exercise

We shall copy text from REST.DOC to the WINE_REP.PPT presentation.

Procedure:

1 Activate PowerPoint and the WINE_REP.PPT document.

2 Activate the Slide Sorter View and select slide 2. Click on the figure on the slide to activate it and reduce it in size by dragging the sizing handles.

3 Centre the figure in the lower part of the slide.

Text

4 Click on the *Text Tool* button on the Drawing toolbar flanking the left side of the screen.

5 Drag the mouse pointer (an arrow pointing downwards) across the slide to create a box in which the required text can be inserted.

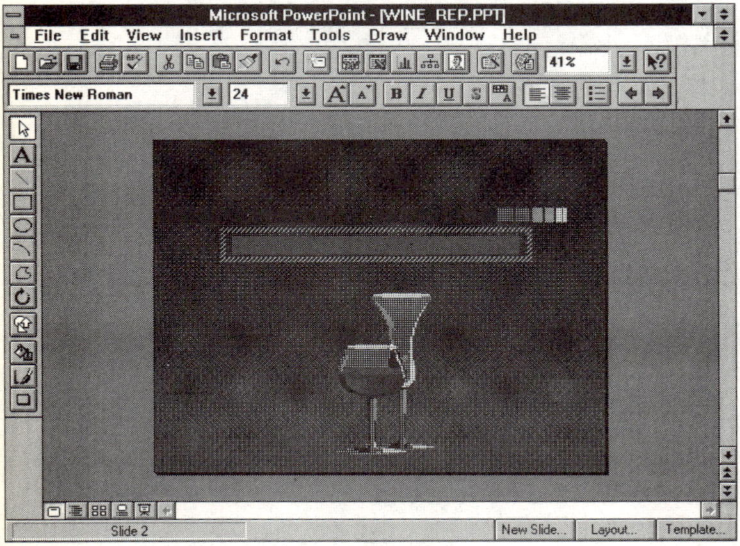

6 Activate Word, open REST.DOC and select the title of the document, 'The Scalded Rat Restaurant, Annual Report 1994'.

Copy

7 Click on the *Copy* button on the Standard toolbar or select *Copy* from the *Edit* menu.

8 Activate PowerPoint and place the insertion point in the new text box.

Paste

9 Click on the *Paste* button on the Standard toolbar, or select *Paste* from the *Edit* menu.

10 Click anywhere outside the text box.

The Word text is now displayed on the slide.

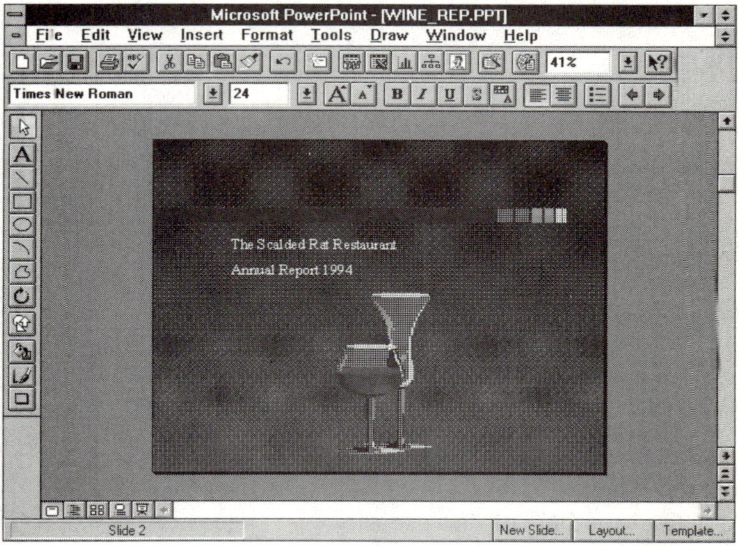

12.1.4 Linking Word data to a presentation

If you wish the Word data you have copied to a slide to be automatically updated when the source data in Word are modified, you should link the text to the presentation.

To do this, proceed as described above, but select *Paste Special* from the *Edit* menu instead of *Paste*. Then, in the *Paste Special* dialog window, activate the *Paste Link* option button. Select *Microsoft Word 6.0 Document Object* from the list and click on *OK*.

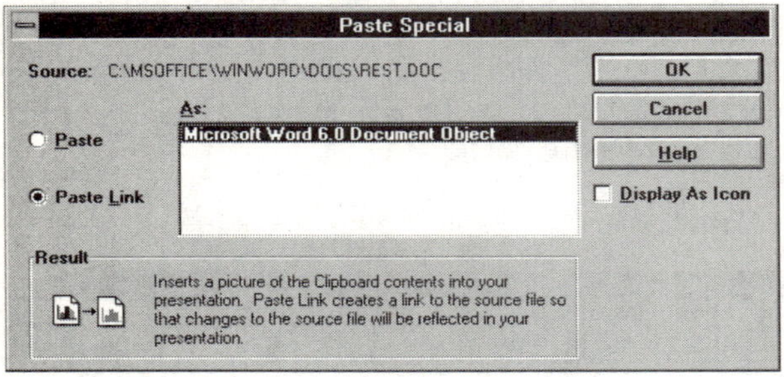

Exercise
We shall now link data from the REST.DOC Word document to the WINE_REP.PPT PowerPoint presentation. We shall create a new slide to contain this data.

Procedure:

1. Activate PowerPoint and the WINE_REP.PPT presentation.
2. Activate slide 3 and click on the *New Slide* button. The new slide will be inserted after this slide. The *New Slide* dialog window appears. Choose the second option, Bulleted List, in the *AutoLayout* list. Click on *OK*. The new slide appears on the screen.
3. Activate Word and the REST.DOC document.
4. Select the text under the first heading 'Staff 1994'.
5. Click on the *Copy* button on the Standard toolbar or select *Copy* from the *Edit* menu.
6. Switch to PowerPoint and click on the *Click to add title* box to activate that box.
7. Click on the *Paste* button to place the heading in the title box.

8 Switch to Word and select the rest of the text from the 'Staff 1994' section.

9 Click on the *Copy* button or select *Copy* from the *Edit* menu.

10 Switch to PowerPoint and click on the *Click to add text* box to activate it. Press the spacebar to remove this text.

Bullet On/Off

7 Click on the *Bullet On/Off* button on the Formatting toolbar to switch the bulleting function off.

8 Open the *Edit* menu and select *Paste Special*.

9 Activate the *Paste Link* option button, select *Microsoft Word 6.0 Document Object* from the list and click on *OK*.

10 The text is imported as linked object into the slide. Click anywhere outside the slide to remove the frame around the text.

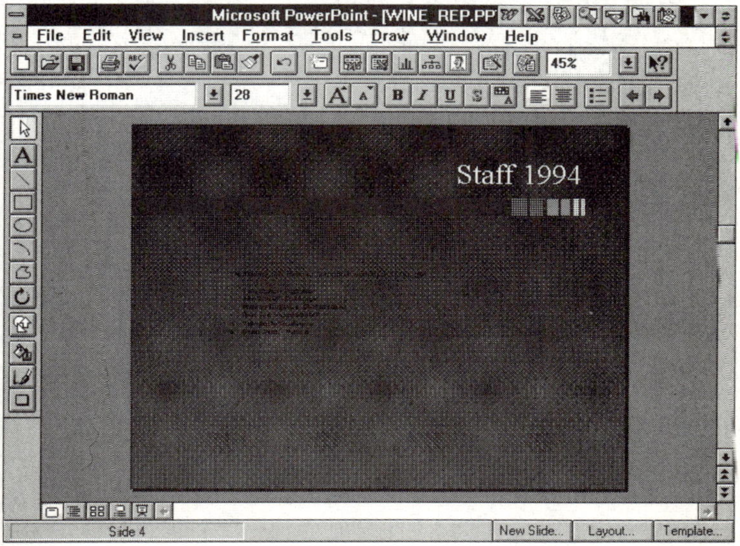

As you see, the text retains the initial Word format. You can change this in the original document by double clicking on the imported text. The source document is opened. There, you can increase the font size of the selected text (to size 24 for example).
In our example, the text, being dark, is not very legible. You can change this by selecting the text box by clicking on it, opening the *Tools* menu and selecting *Recolor*. Choose a suitable colour from the *New* drop-down list.

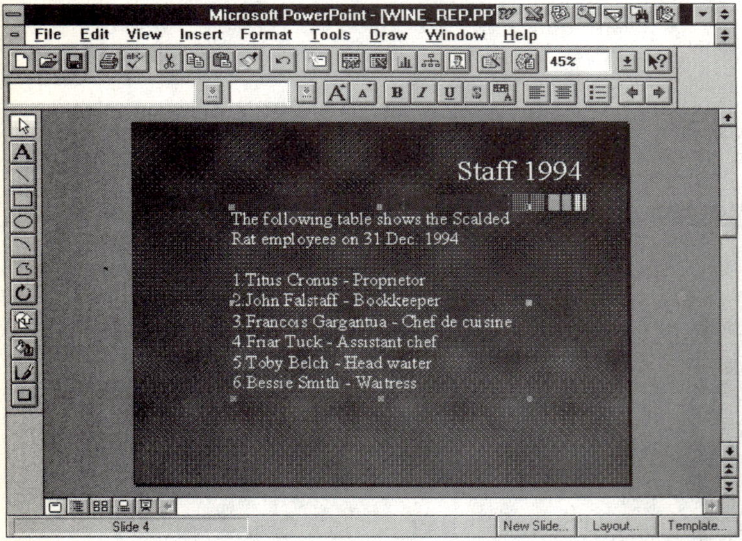

12.1.4 Inserting a new Word table

Insert Microsoft Word table

You can make use of the *Insert Microsoft Word Table* button on the PowerPoint Standard toolbar to create a new table on a slide. When you click on this button, a grid appears, enabling you to specify how large the new table is to be. Drag the mouse pointer across the rows and columns of the grid to indicate the required size. This function is very convenient if you wish to place text in table layout on a new slide and if you wish to make use of Word formatting features for the table layout.

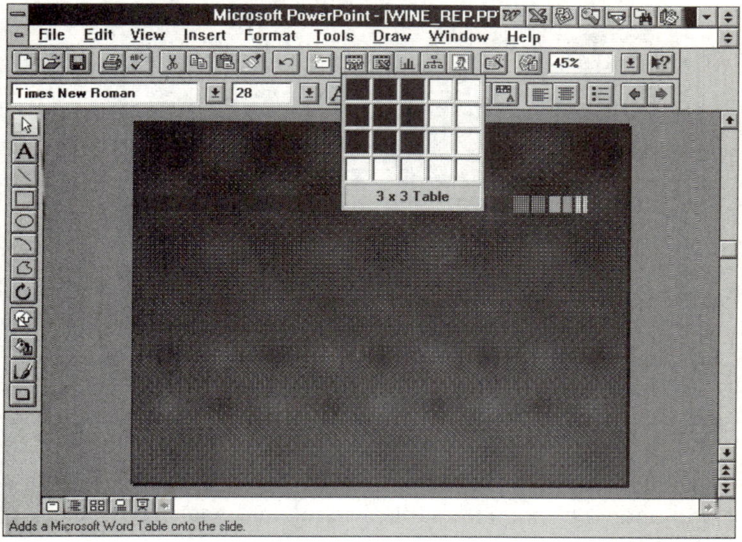

A Word table appears on the slide. You can create and edit the data here by means of the Word menus and toolbars which are shown in the window. When you have finished, click outside the slide to return to the normal PowerPoint work area.

You can also insert a new Word table by clicking on the *New Slide* button in the PowerPoint window. The *New Slide* dialog window is opened. Select the Table slide type (the 9th option) and click on *OK*.

The new layout appears on the screen.

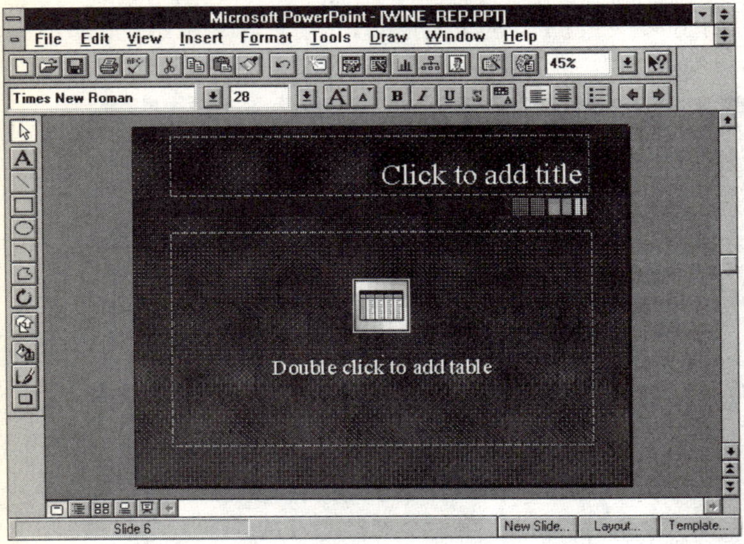

If you double click on the table symbol, the *Insert Word Table* appears.

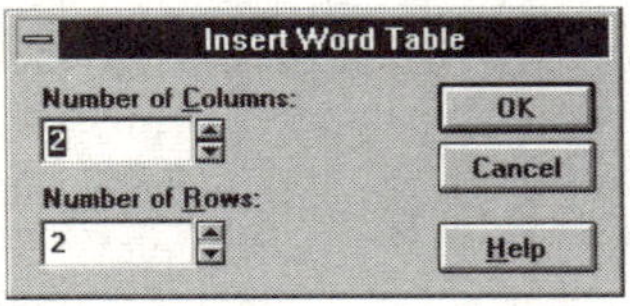

Specify the number of rows and columns required and click on *OK*.

If you wish to edit a Word table later, double click on the table object to activate the Word menus and toolbars.

12.2 Adopting Excel data into a PowerPoint presentation

You can also insert data from an Excel worksheet into a PowerPoint presentation. Numerical data often help to support the presentation. You can embed or link data, such as charts or cells, or simply copy text or pictures.

12.2.1 Embedding Excel data in PowerPoint

If you wish to use Excel data in a PowerPoint presentation and these data do not have to be directly modified when the source data are updated, the best thing to do is to embed them in the presentation. You can then modify them as you wish.

Exercise
We shall embed a range of cells from the BOTTLES.XLS document in WNE_REP.PPT.

Procedure:

1 Start up Excel, open BOTTLES.XLS and activate the *quantity 1994* worksheet.
2 Select the cell range A4:G19.

Copy

3 Click on the *Copy* button on the Standard toolbar, or select *Copy* from the *Edit* menu.
4 Activate PowerPoint, activate the WINE_REP.PPT presentation if necessary and select slide 9, 'Sales according to type'.
5 Click on the *Click to add text* box and press the spacebar to remove this text.
6 Open the *Edit* menu and select *Paste Special.*

The *Paste Special* window appears.

7 Select *Microsoft Excel 5.0 Worksheet Object* and ensure that the *Paste* option button is activated. Click on *OK.*

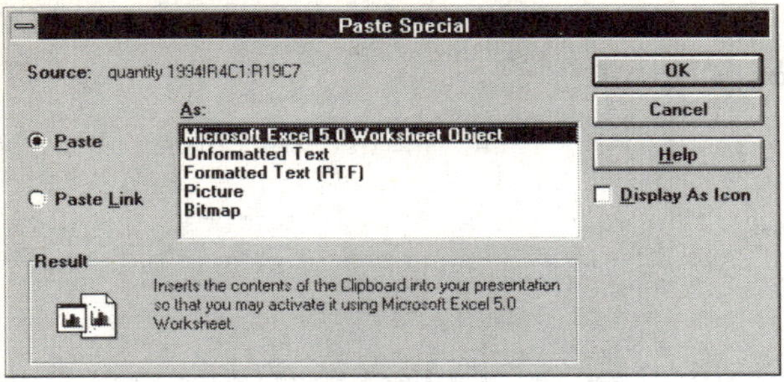

The Excel data are embedded in the slide. The text may not be very legible due to the dark background of the slide. You can change the background (*Format, Slide Background, Change Colour* button) to improve this. You can also enlarge the data a little in the source document to make them more legible.

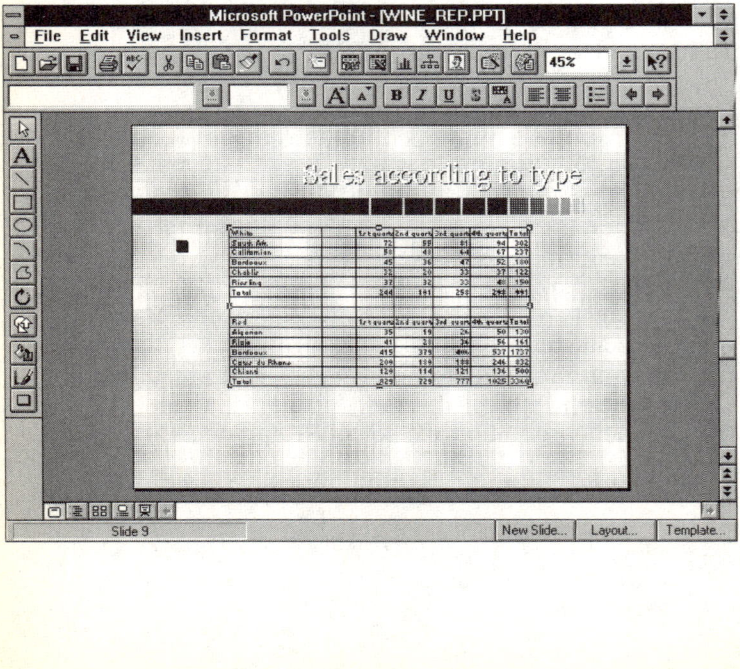

Note
You can also use the drag-and-drop method to embed Excel data in PowerPoint slides. In that case, it is advisable to place both windows adjacent to one another on the screen. (Open one application, press and hold down Shift and click on the button of the other application on the Microsoft Office toolbar.)

12.2.2 Embedding a chart in a slide

In the following exercise we shall embed a chart from BOTTLES.XLS in a new slide.

Exercise
We shall create a new slide and embed an Excel chart in it.

Procedure:

1. Activate PowerPoint and WINE_REP.PPT.

2. Activate slide 9 and click on the *New Slide* button at the bottom of the PowerPoint window.
3. Select the second last type of slide (Title Only) in the *New Slide* dialog window. Click on *OK*.
4. Click in the *Click to add title* box and type **Sales according to sort**.
5. Click anywhere outside this box.
6. Activate Excel, the BOTTLES.XLS workbook and the *quantity 1994 (chart)* chart.
7. Activate the chart by clicking on it.

Copy

8. Click on the *Copy* button or select *Copy* from the *Edit* menu.
9. Activate PowerPoint and the new slide (number 10).
10. Open the *Edit* menu and select *Paste Special*.
11. Activate the *Paste* option button and select *Microsoft Excel 5.0 Chart Object* from the list. Click on *OK*.
12. The chart is embedded in the slide.

You can increase the size of the chart by dragging the sizing handles to make the chart more legible.

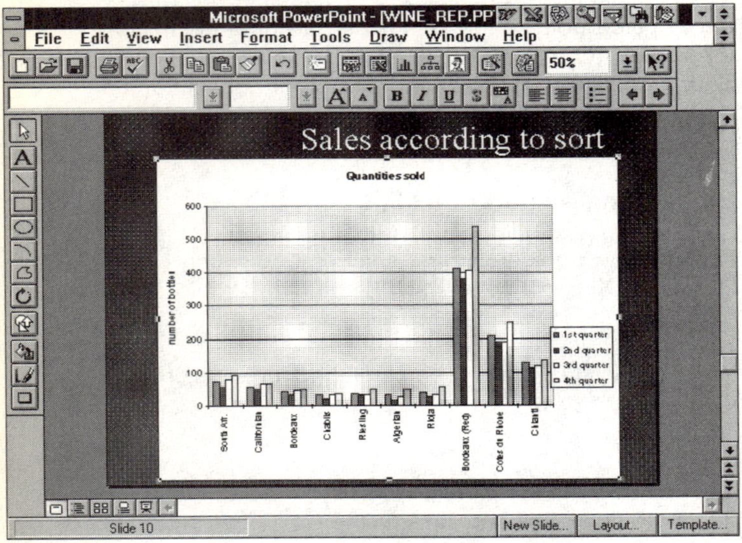

12.2.3 Linking Excel data to a PowerPoint presentation

If you wish to copy Excel data to PowerPoint in such a way that they are automatically updated when the source data are altered, you can link the two documents in question.

Exercise

We shall now link data from the *returns 1994* worksheet to the PowerPoint presentation.

Procedure:

1 Activate Excel, the BOTTLES.XLS workbook and the *returns 1994* worksheet.

2 Select the range A4:G19.
3 Click on the *Copy* button on the Standard toolbar, or select *Copy* from the *Edit* menu.
4 Activate PowerPoint and select slide 11 (with the title Returns).
5 Click on the *Layout* button at the bottom of the screen, select the *Title Only* type (second last) in the *Slide Layout* dialog window, and click on the *Apply* button.
6 Open the *Edit* menu and select *Paste Special*.
7 Activate the *Paste Link* option button and select *Microsoft Excel 5.0 Worksheet Object*. Click on *OK*.

The worksheet data are inserted and linked to the slide. You can enlarge the inserted table by dragging the sizing handles. You can also change the slide background colour so that the data in the worksheet become more legible.

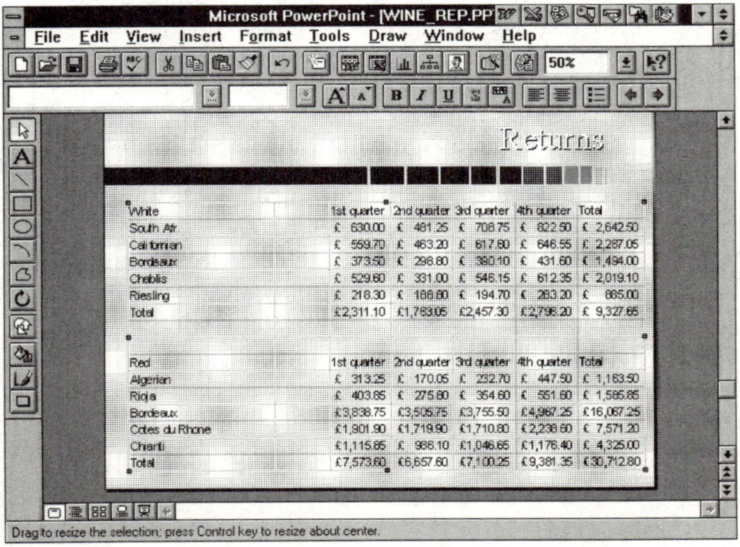

12.2.4 Inserting Excel data as text

If you wish to insert Excel data in a PowerPoint presentation and you wish to be able to edit it as PowerPoint text, you can insert it as text.

Exercise
We shall now insert a range from an Excel worksheet as text in PowerPoint.

Procedure:

1 Activate Excel, the BOTTLES.XLS workbook and the *purchase 1994* worksheet.
2 Select the range A4:G19.

Copy

3 Click on the *Copy* button on the Standard toolbar, or select *Copy* from the *Edit* menu.
4 Activate PowerPoint and select slide 10 (with the title Costs).

Bullet On/Off

5 Click on the *Click to add text* box and press the spacebar to remove this text. Now click on the *Bullet On/Off* button on the Formatting toolbar to switch the bullets off.
6 Open the *Edit* menu and select *Paste Special.*
7 Activate the *Paste* option button and select *Formatted Text (RTF)*. Click on *OK*.

The worksheet data are inserted on the slide. You can reduce the font size to a suitable format by marking the text and selecting an applicable font size, such as 14 pts. You can also change the slide colours to make the data more legible if required.

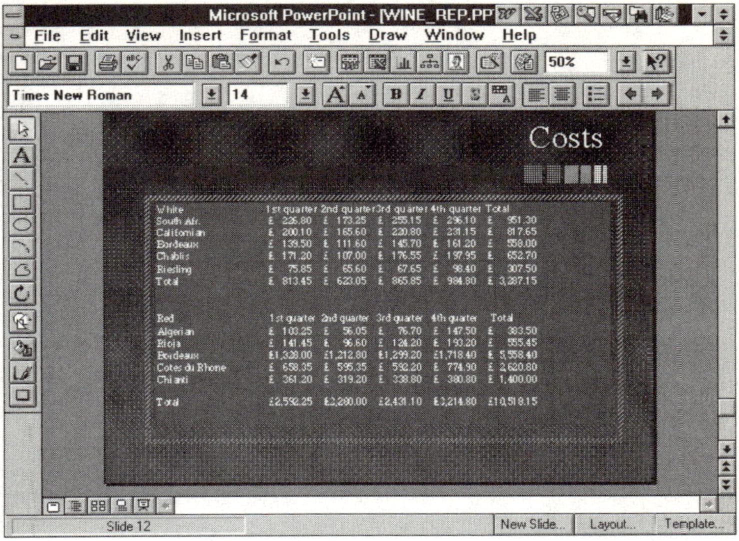
Microsoft PowerPoint - [WINE_REP.PP
File Edit View Insert Format Tools Draw Window Help
50%
Times New Roman
14
Costs
White 1st quarter 2nd quarter 3rd quarter 4th quarter Total
South Afr. £ 226.80 £ 173.25 £ 255.15 £ 296.10 £ 951.30
Californian £ 200.10 £ 165.60 £ 220.80 £ 231.15 £ 817.65
Bordeaux £ 139.50 £ 111.60 £ 145.70 £ 161.20 £ 558.00
Chablis £ 171.20 £ 107.00 £ 176.55 £ 197.95 £ 652.70
Riesling £ 75.85 £ 65.60 £ 67.65 £ 98.40 £ 307.50
Total £ 813.45 £ 623.05 £ 865.85 £ 984.80 £ 3,287.15
Red 1st quarter 2nd quarter 3rd quarter 4th quarter Total
Algerian £ 103.25 £ 56.05 £ 76.70 £ 147.50 £ 383.50
Rioja £ 141.45 £ 96.60 £ 124.20 £ 193.20 £ 555.45
Bordeaux £1,328.00 £1,212.80 £1,299.20 £1,718.40 £ 5,558.40
Cotes du Rhone £ 658.35 £ 595.35 £ 592.20 £ 774.90 £ 2,620.80
Chianti £ 361.20 £ 319.20 £ 338.80 £ 380.80 £ 1,400.00
Total £2,592.25 £2,280.00 £2,431.10 £3,214.80 £10,518.15
Slide 12
New Slide...
Layout...
Template...

13 Integration: adopting data into Access databases

You can also integrate data from other Microsoft Office applications in Access databases. In this chapter, we shall discuss how you can use various integration techniques to insert data from Word and Excel into Access.

13.1 Adopting Word data into a database

Imagine that you have a Word table that you wish to insert into a database table in Access. You can either export a Word table to a new Access table or integrate it in an existing Access table.

Text which is laid out with separating characters can be imported from Word into an Access table. If you wish to import a Word table, you must first export the Word table to a text file with separating characters. This layout is then suitable for import into Access.

Each field in the Word table must be of the same data type as the corresponding field in the Access table. If you wish to use the first row from the Word table as field names, these field names must correspond exactly to the field names in the Access table. You can examine the field names by opening the Design View in Access. If you do not want to use the first row of the Word table as field names, the fields in the Word table must be in the same order of sequence as the fields in the Access table so that you can be sure that the data will be placed at the correct positions in the Access table.

Exercise
We shall import the table from the NEWFAC.DOC we created in section 3.11 into a new table in Access.

Procedure:

1 Start up Word and open NEWFAC.DOC. This opens the document you created in section 3.11.

If you export data, the entire file is exported. This is not what we wish in this example so we shall create a new file containing only the data from the Word table.

2 Change the column width if necessary so that all cells are shown neatly on the screen. Place the cursor in the table and open the *Table* menu. Click on *Select Table*. The entire table is selected.

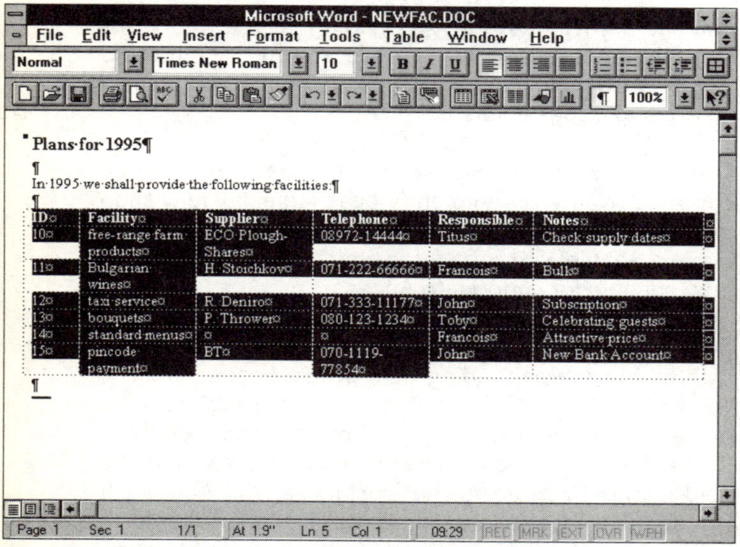

Copy

3 Click on the *Copy* button on the Standard toolbar or select *Copy* from the *Edit* menu.

4 Open the *File* menu and select *New*. Ensure that the *Document* option button is activated in the *New* dialog window and click on *OK*.

Paste

5 A new empty document window appears. Click on the *Paste* button or select *Paste* from the *Edit* menu. The marked data are copied to the new document.

6 Place the cursor in the table again and select *Select Table* from the *Table* menu. The entire table is marked.

7 Open the *Table* menu again and select *Convert Table to Text*. The dialog window of the same name appears.

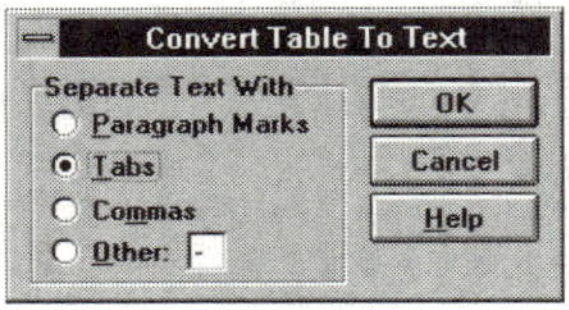

8 Activate the *Tabs* option button if necessary and click on *OK*.

The table is converted to text with tabs.

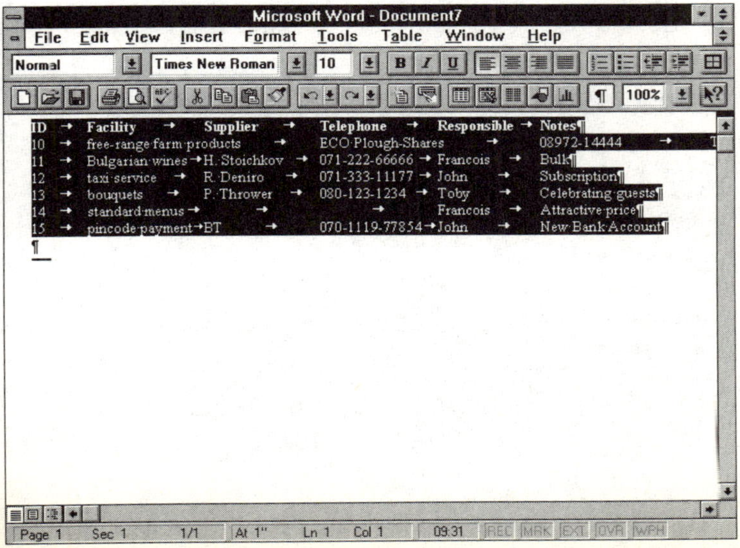

9 Open the *File* menu and select *Save As*.
10 In the *Save As* dialog window, open the *Save File as Type* drop-down list and select *Text Only with Line Breaks*. Assign the name NEWFACIL and click on *OK*.
11 Close the document.

You must close a document before it can be imported into a different application.

12 Switch to Access and open the RESTAUR.MDB database.
13 Open the *File* menu and select *Import*. The *Import* dialog window appears.
14 Select *Text (Delimited)* and click on *OK*.
15 The *Select File* dialog window appears.
16 Select the NEWFACIL.TXT file from the list and click on *Import*. The *Import Text Options* dialog window appears.
17 Ensure that a cross has been placed in the *First Row Contains Field Names* check box. Activate the *Create New Table* button and click on the *Options* button.
18 Set the *Text Delimiter* to *(none)* and the *Field Separator* to *(tab)*. Click on *OK*.

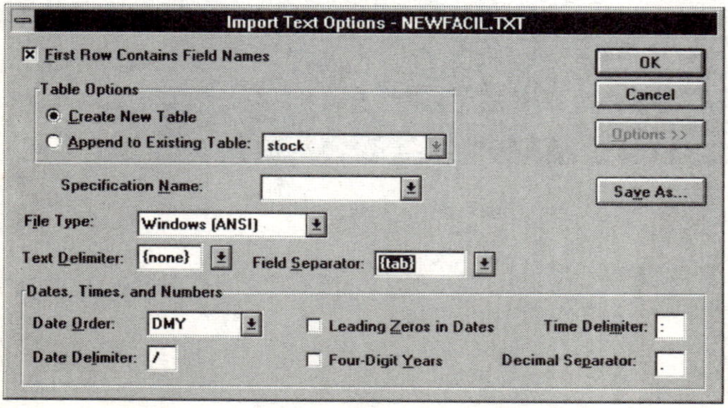

19 A dialog window informs you that the records have been imported without any problems arising. Click on *OK* to acknowledge this and then on *Close* in the *Select File* window.

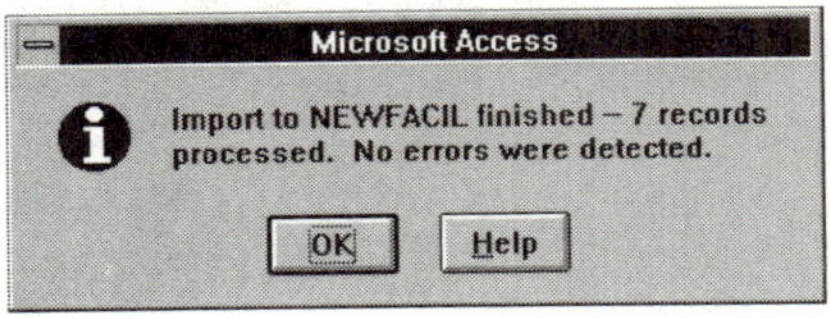

20 When the *Select File* window appears, click on the *Close* button.

You will see that the NEWFACIL file has been adopted as a table into the database.

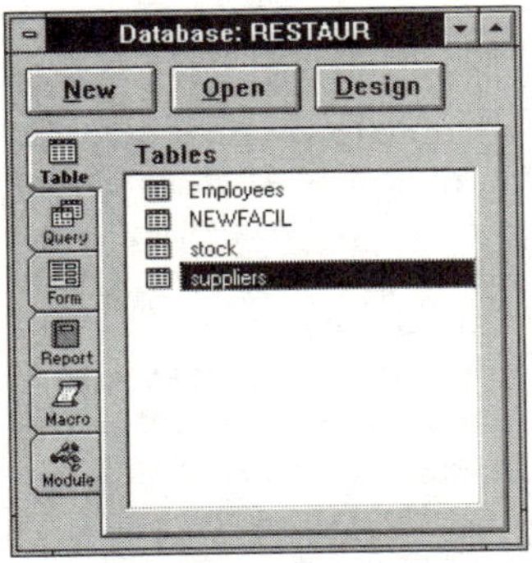

You can now open the new table to examine the records. Increase the column width to get a better overview.

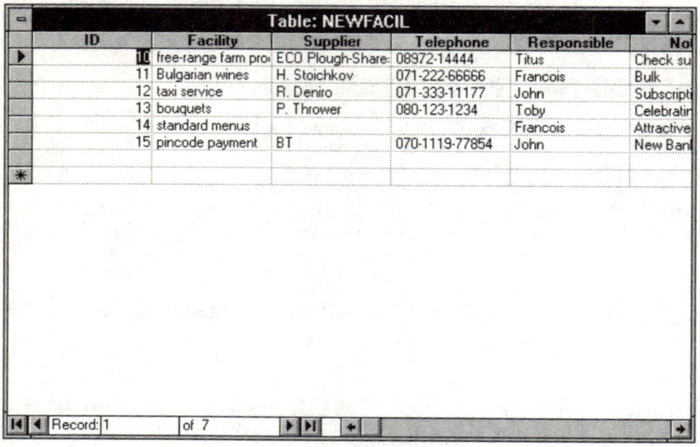

Note

If you want to append the Word table to an existing table, you should proceed as described above. At step 17, you should activate the *Append to Existing Table* option button in the *Import Text Options* dialog window and specify the required table. As mentioned, when appending to an existing table, the data types should exactly correspond in the existing table and the table being imported, and if you want to use the first row of the Word table as field names, these names have to be exactly the same as those in the Access table; in addition, they must be in the same order of sequence.

13.2 Adopting Excel data into a database

You can easily insert Excel workbook data into a database. You can import or embed the data into an Access table, or insert them into an Access form.

13.2.1 Importing Excel data into a new Access table

You can import Excel data into a new table or into an existing table. In the following exercise, we shall illustrate how to create a new Access table based on Worksheet data from Excel.

Exercise

We shall create a new database table based on the *returns 1994* Excel worksheet. The Excel worksheet must be adjusted first so that the first row contains the field names in the new database table.

Procedure:

1 Start up Excel, open the BOTTLES.XLS document and select the *returns 1994* worksheet.

Copy

2 Select the entire worksheet by clicking on the *Select All* button (upper left-hand corner of the work area). Click on the *Copy* button on the Standard toolbar or select *Copy* from the *Edit* menu.

3 Select the *purchase 1994* worksheet and open the *Insert* menu. Select *Worksheet*.

Paste

4 When the new worksheet appears, click on the *Paste* button or select *Paste* from the *Edit* menu. The data are copied to the new worksheet.

5 Change the data in the worksheet so that the layout is as follows:

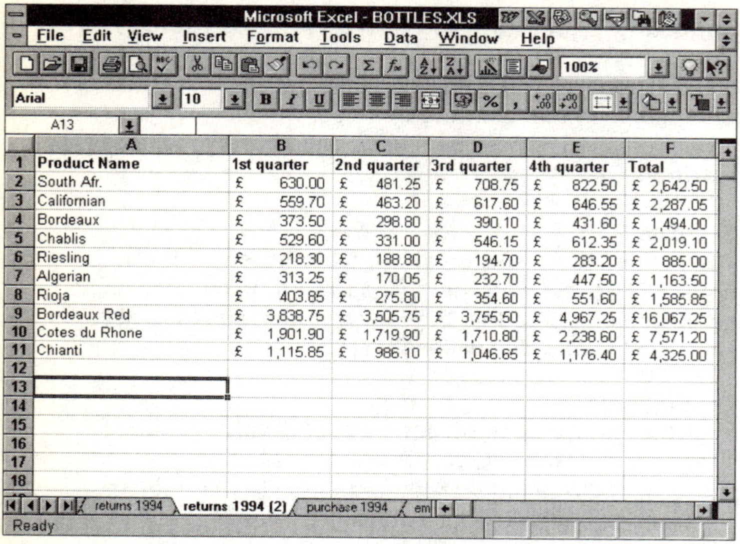

	A	B	C	D	E	F
1	Product Name	1st quarter	2nd quarter	3rd quarter	4th quarter	Total
2	South Afr.	£ 630.00	£ 481.25	£ 708.75	£ 822.50	£ 2,642.50
3	Californian	£ 559.70	£ 463.20	£ 617.60	£ 646.55	£ 2,287.05
4	Bordeaux	£ 373.50	£ 298.80	£ 390.10	£ 431.60	£ 1,494.00
5	Chablis	£ 529.60	£ 331.00	£ 546.15	£ 612.35	£ 2,019.10
6	Riesling	£ 218.30	£ 188.80	£ 194.70	£ 283.20	£ 885.00
7	Algerian	£ 313.25	£ 170.05	£ 232.70	£ 447.50	£ 1,163.50
8	Rioja	£ 403.85	£ 275.80	£ 354.60	£ 551.60	£ 1,585.85
9	Bordeaux Red	£ 3,838.75	£ 3,505.75	£ 3,755.50	£ 4,967.25	£ 16,067.25
10	Cotes du Rhone	£ 1,901.90	£ 1,719.90	£ 1,710.80	£ 2,238.60	£ 7,571.20
11	Chianti	£ 1,115.85	£ 986.10	£ 1,046.65	£ 1,176.40	£ 4,325.00

6 Change the name of the worksheet to *returns 1994 (2)* by double clicking on the sheet tab and typing the new name.

7 Close BOTTLES.XLS and save the changes.

8 Start up Access and activate the RESTAUR.MDB database window.

9 Open the *File* menu and select *Import*.

10 Select *Microsoft Excel 5.0* from the *Data Source* list in the *Import* dialog window and click on *OK*.

11 The *Select File* window appears. Select the BOTTLES.XLS file and click on the *Import* button.

The *Import Spreadsheet Options* dialog window appears.

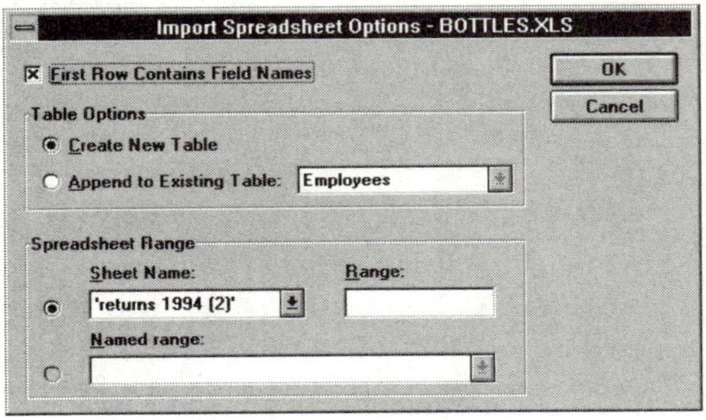

12 Activate the *Create New Table* option button, place a cross in the *First Row Contains Field Names* check box, specify the *returns 1994 (2)* sheet name and click on *OK*.

A small message box appears informing you that the import process has taken place.

13 Click on *OK* to acknowledge this and click on *Close* to close the *Select File* window.

The new BOTTLES table is displayed in the list.

14 Select the new table and click on *Open* to examine it.

The values may not be shown in the correct currency notation. If so, click on the *Design View* button and change the Data Type of each of the fields to *Currency*.

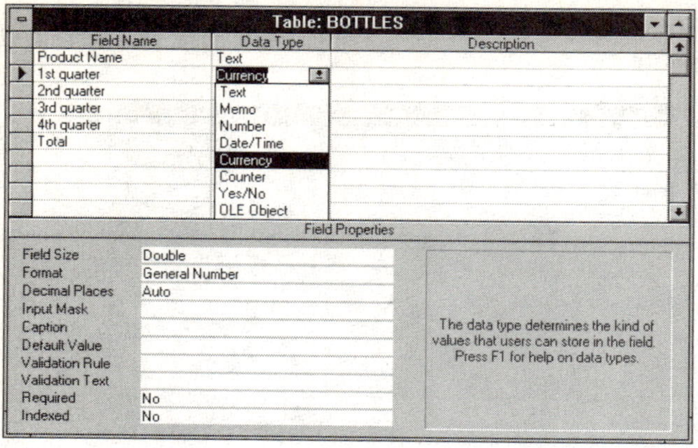

Click in the *Format* box in the *Properties* section to select the appropriate currency notation.

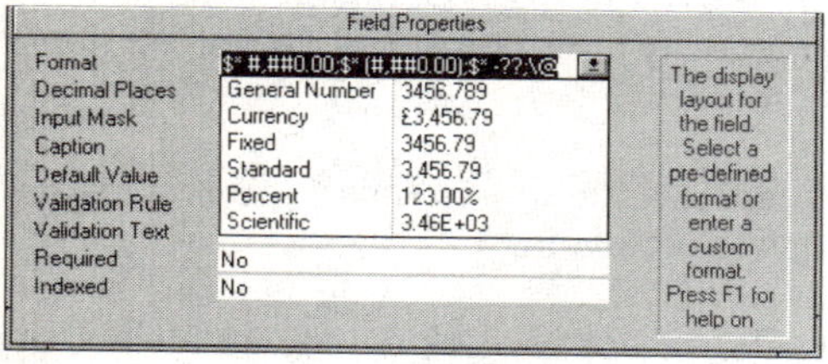

When all the required adjustments have been made, the table will look something like this:

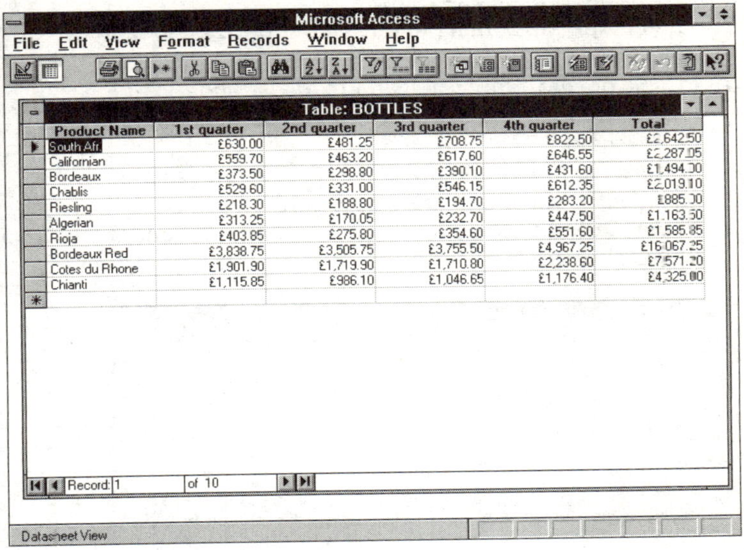

Product Name	1st quarter	2nd quarter	3rd quarter	4th quarter	Total
South Afr.	£630.00	£481.25	£708.75	£822.50	£2,642.50
Californian	£559.70	£463.20	£617.60	£646.55	£2,287.05
Bordeaux	£373.50	£298.80	£390.10	£431.60	£1,494.00
Chablis	£529.60	£331.00	£546.15	£612.35	£2,019.10
Riesling	£218.30	£188.80	£194.70	£283.20	£885.00
Algerian	£313.25	£170.05	£232.70	£447.50	£1,163.50
Rioja	£403.85	£275.80	£354.60	£551.60	£1,585.85
Bordeaux Red	£3,838.75	£3,505.75	£3,755.50	£4,967.25	£16,067.25
Cotes du Rhone	£1,901.90	£1,719.90	£1,710.80	£2,238.60	£7,571.20
Chianti	£1,115.85	£986.10	£1,046.65	£1,176.40	£4,325.00

13.2.2 Embedding data from an Excel worksheet as an object

You can embed (part of) an Excel worksheet as an object in an Access database. In this database object, you will then be able to make use of a number of Excel functions to edit the data in the database; this is done by double clicking on the object. When you edit these data, the data in the original Excel version remain unchanged.

Exercise
We shall now embed the *quantity 1994* worksheet in the *stock* database table.

Procedure:

1 Activate Microsoft Access and open the RESTAUR.MDB database window.

2 Select the *stock* table and click on the *Design* button.

3 Click on the empty field under *Illustration* in the *Field Name* column and type **Sales** as the name of a new field.

4 Press Tab to move to the *Data Type* column and select OLE object from the drop-down list.

5 Type **Quantities sold** in the *Caption* box under *Field Properties*.

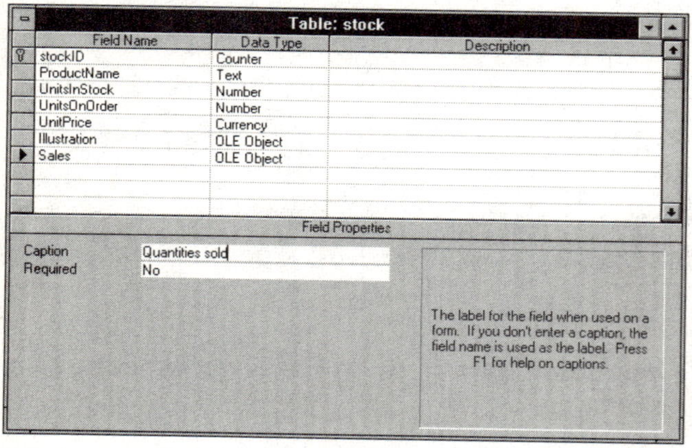

Datasheet View

6 Click on the *Datasheet View* button on the toolbar and click on *OK* if you are asked if you wish to save the table.

7 The new *Quantities sold* column is displayed in the table at the extreme right-hand side.

8 Click in record 1 of the new field.

9 Open the *Edit* menu and select *Insert Object*.

The *Insert Object* dialog window opens.

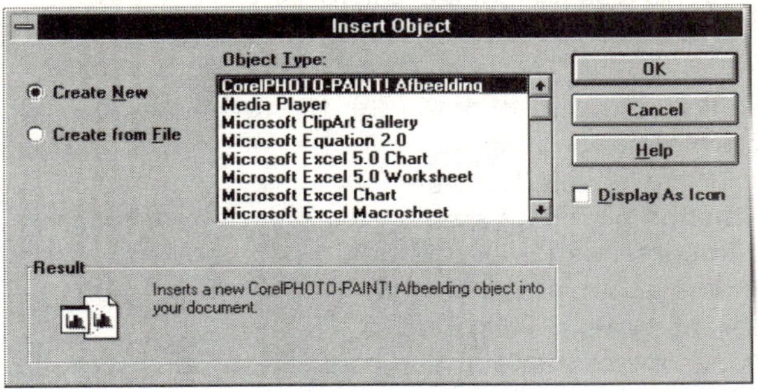

10 Activate the *Create from File* option button, select BOTTLES.XLS (by clicking on the *Browse* button if necessary) and click on *OK*.

Copy

Paste

The first record displays the text 'Microsoft Excel 5.0 Worksheet' in the *Quantities sold* field. You can now copy the embedded object to the other records by selecting the first record, clicking on the *Copy* button, selecting the destination cell and clicking on the *Paste* button.

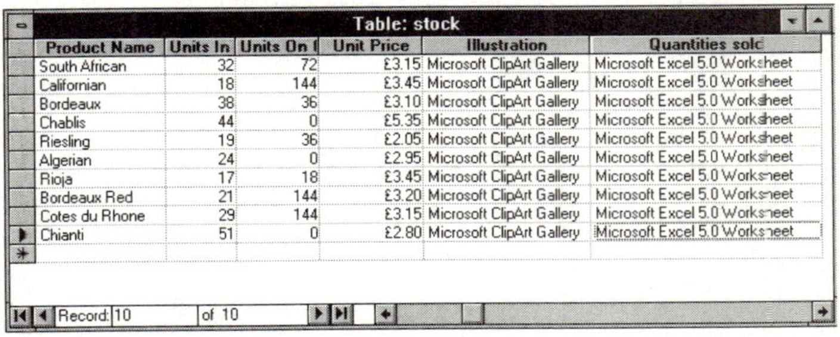
Table: stock

Product Name	Units In	Units On (	Unit Price	Illustration	Quantities sold
South African	32	72	£3.15	Microsoft ClipArt Gallery	Microsoft Excel 5.0 Worksheet
Californian	18	144	£3.45	Microsoft ClipArt Gallery	Microsoft Excel 5.0 Worksheet
Bordeaux	38	36	£3.10	Microsoft ClipArt Gallery	Microsoft Excel 5.0 Worksheet
Chablis	44	0	£5.35	Microsoft ClipArt Gallery	Microsoft Excel 5.0 Worksheet
Riesling	19	36	£2.05	Microsoft ClipArt Gallery	Microsoft Excel 5.0 Worksheet
Algerian	24	0	£2.95	Microsoft ClipArt Gallery	Microsoft Excel 5.0 Worksheet
Rioja	17	18	£3.45	Microsoft ClipArt Gallery	Microsoft Excel 5.0 Worksheet
Bordeaux Red	21	144	£3.20	Microsoft ClipArt Gallery	Microsoft Excel 5.0 Worksheet
Cotes du Rhone	29	144	£3.15	Microsoft ClipArt Gallery	Microsoft Excel 5.0 Worksheet
Chianti	51	0	£2.80	Microsoft ClipArt Gallery	Microsoft Excel 5.0 Worksheet

Record: 10 of 10

If you base a new form on this table, the embedded Excel object is also included in the form. You can therefore open and edit this OLE object from the form.

When working with forms in the Design View, you can create a frame for an unbound object or for a bound object.
An unbound object frame is a control on a form or report used to contain an unbound object. An unbound object is an object, such as a picture, whose value is not derived from data stored in a table.
A bound object frame is a control on a form or report used to display and manipulate OLE objects that are stored in tables.

We dealt with how to insert an object frame in a form in section 9.4.1.

Appendix A
Codes for the more common special characters in Word

(NumLock on)

Alt-0163	£
Alt-0188	1/4
Alt-0189	1/2
Alt-0224	à
Alt-0225	á
Alt-0226	â
Alt-0228	ä
Alt-0232	è
Alt-0233	é
Alt-0234	ê
Alt-0235	ë
Alt-0238	î
Alt-0241	ñ
Alt-0244	ô
Alt-0246	ö

Appendix B
Terminology

application A program written to execute a specific task, such as word processing or data management.

application window The window in which an application is displayed on the screen.

cell A box in a table or worksheet, at the intersection of a row and column. In Excel, a cell is referred to by naming the column letter and row number.

Clipboard A temporary buffer for text or pictures, used to store data that are being copied or moved from one position to another.

control A graphic object in a form or report, such as a text box, a frame for a bound (or unbound) object or a command button. The control enables you to implement an action or increase the readability of a report or form.

database object A component of a database, such as a table, query, form, report, macro or module.

DDE (Dynamic Data Exchange) A series of commands which ensures that the exchange of data between Microsoft applications is possible.

document window The window in which a document is displayed on the screen.

dynaset The result of a query or filter; the records which are the result of implementing a query or application of a filter.

embedding Inserting data from one application into another in such a way that they form part of the destination document. Double clicking on the embedded object activates the functions of the application used to create the source document.

export Storing data in an application in a different file structure so that they can be read and modified by a different application.

expression A combination of operators, fixed values, character strings, functions, fields, controls and properties which are combined in such a way that the result is a single value.

field (in Word) A series of codes by which elements are automatically inserted into a document. These elements can be figures, text or page numbers for example.

field selector The box above a column in a datasheet, upon which you can click to select the column.

file type The specific way in which an application codes and stores the input.

fill handle The small black block at the bottom right-hand side of a selected cell or range in Excel, used for *relative* copying of data. If you place the mouse pointer on the block, the pointer assumes the shape of a plus sign. The AutoFill function is activated. The contents of the first cell in the row or column is taken to be the source of the values to be placed.

filter A series of criteria used to generate or sort a subset of records.

import Adopting data into an application which were not created in that application.

input mask A specific layout structure which determines and facilitates the input of data.

insertion point The symbol on the screen which indicates where the current input will be placed.

link Inserting data from one application into another in such a way that a link exists between the source and the destination files. If the data in the source file are altered, the data are automatically updated in the destination file.

mouse pointer The symbol on the screen which indicates the currently active mouse position; may assume various shapes.

object Data, such as a table or chart, which are created as a unit in one application and which may be inserted and stored in another.

object button One of the six buttons in the Access database window providing access to tables, queries, forms, reports, macros and modules in an opened database.

OLE Object Linking and Embedding; a method of establishing a connection between data created in one application and copied to another.

pivot table A table in an Excel worksheet which enables you to summarise and analyse data from a list or table.

primary key A field or combination of fields uniquely identifies each record in a table. As the main index for the table it is used to associate data between tables.

query A method of selecting data from a table which conform to specified criteria. You can use the query to examine and edit data from several tables. A query can be used as the basis of a form, report or chart.

Index

General

Access

Excel

Word